John Dewey

The Later Works, 1925–1953

Volume 4: 1929

EDITED BY JO ANN BOYDSTON

TEXTUAL EDITOR, HARRIET FURST SIMON

With an Introduction by Stephen Toulmin

Southern Illinois University Press

Carbondale and Edwardsville

COMMITTEE ON
SCHOLARLY EDITIONS

AN APPROVED EDITION

MODERN LANGUAGE
ASSOCIATION OF AMERICA

The text of this reprinting is a photo-offset reproduction of the original cloth
edition that contains the full apparatus for the volume awarded the seal of the
Committee on Scholarly Editions of the Modern Language Association.

The paperbound edition has been made possible by a special subvention from
the John Dewey Foundation.

The Library of Congress catalogued the first printing of this work (in cloth) as
follows:

Dewey, John, 1859–1952.
  The later works, 1925–1953.

  Vol. 4 has introd. by Stephen Toulmin.
  Continues The middle works, 1899–1924.
  Includes bibliographies and indexes.

  CONTENTS: v. 1. 1925—   —v. 4. 1929.
  1. Philosophy—Collected works.   I. Boydston, Jo Ann, 1924-.   II.
B945.D41   1981   191   80-27285
ISBN 0-8093-1162-3 (v. 4)

ISBN 0-8093-1493-2 (paperback)

Contents

Introduction
By Stephen Toulmin

"Yesterday evening," reported the *Scotsman* of Edinburgh
on Thursday, April 18, 1929, "Professor John Dewey delivered the first of his lectures in the Music Classroom of the
University.

"Extraordinary scenes were witnessed. There was not an
available seat in the hall, while the platform at the back was
crowded with people standing. Many were unable to gain admission to the hall itself, and stood on the stairway leading
to it, where they could have heard little."[1]

So began the series of Gifford Lectures which were the basis of
Dewey's book, *The Quest for Certainty.*

The occasion which the *Scotsman* described was a notable one
in several ways. Few of us think of John Dewey as a theologian;
yet on that April day in 1929 he spoke as "Gifford Lecturer in
Natural Theology" at the University of Edinburgh, and these unfamiliar robes sat quite comfortably on his shoulders. Nor was
it the first time that an American pragmatist had filled this
role. Some thirty years before, as the Principal of the University
pointed out in his opening remarks, William James had delivered
at Edinburgh the Gifford Lectures we still know as *The Varieties
of Religious Experience*; and James's was a very hard act to follow. Finally, Dewey's international reputation, which did much
to pack the hall and stairway of the Edinburgh Music Classroom, was above all a reputation as an educational reformer,
earned first by his work at the Laboratory School of the University of Chicago, later through his association with the Teachers
College at Columbia University. But, as Dewey was at some pains

1. *Scotsman* (Edinburgh), April 18, 1929, reporting the lecture of Wednesday,
April 17, under the headlines: "Adjusting Beliefs/Influence of Science/Edin-
burgh Gifford Lectures."

to make clear on this particular occasion, he was first and fore-most a philosopher, not an "educationist."

The annual "Gifford Lectures" are a long-established feature of Scottish intellectual life. They bring to each of the major Scottish universities in turn a distinguished scholar—usually, but not invariably, a philosopher or theologian—who spends some time at the University, and gives a series of public lectures extending over a month or more. (The ten lectures embodied in John Dewey's *The Quest for Certainty* were delivered twice weekly from April 17 to May 17, 1929.)

By the original terms of the Gifford bequest, the subject of the Gifford Lectures is specified as *natural theology*. In British usage especially, the idea of a "natural theology" has always been elastic; so, by longstanding practice, the Gifford Trustees have been content to see the phrase interpreted broadly, to cover any discussion of the larger implications of human knowledge and experience, whether from a philosophical, a psychological or a theological standpoint. The breadth and scope of the arguments in *The Quest for Certainty* thus placed them squarely in the tradition of the Giffords; and, while they did not serve to turn Dewey into a professional theologian, they certainly helped to "place" his pragmatism in its genealogy, as a major contribution to the historical debate about human knowledge and practice, which forms the heart of the Western philosophical tradition.

The Quest for Certainty is also a key work in Dewey's own development. Herbert Schneider, his student and colleague, used to speak of this book (echoing Woodbridge) as "the best statement of Dewey's fundamental position": a position which, as Schneider put it in conversation,

> took naturalistic philosophy for granted and wasn't inter-ested in the problem of "the external world" any more, the way the old-fashioned idealists were.[2]

Half a century on, we are in a better position to see just how remarkable a statement Dewey succeeded in making in the course of these Gifford Lectures.

The lectures display, of course, all of that robust vigor and

2. Oral interview with Herbert W. Schneider at the Center for Dewey Studies, Southern Illinois University at Carbondale, June 29, 1967.

good sense which are evident in so much of Dewey's writing. But they display also farsightedness, perception and originality of a kind that could hardly be recognized when they were first delivered in 1929. In the first place, they set out Dewey's interpretation of the traditional distinction between *theoria* and *praxis* in clearer and sharper terms than any of his other books. In the second place, they show us just how different John Dewey's philosophical methods and arguments were from those of William James or Charles Sanders Peirce, and so how misleading it can be to lump them all together, as the single school of "pragmatists." Yet, above all, they show us Dewey at his best, in his delicate feeling for the intellectual relations between philosophy and the natural sciences. In particular: the first appearance of Werner Heisenberg's "uncertainty principle" in 1927 at once gave rise to lively philosophical controversy, but nobody in the resulting debate spoke or wrote more profoundly about the epistemological meaning of Heisenberg's work than Dewey did in these lectures.[3]

In these introductory pages, we may look at two main sets of topics. (1) To begin with, we may consider Dewey's criticism of the ways in which central problems in the theory of knowledge have been posed, at least since René Descartes and John Locke. By putting John Dewey's arguments alongside those of his younger contemporaries, Ludwig Wittgenstein and Martin Heidegger, we can see just how deeply his critique of traditional epistemology was capable of cutting. Yet Dewey's critique was not intended to be merely destructive. It offered also, in outline, a positive view about "the relation of knowledge and action"—to quote Dewey's own subtitle for the book; and this view too (we shall see) has been only reinforced by subsequent developments within the natural sciences themselves.

(2) Secondly, we may seek to place John Dewey's philosophy in the longerstanding debate about "knowledge," as it has been carried on ever since the time of Plato. Some readers are still misled by the apparently homespun instrumentalism of Dewey's work on *experimental logic*, and the unduly "scientistic" language he sometimes used in writing about it. As a result, the

3. See *The Quest for Certainty* (New York: Minton, Balch and Co., 1929; *The Later Works of John Dewey, 1925–1953*, vol. 4, ed. Jo Ann Boydston [Carbondale: Southern Illinois University Press, 1984]), esp. Chapter 8, pp. 160–63. Page numbers refer to the present edition.

force of his argument is needlessly blunted, and it is harder to recognize just how central a position he occupies in one of the classical traditions of philosophy. Here, therefore, we should take care to consider, first, Dewey's relations to the *classical skepticism* of such Pyrrhonists as Sextus Empiricus; and, second, the more positive contributions made by his ideas about *praxis*. As we shall see, his emphasis on the presence of *experiential* elements in our methods of argument took one step further the debate about practical reasoning which had been initiated in Aristotle's *Topics*, and developed by the rhetoricians of late antiquity and the Renaissance.

In claiming that *logic* should be "experimental," Dewey was of course separating himself from traditional Platonism. He did so, not through an unwitting lapse into *psychologism*, as Frege's successors clearly assumed, but knowingly and deliberately. If Dewey was right, the charge of psychologism cut both ways. He saw the Platonist demand for certainty and necessity as having its own emotional origins: it was an "escape from peril." These origins were partly cultural, being the product of superstitions that went back ultimately to the astrotheology of the Ancient Empires, but they were also partly personal—an expression of an urge for a psychological security which the world of practical life does not provide.[4]

Dewey begins his radical dismantling of the epistemological tradition in the very first chapter. From the start (he argues) philosophers in this tradition assumed that the "knower" is in the position of a *spectator*, who makes judgments or discovers facts about the world without otherwise acting on it. Correspondingly, they thought of the process of "knowing" on the model of *vision*—or, to speak more exactly,

> modeled after what was supposed to take place in the act of vision. The object refracts light to the eye and is seen; it makes a difference to the eye and to the person having an optical apparatus, but none to the thing seen.[5]

4. Chapter 1, esp. pp. 15–18.
5. Chapter 1, p. 19.

At first glance, one might think that this criticism could be brought to bear only against empiricist theories of knowledge, but (Dewey argues) it holds good equally against the idealists:

> They all hold that the operation of inquiry excludes any element of practical activity that enters into the construction of the object known. Strangely enough this is as true of idealism as of realism, of theories of synthetic activity as of those of passive receptivity. For according to them [sc., idealists] "mind" constructs the known object not in any observable way, or by means of practical overt acts having a temporal quality, but by some occult internal operation.[6]

In response, Dewey asserts that "knowing" is intelligible only as the outcome of the activities by which we "come to know" the things we do; and all the different ways of "coming to know" involve corresponding methods of *operating on* the world. Indeed, as Heisenberg had now confirmed:

> What is known is seen to be a product in which the act of observation plays a necessary role. Knowing is seen to be a participant in what is finally known. . . . one kind of interaction which goes on within the world.[7]

In the fifty years since Dewey gave his Gifford Lectures, some philosophers have been tempted to underrate the force and depth of his epistemological critique. There are two reasons for this. On the one hand, Dewey's literary style was misleadingly loose-limbed and colloquial; and, in a period when logical rigor and formality were the professional mode, his colleagues could disregard arguments presented as discursively as his. He did not refute his opponents' positions by finding formal fallacies in their published papers; nor did he accuse them of falling into outright nonsense as a result of committing "category mistakes." More fundamentally, he called in question the intellectual models which shaped their ways of stating their initial problems; and somehow, having been found "not guilty" of formal errors, they found it easier to overlook Dewey's more radical, and substantive criticisms.

6. Chapter 1, pp. 18–19.
7. Chapter 8, p. 163.

In the second place, the very features which stamped Dewey's positions (and his prose) as *American* apparently gave his readers an excuse to underestimate the power of his arguments. Instead of dealing in the grand, mysterious abstractions which would at once have earned him renown as a truly profound metaphysician, Dewey always took care to prick the hot-air balloons of the traditional philosophers, and bring their issues down to earth. His reward was to be criticized as shallow, or as a popularizer; and matters were not improved by the praise he was willing to give to such "amateur" philosophical writers as P. W. Bridgman. In this criticism, Dewey encountered an age-old prejudice among the audience for philosophical writings, who see obscurity as a sign of depth, and who—in accordance with the old Latin tag, *omne ignotum pro magnifico*—regard anything unintelligible as being that much the grander.

Would it have been better for John Dewey if he had worked in Europe? Certainly (one can now see) the thrust of his arguments paralleled that to be found in some of the "profoundest" European philosophers of his time: e.g., Martin Heidegger and Ludwig Wittgenstein. In different ways, both Heidegger and Wittgenstein were concerned to undermine the epistemological heritage of the Cartesian and Lockean traditions. As Heidegger put the point, epigrammatically, we can no longer regard the world *as a view*; a "view" being something that a spectator can contemplate without intervening in. Rather, Heidegger was preoccupied with the ways in which we "constitute" the objects of our experience through being involved with them less detachedly and impersonally. Our knowledge of the world thus springs from our involvement with it, and the world *as we know it* is always a world which is "to hand," and a world with which we deal. (In this respect, of course, the arguments of Jürgen Habermas preserve something of Heidegger's vision: the essential insight that objects are "constituted" by being the objects of human interests, and that "knowledge of objects" is available to us only where those interests are engaged, links the two philosophers.)[8]

There are still closer parallels between the mature position of John Dewey, as captured in *The Quest for Certainty*, and the

8. The parallels between the ideas of John Dewey and those of Wittgenstein and Heidegger have been pointed out also by Richard Rorty: see *Philosophy and the Mirror of Nature* (Princeton, N.J.: Princeton University Press, 1979).

views that Ludwig Wittgenstein began to develop from 1927 on. In particular, both men were equally opposed to the theory of *sense data*, which had been launched by Ernst Mach in his book, *Die Analyse der Empfindungen* (1885), popularized in English by Karl Pearson, and later adopted in one form or another by such influential neo-empiricists as Bertrand Russell and G. E. Moore. This whole approach to the problem of perception, as Dewey saw, represented a revival of the "sensationalist" methods of the eighteenth-century British empiricists, and so was deeply committed to that *spectator's* point of view which he so emphatically rejected. To that conclusion Wittgenstein would have said, "Amen"; with the one addition that a sensationalist approach places the alleged objects of direct knowledge essentially "in our heads," and so destroys all our hopes of bringing language to bear on them. So, paradoxically, the direct objects of our experience, from which all other knowledge was supposedly inferred or constructed, were "purely private," and beyond the scope of meaningful description.

To take this parallel one stage further: some have argued that Wittgenstein himself was—in effect—putting forward a pragmatist version of the Kantian philosophy, in which the scope and limits of the Reason were reinterpreted as the scope and limits of Language. (This reading of Wittgenstein has been put forward both by those who sympathize with the position, as demystifying Kant's position, and also by those who oppose it, on the grounds that it distracts us from the true character of thought, language and experience.)

Viewing Wittgenstein as a pragmatist of a sophisticated kind can certainly be helpful. In particular, his use of the notions of "language games" and "forms of life" serves to focus attention directly on the question of *praxis*. Whereas Dewey spoke in rather broad terms of knowledge as rooted in "action," and did not give us a technique for analysing action in any systematic way, the ideas of the later Wittgenstein have stimulated a great deal of thought about the *taxonomy* of human actions. We can see their longterm influence on human science in the cross-cultural psychology of Eleanor Rosch and her colleagues, whose studies of categorization have picked up Wittgenstein's notion of "family resemblances"; and it is apparent also in the micro-sociological analysis of Erving Goffman and his successors.

Thus, Goffman's dramaturgical model for the analysis of human conduct gives us a way of dissecting out and describing the individual "forms of life" which enter into human social life and learning. In all these areas of research (we may say) John Dewey's insistence on the *active* character of human knowledge is now bearing fruit, and the combined heritage of Dewey and Wittgenstein is giving us a new command over psychology and social theory.

Dewey's insistence on the relation between knowledge and action throws light on twentieth-century natural science, as well as on philosophy. In particular, his criticism of the picture of the "knower" as a kind of *spectator* goes far beyond Heisenberg's principle, and is relevant to much of contemporary science.

The spectator model of knowing originated, of course, with the classical Greek philosophers. The primary meaning of *theoria* was, for them, "being an onlooker"; and the *episteme* at which they aimed was to be the genteel, aristocratic understanding of those who did not actively seek to manipulate, exploit or change the world of Nature. To say this is not to endorse the Marxist interpretation of Greek philosophy, as requiring one to despise the manual labor of the proletariat. It is to recall only that, for the Greeks, success in philosophy rested on the ability to consider issues in abstract, general terms, not merely as they related to particular, material instances; and this implied the ability to view the world from a detached point of view, i.e. to observe it, without influencing it. That was ideally possible, of course, only for the Immutable God, who understood and brought about change in the cosmos, without himself being changed (the famous "Unmoved Mover"); but the posture was one toward which human thinkers too could and should aim, in their attempts to approximate the detachment of Divinity.

At the time, nobody had occasion to ask whether this posture was subject to *intrinsic* limits: whether there was not a point beyond which detachment could not reach, without destroying the very possibility of acquiring knowledge. In all the fields of scientific investigation which actively concerned the Greeks, it seemed possible to increase without limit one's ability to arrive at objective (or spectator's) knowledge; and this remained true some nineteen hundred years later, when Galileo, Descartes and Newton adopted the same ideal as a foundation for modern science. In launching mathematical physics, especially the mathematical theory of planetary astronomy, they took it for granted that human observers could discover the laws of motion without changing the motions to which those laws applied. For all their disagreements with Aristotle, the "new, mathematical and experimental philosophers"—as the seventeenth-century scientists called themselves—continued in this one, crucial respect to work within his tradition.

This scientific ideal of detachment and "objectivity" is best expressed, perhaps, in the famous image devised by the French astronomer Laplace. For Laplace, the complete knowledge of Nature at which the Newtonian scientist aimed was like that which would be possessed by a Calculator of unlimited capacity, who was given the initial positions and velocities of every particle in the universe at the moment of Creation, and used Newton's laws of motion to compute the entire subsequent history of the world. Such an Omniscient Calculator could know all there was to be known about Nature, without affecting the actual course of natural processes in any way; and human scientists, too, could hope to approximate this kind of knowledge by progressively reducing their influence on their objects of investigation.

How far can this be done? The limits to the Laplacean ideal of detachment and objectivity have become clearly apparent only in the course of the twentieth century, and they have done so in two distinct ways. On the one hand—as Dewey himself insists in his eighth chapter on "The Naturalization of Intelligence"—the principle of indeterminacy reveals a limit on the extent to which we can realistically cleave to that ideal, even in dealing with the world of physical objects. There, it is now apparent that the nature of things (specifically, the nature of *quanta*) limits the extent to which we can in fact reduce our influence on the objects that we study: even on the purely physical level, that is to say, *observing* any natural system always involves *acting on* it also. On the other hand—to carry Dewey's argument further, in a direction that Karl Popper has pursued—the scope of twentieth-century science has expanded beyond the realm of physical objects and physiological phenomena, which are by nature indifferent to the fact that we are studying them, into psychology and the other human sciences, where our "research subjects" are normally aware of being observed, and are liable to react countersuggestibly to our scrutiny. Whereas Descartes and Kant alike saw the human mind as lying beyond the scope of science, we now seek to bring it into the scientific fold.

The Cartesian and Newtonian "modern scientists," whose ideas dominated European thinking about Nature from the mid-seventeenth to the early twentieth century, had thus refined the Greek ideal of *theoria* to the point of cutting it off entirely from *praxis*. The "natural philosopher" was not just a spectator but an essentially unseen spectator. The interaction between human observers and natural objects was a one-way interaction, in which the "external" world affected the "internal" mind, without being affected in return. So the physical world would continue to operate unchangingly, like a clock mechanism, regardless of whether the human scientist was observing it or not.

The move away from a *detached* view of "objectivity"—as symbolized by Heisenberg's indeterminacy principle—has gone much further since 1929. By the 1980s, the idea that we interact with (and modify) the behavior of the natural systems we study, is a commonplace throughout the natural sciences and technology. On the one hand, psychiatrists can learn about their individual patients' distresses, and so about mental disorder in general, only if they allow themselves to interact with patients on a *two-way* basis: on the other hand, the development of ecology has focussed new attention on the natural systems which link human beings to the other elements in their environments in self-sustaining ways. So, whether we consider the mental lives and activities of individuals or the collective activities of social groups and settlements, the new "human sciences" have been forced to move far away from the detachment of traditional scientific "objectivity" and to develop novel *interactive* methods of investigation and thought. During the fifty years since Dewey wrote his Gifford Lectures, his critique of the "modern" sciences, and of the epistemology associated with them, has become all the more relevant to our actual situation; and the separation of Human Observers and Agents from their Natural Objects of study, which had formed a crucial element in seventeenth-century thought, has lost its central place in scientific method.

Even if Heisenberg had not written as he did, in the year 1927, Dewey could thus have found other reasons to attack the opposition between *theoria* and *praxis* as artificial. The fact that quantum mechanics made its appearance just when it did no doubt helped to reinforce his basic argument; but the central point of his pragmatist thesis was not conditional on the validity of quantum physics. On the contrary: from the start, the Newtonian assumption that a scientist can—at least in principle—reduce the extent of his influence on natural objects and processes without limit had been artificial and idealized. Dewey was also right to insist that the basic image of the knower and the known which had underlain the philosophical debate from the time of Descartes and Locke took for granted the seventeenth-century mechanical world view. Instead of giving an *analytical* account of knowledge and perception, which could be accepted or rejected regardless of all scientific considerations, the seventeenth-century epistemologists had presented a *hypothetical* theory of cognition, vision and other mental operations, whose plausibility depended on the continued acceptance of a mechanistic physics. It was, thus, not just Heisenberg, but the whole thrust of physics from James Clerk Maxwell on, which had called the older model of knowledge in doubt, and paved the way for Dewey and other recent philosophers to start building afresh.

From the new point of view—which Dewey shared with both Heidegger and Wittgenstein—the traditional image of the human thinker or "knower," as removed from the objects and processes he observes, has to be set aside. Instead of mental activities going on entirely within the special, "internal" realm of the *sensorium*, and so being essentially separated, hidden away from the physical, or "external" world, we must now regard them all as involving interactions between the knower and the known; and recognize that any attempt at defining a realm of contemplative theory quite devoid of all overt expression in practice will lead philosophers and scientists alike into a dead end.

In this respect, Dewey openly allied himself with those philosophers of twentieth-century physics (e.g. P. W. Bridgman and A. S. Eddington) who emphasized the *operational* character of scientific ideas. For Dewey as for them, "ideas" have the meanings they do only to the extent that they are *put to work*. Human beings show rational command over their lives through the *sets of operations* which they devise and put to work. To use Witt-

genstein's image, an "idea" or a "thought" which is not associated with such sets of operations serves no more purpose (and
so has no more *meaning*) than an "idle wheel" added to a clock
mechanism, which drives nothing and so has no intelligible
effect.

Taking these arguments as a model, Dewey saw "the critical
task imposed on contemporary thought" as a twofold task. On
the negative side, it required a "thoroughgoing revision" of
"ideas of mind and thought": on the positive side, one must consider extending "the method of operative intelligence" to "direction of life in other fields." What did this imply for philosophy?
From now on (he argued) the authority of the intellect would
rest less on a capacity for passive observation than on the em-
ployment of active method. Still, in this respect, Dewey's answer
remains programmatic rather than substantive: he scarcely goes
beyond the critical rejection of the Old, and leaves us to imagine
for ourselves what will be the actual content of the New.

With *The Quest for Certainty* before us, we may also address
two historical questions. To begin with, how does John Dewey's
philosophical work appear in retrospect, when placed alongside
that of his two pragmatist colleagues, William James and Charles
Sanders Peirce? If we pursue this question, we shall see just how
systematically Dewey carried through his pragmatist program
for the analysis of knowledge.

James had a lifelong commitment to psychology as well as philosophy, and his epistemological theories were a compromise
between empiricist and Kantian ideas: we do not find in his writings the same thoroughgoing rejection of the traditional "spectator" view as Dewey presents in his Gifford Lectures. For his part,
C. S. Peirce retained a mathematician's lingering fondness for
formal analysis: many of the ideas he put forward in his theory
of language (e.g. the "type"/"token" distinction) were picked
up by subsequent formal logicians, from Bertrand Russell to
Willard Van Orman Quine, and Peirce himself is still regarded as
one of the forefathers of semiotics. John Dewey alone enunciated
the program for a *thoroughly* "pragmatist" account of science
and philosophy.

In this account, the continuing legacy of the seventeenth-century debate was finally disowned. So, all questions about language and thought, meaning and reason, were taken back, out of the Private World of the *sensorium,* and set once again in their proper context, in the Public World of *praxis*—i.e. practical operations and overt procedures. Hence, for instance, Dewey's scorn for "subjectivism," which once again anticipated ideas developed later by his younger contemporaries. His criticisms of a "sensationalist" approach to epistemology, as too "subjective," thus foreshadow Ludwig Wittgenstein's later attack on any attempt to build a theory of mind on the basis of "essentially private" experiences and meanings.

Going further, we may ask, also, about John Dewey's place in a longer historical perspective. How will the pragmatist ideas put forward in *The Quest for Certainty* and elsewhere stand, when viewed against the whole history of philosophy? Here, we shall look at Dewey's affinity with two longerstanding traditions of philosophical argument: (1) the classical skepticism of such men as Pyrrho and Sextus Empiricus, and (2) the approaches to practical reasoning inaugurated in Aristotle's *Topics* and developed by the rhetoricians from late antiquity on.

In the modern philosophical debate (we must remark) the term "skepticism" has become devalued, or at least confused. These days, David Hume is viewed as the type example of a skeptic: his skepticism is seen in all his negative assertions about the apparent impossibility of knowledge. Here, however, a crucial ambiguity enters the debate. For the force of all those negative assertions was hypothetical. Suppose that we took the empiricist axioms—"sense impressions" and "demonstrative reasoning"—as starting points: by doing so, we should condemn ourselves to irremediable ignorance. But, if we assume instead that humans bring to bear on their experience principles of human nature (and of interpretation) which are not themselves *derived from* their experience, the possibility of knowledge will be less mysterious. What we call our "knowledge" will then be what those principles lead us, as humans, to *make of* our experience.

By the standards of the times, this was of course a radical argument. For most of Hume's immediate predecessors, the motto *nihil est in intellectu quod non prius fuerit in sensu*—the view that all the instruments of the mind are derived from the senses—

had been an axiom. But, properly understood, Hume's was not a skeptical argument. To the extent that he was inclined to accept the empiricist starting points for himself, his claims about the impossibility of knowledge were those, not of a skeptic, but of a *dogmatist*. If there is a residual skepticism in Hume, we must look for it elsewhere. As Pyrrho and Sextus understood the skeptical position—which was their own—no true skeptic would deny the possibility of knowledge, any more than he would assert it; for either course would be excessively dogmatic. Wisdom consisted in seeing that we can, in general, prove neither the possibility nor the *im*possibility of knowledge: instead, we must make do with whatever more-or-less reliable convictions we arrive at, and find substantial support for, as we go along. So, it was in Hume's tentative commitment to the empirical human sciences—in his essays on economics, ethics and anthropology, for instance—that the true skeptic found expression.[9]

The targets of classical "skepticism" were, thus, the Platonist ideals of *episteme* and quasi-geometrical *proof*: the pursuit of these ideals had led philosophy—in Hume's famous phrase—into a world of "sophistry and illusion." Instead of vainly pursuing *episteme* at the expense of *doxa*, the way ahead was to focus on the difference between well-founded opinions and baseless ones. So, skepticism led on into the study of rhetoric, or *practical reasoning*: once the skeptical move had been made, the way was opened up to examine opinions (*doxai*) in substantive rather than geometrical terms, and to see how claims of different kinds could be supported by evidence and arguments of *non*-geometrical kinds.

John Dewey took both of these steps. In the epistemology of *The Quest for Certainty*, he rejected the standard model of "sense experience" and "knowledge" which had misled philosophy from the time of Descartes on: in the *Essays in Experimental Logic*, he took the further step on into the field of "practical reasoning." Methods of reasoning are not criticized, in practice, by formal, *a priori* standards alone: they are judged by their fruits. Here again, Dewey took up a position that many of his professional colleagues were not ready to grasp, still less ap-

9. Our view of classical skepticism has been much refined in recent years by the work of such scholars as Miles Burnyeat and Richard Popkin; I have learned much about the subject from discussions with Dr. Avner Cohen.

preciate. As a result of the work of Gottlob Frege and Bertrand Russell, they had seen logic take on new vigor, and they were not happy at the prospect of any threat to the *formal* achievements of the new twentieth-century "symbolic logic."

It was not generally noticed just what severe limits Frege and Russell had placed on the scope of logic. For Aristotle and his successors, logic had been the study of *reasoning*. As such, it comprised two main parts: "analytics," which concerned itself with the formal structures of arguments, and "topics," which considered their varied functions. The anatomical investigation of formal structures could, to a great extent, be carried on in terms that were indifferent to the practical subject matter; so there was no problem about handling *analytics* in a purely formal, even a quasi-mathematical manner, as is of course done in modern "mathematical logic." But it was clear to students of practical reasoning—beginning with Aristotle himself—that functional issues can be addressed only with an eye to "the nature of the case."

At the very beginning of the *Nicomachean Ethics*, for example, Aristotle rejects any assumption that moral reasoning can aim at the kind of "geometrical" structure which Plato gave to planetary theory, and dreamed of extending into ethics: if you understand the special character of moral problems, you must see that this sort of structure is inappropriate to ethical, legal and similar issues. And, in other works—notably, the *Topics*, the *Politics* and the *Rhetoric*—Aristotle goes on to explore the rational functions, methods of argument and criteria of judgment relevant to practical argumentation in other fields. In all these works, he approaches questions of rational analysis and criticism in functional terms, as arising from the basic purposes of reasoning in different human activities and areas of experience.

In this way, Aristotle laid the groundwork for the students of *rhetoric* who succeeded him—from Hermagoras to Cicero in antiquity, by way of Aquinas and the medieval causists and common lawyers, up to Adam Smith and William Whewell in the eighteenth and nineteenth centuries. The philosophical significance of this tradition has been eclipsed, among many twentieth-century philosophers, by the charms of mathematical logic, but it still has important lessons today. For there is no way (Aristotle argues) in which one can discuss the functional aspects of argument in general, abstract, theoretical, formal or *a priori* terms: instead, they must be dealt with in specific, concrete, practical, substantive terms, in the light of our experience. In that sense, the "topical" part of logic cannot help being empirical—or, to use Dewey's word, "experimental."

The Quest for Certainty thus sets out one part—though the most original and productive part—of Dewey's overall position. In it, we are given his pragmatist account of thinking, which he defines as

> the actual transition from the problematic to the secure, as far as that is intentionally guided. . . . that mode of serial responsive behavior to a problematic situation in which transition to the relatively settled and clear is effected;[10]

and we are shown how this conception permits us to transcend the paradoxes with which the "subjectivist" models of the empiricists and the idealists had plagued the theory of knowledge for some three hundred years.

Still, it is necessary to view the argument of Dewey's Gifford Lectures in their larger context. As a topic for philosophical discussion, the study of thinking needs to be supplemented by a theory of reasoning; and that is what Dewey gives us in his *Essays in Experimental Logic*. Taken together, the two books survey the central territory of philosophy from two complementary points of view. The skeptic in Dewey rejects any *a priori* model of knowledge, as a variety of "seeing," in favor of an account of perception and discovery which respects the most reflective and up-to-date results of scientific analysis; while the pragmatist in him finds the primary subject matter for theory of knowledge ("what guarantees our knowledge") in the actual reasoning practices of human thinkers ("how we in fact think"). So, between them, the two halves of Dewey's philosophy dovetail to provide a complete system, on which the functional analysis of cognition, reasoning and knowledge can safely build.

10. *The Quest for Certainty*, Chapter 9, p. 181.

The Quest for Certainty

A Study of the Relation of Knowledge and
Action

I. Escape from Peril

Man who lives in a world of hazards is compelled to
seek for security. He has sought to attain it in two ways. One of
them began with an attempt to propitiate the powers which en-
viron him and determine his destiny. It expressed itself in supplication, sacrifice, ceremonial rite and magical cult. In time
these crude methods were largely displaced. The sacrifice of a
contrite heart was esteemed more pleasing than that of bulls and
oxen; the inner attitude of reverence and devotion more desirable than external ceremonies. If man could not conquer destiny
he could willingly ally himself with it; putting his will, even
in sore affliction, on the side of the powers which dispense fortune, he could escape defeat and might triumph in the midst of
destruction.

The other course is to invent arts and by their means turn the
powers of nature to account; man constructs a fortress out of the
very conditions and forces which threaten him. He builds shel-
ters, weaves garments, makes flame his friend instead of his en-
emy, and grows into the complicated arts of associated living.
This is the method of changing the world through action, as the
other is the method of changing the self in emotion and idea. It is
a commentary on the slight control man has obtained over himself by means of control over nature, that the method of action
has been felt to manifest dangerous pride, even defiance of the
powers which be. People of old wavered between thinking arts to
be the gift of the gods and to be an invasion of their prerogatives.
Both versions testify to the sense of something extraordinary in
the arts, something either superhuman or unnatural. The souls
who have predicted that by means of the arts man might establish a kingdom of order, justice and beauty through mastery of
nature's energies and laws have been few and little heeded.

Men have been glad enough to enjoy the fruits of such arts as they possess, and in recent centuries have increasingly devoted themselves to their multiplication. But this effort has been conjoined with a profound distrust of the arts as a method of dealing with the serious perils of life. Doubt as to the truth of this statement will be dispelled if one considers the disesteem in which the idea of practice has been held. Philosophers have celebrated the method of change in personal ideas, and religious teachers that of change in the affections of the heart. These conversions have been prized on their own account, and only incidentally because of a change in action which would ensue. The latter has been esteemed as an evidence of the change in thought and sentiment, not as a method of transforming the scene of life. The places in which the use of the arts has effected actual objective transformation have been regarded as inferior, if not base, and the activities connected with them as menial. The disparagement attending the idea of the material has seized upon them. The honorable quality associated with the idea of the "spiritual" has been reserved for change in inner attitudes.

The depreciation of action, of doing and making, has been cultivated by philosophers. But while philosophers have perpetuated the derogation by formulating and justifying it, they did not originate it. They glorified their own office without doubt in placing theory so much above practice. But independently of their attitude, many things conspired to the same effect. Work has been onerous, toilsome, associated with a primeval curse. It has been done under compulsion and the pressure of necessity, while intellectual activity is associated with leisure. On account of the unpleasantness of practical activity, as much of it as possible has been put upon slaves and serfs. Thus the social dishonor in which this class was held was extended to the work they do. There is also the age-long association of knowing and thinking with immaterial and spiritual principles, and of the arts, of all practical activity in doing and making, with matter. For work is done with the body, by means of mechanical appliances and is directed upon material things. The disrepute which has attended the thought of material things in comparison with immaterial thought has been transferred to everything associated with practice.

One might continue in this strain. The natural history of conceptions about work and the arts if it were traced through a succession of peoples and cultures would be instructive. But all that is needed for our purpose is to raise the question: Why this invidious discrimination? A very little reflection shows that the suggestions which have been offered by way of explanation themselves need to be explained. Ideas derived from social castes and emotional revulsions are hardly reasons to be offered in justification of a belief, although they may have a bearing on its causation. Contempt for matter and bodies and glorification of the immaterial are affairs which are not self-explanatory. And, as we shall be at some pains to show later in the discussion, the idea which connects thinking and knowing with some principle or force that is wholly separate from connection with physical things will not stand examination, especially since the whole-hearted adoption of experimental method in the natural sciences.

The questions suggested have far-reaching issues. What is the cause and the import of the sharp division between theory and practice? Why should the latter be disesteemed along with matter and the body? What has been the effect upon the various modes in which action is manifested: industry, politics, the fine arts, and upon morals conceived of as overt activity having consequences, instead of as mere inner personal attitude? How has the separation of intellect from action affected the theory of knowledge? What has been in particular the effect upon the conception and course of philosophy? What forces are at work to break down the division? What would the effect be if the divorce were annulled, and knowing and doing were brought into intrinsic connection with one another? What revisions of the traditional theory of mind, thought and knowing would be required, and what change in the idea of the office of philosophy would be demanded? What modifications would ensue in the disciplines which are concerned with the various phases of human activity?

These questions form the theme of this book, and indicate the nature of the problems to be discussed. In this opening chapter we shall consider especially some historic grounds for the elevation of knowledge above making and doing. This phase of the discussion will disclose that exaltation of pure intellect and its activity above practical affairs is fundamentally connected with the quest for a certainty which shall be absolute and unshakeable. The distinctive characteristic of practical activity, one which is so inherent that it cannot be eliminated, is the uncertainty which attends it. Of it we are compelled to say: Act, but act at your peril. Judgment and belief regarding actions to be performed can never attain more than a precarious probability. Through thought, however, it has seemed that men might escape from the perils of uncertainty.

Practical activity deals with individualized and unique situations which are never exactly duplicable and about which, accordingly, no complete assurance is possible. All activity, moreover, involves change. The intellect, however, according to the traditional doctrine, may grasp universal Being, and Being which is universal is fixed and immutable. Wherever there is practical activity we human beings are involved as partakers in the issue. All the fear, disesteem and lack of confidence which gather about the thought of ourselves, cluster also about the thought of the actions in which we are partners. Man's distrust of himself has caused him to desire to get beyond and above himself; in pure knowledge he has thought he could attain this self-transcendence.

There is no need to expatiate upon the risk which attends overt action. The burden of proverbs and wise saws is that the best laid plans of men as of mice gang agley. Fortune rather than our own intent and act determines eventual success and failure. The pathos of unfulfilled expectation, the tragedy of defeated purpose and ideals, the catastrophes of accident, are the commonplaces of all comment on the human scene. We survey conditions, make the wisest choice we can; we act, and we must trust the rest to fate, fortune or providence. Moralists tell us to look to the end when we act and then inform us that the end is always uncertain. Judging, planning, choice, no matter how thoroughly conducted, and action no matter how prudently executed, never are the sole determinants of any outcome. Alien and indifferent natural forces, unforeseeable conditions enter in and have a decisive voice. The more important the issue, the greater is their say as to the ulterior event.

Hence men have longed to find a realm in which there is an activity which is not overt and which has no external consequences. "Safety first" has played a large role in effecting a preference for knowing over doing and making. With those to whom the process of pure thinking is congenial and who have the leisure and the aptitude to pursue their preference, the happiness attending knowing is unalloyed; it is not entangled in the risks which overt action cannot escape. Thought has been alleged to be a purely inner activity, intrinsic to mind alone; and according to traditional classic doctrine, "mind" is complete and self-sufficient in itself. Overt action may follow upon its operations but in an external way, a way not intrinsic to its completion. Since rational activity is complete within itself it needs no external manifestation. Failure and frustration are attributed to the accidents of an alien, intractable and inferior realm of existence. The outer lot of thought is cast in a world external to it, but one which in no way injures the supremacy and completeness of thought and knowledge in their intrinsic natures.

Thus the arts by which man attains such practical security as is possible of achievement are looked down upon. The security they provide is relative, ever incomplete, at the risk of untoward circumstance. The multiplication of arts may even be bemoaned as a source of new dangers. Each of them demands its own measures of protection. Each one in its operation brings with it new and unexpected consequences having perils for which we are not prepared. The quest for certainty is a quest for a peace which is assured, an object which is unqualified by risk and the shadow of fear which action casts. For it is not uncertainty *per se* which men dislike, but the fact that uncertainty involves us in peril of evils. Uncertainty that affected only the detail of consequences to be experienced provided they had a warrant of being enjoyable would have no sting. It would bring the zest of adventure and the spice of variety. Quest for complete certainty can be fulfilled in pure knowing alone. Such is the verdict of our most enduring philosophic tradition.

While the tradition has, as we shall see later, found its way into all themes and subjects, and determines the form of current problems and conclusions regarding mind and knowledge, it may be doubted whether if we were suddenly released from the burden of tradition, we should, on the basis of present experience take the disparaging view of practice and the exalted view of knowledge apart from action which tradition dictates. For man, in spite of the new perils in which the machinery of his new arts of production and transportation have involved him, has learned to play with sources of danger. He even seeks them out, weary of the routine of a too sheltered life. The enormous change taking place in the position of women is itself, for example, a

commentary on a change of attitude toward the value of protection as an end in itself. We have attained, at least subconsciously,
a certain feeling of confidence; a feeling that control of the main
conditions of fortune is to an appreciable degree passing into our
own hands. We live surrounded with the protection of thousands
of arts and we have devised schemes of insurance which mitigate
and distribute the evils which accrue. Barring the fears which
war leaves in its train, it is perhaps a safe speculation that if contemporary western man were completely deprived of all the old
beliefs about knowledge and action he would assume, with a fair
degree of confidence, that it lies within his power to achieve a
reasonable degree of security in life.

This suggestion is speculative. Acceptance of it is not needed
by the argument. It has its value as an indication of the earlier
conditions in which a felt need for assurance was the dominant
emotion. For primitive men had none of the elaborate arts of
protection and use which we now enjoy and no confidence in his
own powers when they were reinforced by appliances of art. He
lived under conditions in which he was extraordinarily exposed
to peril, and at the same time he was without the means of defense which are to-day matters of course. Most of our simplest
tools and utensils did not exist; there was no accurate foresight;
men faced the forces of nature in a state of nakedness which was
more than physical; save under unusually benign conditions he
was beset with dangers that knew no remission. In consequence,
mystery attended experiences of good and evil; they could not be
traced to their natural causes and they seemed to be the dispensations, the gifts and the inflictions, of powers beyond possibility
of control. The precarious crises of birth, puberty, illness, death,
war, famine, plague, the uncertainties of the hunt, the vicissitudes of climate and the great seasonal changes, kept imagination occupied with the uncertain. Any scene or object that was
implicated in any conspicuous tragedy or triumph, in no matter
how accidental a way, got a peculiar significance. It was seized
upon as a harbinger of good or as an omen of evil. Accordingly,
some things were cherished as means of encompassing safety just
as a good artisan to-day looks after his tools; others were feared
and shunned because of their potencies for harm.

As a drowning man is said to grasp at a straw, so men who
lacked the instruments and skills developed in later days, snatched

at whatever, by any stretch of imagination, could be regarded as a source of help in time of trouble. The attention, interest and care which now go to acquiring skill in the use of appliances and to the invention of means for better service of ends, were devoted to noting omens, making irrelevant prognostications, performing ritualistic ceremonies and manipulating objects possessed of magical power over natural events. In such an atmosphere primitive religion was born and fostered. Rather this atmosphere *was* the religious disposition.

Search for alliance with means which might promote prosperity and which would afford defense against hostile powers was constant. While this attitude was most marked in connection with the recurrent crises of life, yet the boundary line between these crucial affairs with their extraordinary risks and everyday acts was shadowy. The acts that related to commonplace things and everyday occupations were usually accompanied, for good measure of security, by ritual acts. The making of a weapon, the molding of a bowl, the weaving of a mat, the sowing of seed, the reaping of a harvest, required acts different in kind to the technical skills employed. These other acts had a special solemnity and were thought necessary in order to ensure the success of the practical operations used.

While it is difficult to avoid the use of the word supernatural, we must avoid the meaning the word has for us. As long as there was no defined area of the *natural*, that which is over and beyond the natural can have no significance. The distinction, as anthropological students have pointed out, was between ordinary and extraordinary; between the prosaic, usual run of events and the crucial incident or irruption which determined the direction which the average and expected course of events took. But the two realms were in no way sharply demarcated from each other. There was a no-man's land, a vague territory, in which they overlapped. At any moment the extraordinary might invade the commonplace and either wreck it or clothe it with some surprising glory. The use of ordinary things under critical conditions was fraught with inexplicable potentialities of good and evil.

The two dominant conceptions, cultural categories one might call them, which grew and flourished under such circumstances were those of the holy and the fortunate, with their opposites, the profane and the unlucky. As with the idea of the supernatural, meanings are not to be assigned on the basis of present usage. Everything which was charged with some extraordinary potency for benefit or injury was holy; holiness meant necessity for being approached with ceremonial scruples. The holy thing, whether place, object, person or ritual appliance, has its sinister face; "to be handled with care" is written upon it. From it there issues the command: *Noli me tangere.* Tabus, a whole set of prohibitions and injunctions, gather about it. It is capable of transmitting its mysterious potency to other things. To secure the favor of the holy is to be on the road to success, while any conspicuous success is proof of the favor of some overshadowing power—a fact which politicians of all ages have known how to utilize. Because of its surcharge of power, ambivalent in quality, the holy has to be approached not only with scruples but in an attitude of subjection. There are rites of purification, humiliation, fasting and prayer which are preconditions of securing its favor.

The holy is the bearer of blessing or fortune. But a difference early developed between the ideas of the holy and the lucky, because of the different dispositions in which each was to be approached. A lucky object is something to be used. It is to be manipulated rather than approached with awe. It calls for incantations, spells, divinations rather than for supplication and humiliation. Moreover, the lucky thing tends to be a concrete and tangible object, while the holy one is not usually definitely localized; it is the more potent in the degree in which its habitation and form are vague. The lucky object is subject to pressure, at a pinch to coercion, to scolding and punishment. It might be discarded if it failed to bring luck. There developed a certain element of mastery in its use, in distinction from the dependence and subjection which remained the proper attitude toward the holy. Thus there was a kind of rhythm of domination and submission, of imprecation and supplication, of utilization and communion.

Such statements give, of course, a one-sided picture. Men at all times have gone about many things in a matter-of-fact way and have had their daily enjoyments. Even in the ceremonies of which we have spoken there entered the ordinary love of the dramatic as well as the desire for repetition, once routine is established. Primitive man early developed some tools and some modes of skill. With them went prosaic knowledge of the properties of ordinary things. But these beliefs were surrounded by others of an imaginative and emotional type, and were more or less submerged in the latter. Moreover, prestige attached to the latter. Just because some beliefs were matter-of-fact they did not have the weight and authority that belong to those about the extraordinary and unaccountable. We find the same phenomenon repeated to-day wherever religious beliefs have marked vitality.

Prosaic beliefs about verifiable facts, beliefs backed up by evidence of the senses and by useful fruits, had little glamour and prestige compared with the vogue of objects of rite and ceremony. Hence the things forming their subject-matter were felt to be lower in rank. Familiarity breeds a sense of equality if not of contempt. We deem ourselves on a par with things we daily administer. It is a truism to say that objects regarded with awe have perforce a superior status. Herein is the source of the fundamental dualism of human attention and regard. The distinction between the two attitudes of everyday control and dependence on something superior was finally generalized intellectually. It took effect in the conception of two distinct realms. The inferior was that in which man could foresee and in which he had instruments and arts by which he might expect a reasonable degree of control. The superior was that of occurrences so uncontrollable that they testified to the presence and operation of powers beyond the scope of everyday and mundane things.

The philosophical tradition regarding knowledge and practice, the immaterial or spiritual and the material, was not original and primitive. It had for its background the state of culture which has been sketched. It developed in a social atmosphere in which the division of the ordinary and extraordinary was domesticated. Philosophy reflected upon it and gave it a rational formulation and justification. The bodies of information that corresponded to the everyday arts, the store of matter-of-fact knowledge, were things men knew because of what they did. They were products and promises of utilities. They shared in the relatively low esteem belonging to such things in comparison with the extraordinary and divine. Philosophy inherited the realm with which religion had been concerned. Its mode of knowing was different from that accompanying the empirical arts, just because it dealt with a realm of higher Being. It breathed an air purer than that in which exist the making and doing that relate to livelihood, just as the activities which took the form of rites and ceremonies were nobler and nearer the divine than those spent in toil.

The change from religion to philosophy was so great in form that their identity as to content is easily lost from view. The form ceases to be that of the story told in imaginative and emotional style, and becomes that of rational discourse observing the canons of logic. It is well known that that portion of Aristotle's system which later generations have called metaphysics he called First Philosophy. It is possible to quote from him sentences descriptive of "First Philosophy" which make it seem that the philosophic enterprise is a coldly rational one, objective and analytic. Thus he says it is the most comprehensive of all branches of knowledge because it has for its subject-matter definition of the traits which belong to all forms of Being whatsoever, however much they may differ from one another in detail.

But when these passages are placed in the context they had in Aristotle's own mind, it is clear that the comprehensiveness and universality of first philosophy are not of a strictly analytic sort. They mark a distinction with respect to grade of value and title to reverence. For he explicitly identifies his first philosophy—or metaphysics—with theology; he says it is higher than other sciences. For these deal with generation and production, while its subject-matter permits of demonstrative, that is necessary, truth; and its objects are divine and such as are meet for God to occupy himself with. Again, he says that the objects of philosophy are such as are the causes of as much of the divine as is manifest to us, and that if the divine is anywhere present, it is present in things of the sort with which philosophy deals. The supremacy of worth and dignity of these objects are also made clear in the statement that the Being with which philosophy is occupied is primary, eternal and self-sufficient, because its nature is the Good, so that the Good is among the first principles which are philosophy's subject-matter:—yet not, it must be understood, the good in the sense in which it has meaning and standing in human life but the inherently and eternally perfect, that which is complete and self-sufficient.

Aristotle tells us that from remote antiquity tradition has handed down the idea, in story form, that the heavenly bodies are gods, and that the divine encompasses the entire natural world. This core of truth, he goes on to say in effect, was embroidered with myths for the benefit of the masses, for reasons of expediency, namely, the preservation of social institutions. The negative work of philosophy was then to strip away these imaginative accretions. From the standpoint of popular belief this was its chief work, and it was a destructive one. The masses only felt that their religion was attacked. But the enduring contribution was positive. The belief that the divine encompasses the world was detached from its mythical context and made the basis of philosophy, and it became also the foundation of physical science—as is suggested by the remark that the heavenly bodies are gods. Telling the story of the universe in the form of rational discourse instead of emotionalized imagination signified the discovery of logic as a rational science. Conformity on the part of supreme reality to the requirements of logic conferred upon its constitutive objects necessary and immutable characteristics. Pure contemplation of these forms was man's highest and most divine bliss, a communion with unchangeable truth.

The geometry of Euclid doubtless gave the clew to logic as the instrument of translation of what was sound in opinion into the forms of rational discourse. Geometry seemed to reveal the possibility of a science which owed nothing to observation and sense beyond mere exemplification in figures or diagrams. It seemed to disclose a world of ideal (or non-sensible) forms which were connected with one another by eternal and necessary relations which reason alone could trace. This discovery was generalized by philosophy into the doctrine of a realm of fixed Being which, when grasped by thought, formed a complete system of immutable and necessary truth.

If one looks at the foundations of the philosophies of Plato and Aristotle as an anthropologist looks at his material, that is, as cultural subject-matter, it is clear that these philosophies were systematizations in rational form of the content of Greek religious and artistic beliefs. The systematization involved a purification. Logic provided the patterns to which ultimately real objects had to conform, while physical science was possible in the degree in which the natural world, even in its mutabilities, exhibited exemplification of ultimate immutable rational objects. Thus, along with the elimination of myths and grosser superstitions, there were set up the ideals of science and of a life of reason. Ends which could justify themselves to reason were to take the place of custom as the guide of conduct. These two ideals form a permanent contribution to western civilization.

But with all our gratitude for these enduring gifts, we cannot forget the conditions which attended them. For they brought with them the idea of a higher realm of fixed reality of which alone true science is possible and of an inferior world of changing things with which experience and practical matters are concerned. They glorified the invariant at the expense of change, it being evident that all practical activity falls within the realm of change. It bequeathed the notion, which has ruled philosophy ever since the time of the Greeks, that the office of knowledge is to uncover the antecedently real, rather than, as is the case with our practical judgments, to gain the kind of understanding which is necessary to deal with problems as they arise.

In fixing this conception of knowledge it established also, as far as philosophies of the classic type are concerned, the special task of philosophic inquiry. As a form of knowledge it is concerned with the disclosure of the Real in itself, of Being in and of itself. It is differentiated from other modes of knowing by its preoccupation with a higher and more ultimate form of Being than that with which the sciences of nature are concerned. As far as it occupied itself at all with human conduct, it was to superimpose upon acts ends said to flow from the nature of reason. It thus diverted thought from inquiring into the purposes which experience of actual conditions suggest and from concrete means of their actualization. It translated into a rational form the doctrine of escape from the vicissitudes of existence by means of measures which do not demand an active coping with conditions. For deliverance by means of rites and cults, it substituted deliverance through reason. This deliverance was an intellectual, a theoretical affair, constituted by a knowledge to be attained apart from practical activity.

The realms of knowledge and action were each divided into two regions. It is not to be inferred that Greek philosophy separated activity from knowing. It connected them. But it distinguished activity from action—that is, from making and doing. Rational and necessary knowledge was treated, as in the celebrations of it by Aristotle, as an ultimate, self-sufficient and self-enclosed form of self-originated and self-conducted activity. It was ideal and eternal, independent of change and hence of the world in which men act and live, the world we experience perceptibly and practically. "Pure activity" was sharply marked off from practical action. The latter, whether in the industrial or the fine arts, in morals or in politics, was concerned with an inferior region of Being in which change rules, and which accordingly has Being only by courtesy, for it manifests deficiency of sure footing in Being by the very fact of change. It is infected with *non*-being.

On the side of knowledge, the division carried with it a difference between knowledge, in its full sense, and belief. The former is demonstrative, necessary—that is, sure. Belief on the contrary is only opinion; in its uncertainty and mere probability, it relates to the world of change as knowledge corresponds to the realm of true reality. This fact brings the discussion around once more to our special theme as far as it affects the conception of the office and nature of philosophy. That man has two modes, two dimensions, of belief, cannot be doubted. He has beliefs about actual existences and the course of events, and he has beliefs about ends to be striven for, policies to be adopted, goods to be attained and evils to be averted. The most urgent of all practical problems concerns the connection the subject-matter of these two kinds of beliefs sustain to each other. How shall our most authentic and dependable cognitive beliefs be used to regulate our practical beliefs? How shall the latter serve to organize and integrate our intellectual beliefs?

There is a genuine possibility that the true problem of philosophy is connected with precisely this type of question. Man has beliefs which scientific inquiry vouchsafes, beliefs about the actual structure and processes of things; and he also has beliefs about the values which should regulate his conduct. The question of how these two ways of believing may most effectively and fruitfully interact with one another is the most general and significant of all the problems which life presents to us. Some reasoned discipline, one obviously other than any science, should deal with this issue. Thus there is supplied one way of conceiving of the function of philosophy. But from this mode of defining philosophy we are estopped by the chief philosophical tradition. For according to it the realms of knowledge and of practical action have no inherent connection with each other. Here then is the focus to which the various elements in our discussion converge. We may then profitably recapitulate. The realm of the practical is the region of change, and change is always contingent; it has in it an element of chance that cannot be eliminated. If a thing changes, its alteration is convincing evidence of its lack of true or complete Being. What *is*, in the full and pregnant sense of the word, is always, eternally. It is self-contradictory for that which *is* to alter. If it had no defect or imperfection in it how could it change? That which becomes merely *comes* to be, never truly is. It is infected with non-being; with privation of Being in the perfect sense. The world of generation is the world of decay and destruction. Wherever one thing comes into being something else passes out of being.

Thus the depreciation of practice was given a philosophic, an ontological, justification. Practical action, as distinct from self-revolving rational self-activity, belongs in the realm of generation and decay, a realm inferior in value as in Being. In form, the quest for absolute certainty has reached its goal. Because ultimate Being or reality is fixed, permanent, admitting of no change or variation, it may be grasped by rational intuition and set forth in rational, that is, universal and necessary, demonstration. I do not doubt that there was a feeling before the rise of philosophy that the unalterably fixed and the absolutely certain are one, or that change is the source from which comes all our uncertainties and woes. But in philosophy this inchoate feeling was definitely formulated. It was asserted on grounds held to be as demonstrably necessary as are the conclusions of geometry and logic. Thus the predisposition of philosophy toward the universal, invariant and eternal was fixed. It remains the common possession of the entire classic philosophic tradition.

All parts of the scheme hang together. True Being or Reality is complete; in being complete, it is perfect, divine, immutable, the "unmoved mover." Then there are things that change, that come and go, that are generated and perish, because of lack of the stability which participation in ultimate Being alone confers. These changes, however, have form and character and are knowable in the degree in which they tend toward an end which is the fulfillment and completion of the changes in question. Their instability is not absolute but is marked by aspiration toward a goal.

The perfect and complete is rational thought, the ultimate "end" or terminus of all natural movement. That which changes, which becomes and passes away, *is* material; change *defines* the physical. At most and best, it is a potentiality of reaching a stable and fixed end. To these two realms belong two sorts of knowledge. One of them is alone knowledge in the full sense, *science*. This has a rational, necessary and unchanging form. It is *certain*. The other, dealing with change, is belief or opinion; empirical and particular; it is contingent, a matter of probability, not of certainty. The most it can assert is that things are so and so "upon the whole," usually. Corresponding to the division in Being and in knowledge is that in activities. Pure activity is rational; it is theoretical, in the sense in which theory is apart from practical action. Then there is action in doing and making, occupied with the needs and defects of the lower realm of change in which, in his physical nature, man is implicated.

Although this Greek formulation was made long ago and much of it is now strange in its specific terms, certain features of it are as relevant to present thought as they were significant in their original formulation. For in spite of the great, the enormous changes in the subject-matter and method of the sciences and the tremendous expansion of practical activities by means of arts and technologies, the main tradition of western culture has retained intact this framework of ideas. Perfect certainty is what man wants. It cannot be found by practical doing or making; these take effect in an uncertain future, and involve peril, the risk of misadventure, frustration and failure. Knowledge, on the other hand, is thought to be concerned with a region of being which is fixed in itself. Being eternal and unalterable, human knowing is not to make any difference in it. It can be approached through the medium of the apprehensions and demonstrations of thought, or by some other organ of mind, which does nothing to the real, except just to know it.

There is involved in these doctrines a whole system of philosophical conclusions. The first and foremost is that there is complete correspondence between knowledge in its true meaning and what is real. What is known, what is true for cognition, is what is real in being. The objects of knowledge form the standards of measures of the reality of all other objects of experience. Are the objects of the affections, of desire, effort, choice, that is to say everything to which we attach value, real? Yes, if they can be warranted by knowledge; if we can *know objects* having these value properties, we are justified in thinking them real. But as objects of desire and purpose they have no sure place in Being until they are approached and validated through knowledge. The idea is so familiar that we overlook the unexpressed premise upon which it rests, namely that only the completely fixed and unchanging can be real. The quest for certitude has determined our basic metaphysics.

Secondly, the theory of knowledge has its basic premises fixed by the same doctrine. For knowledge to be certain must relate to that which has antecedent existence or essential being. There are certain things which are alone inherently the proper objects of knowledge and science. Things in the production of which we participate we cannot know in the true sense of the word, for such things succeed instead of preceding our action. What concerns action forms the realm of mere guesswork and probability, as distinct from the warrant of rational assurance which is the ideal of true knowledge. We are so accustomed to the separation of knowledge from doing and making that we fail to recognize how it controls our conceptions of mind, of consciousness and of reflective inquiry. For as relates to genuine knowledge, these must all be defined, on the basis of the premise, so as not to admit of the presence of any overt action that modifies conditions having prior and independent existence.

Special theories of knowledge differ enormously from one another. Their quarrels with one another fill the air. The din thus created makes us deaf to the way in which they say one thing in common. The controversies are familiar. Some theories ascribe the ultimate test of knowledge to impressions passively received, forced upon us whether we will or no. Others ascribe the guarantee of knowledge to synthetic activity of the intellect. Idealistic theories hold that mind and the object known are ultimately one; realistic doctrines reduce knowledge to awareness of what exists independently, and so on. But they all make one common assumption. They all hold that the operation of inquiry excludes any element of practical activity that enters into the construction of the object known. Strangely enough this is as true of idealism as of realism, of theories of synthetic activity as of those of passive receptivity. For according to them "mind" constructs the known object not in any observable way, or by means of practical overt acts having a temporal quality, but by some occult internal operation.

The common essence of all these theories, in short, is that what is known is antecedent to the mental act of observation and inquiry, and is totally unaffected by these acts; otherwise it would not be fixed and unchangeable. This negative condition, that the processes of search, investigation, reflection, involved in knowledge relate to something having prior being, fixes once for all the main characters attributed to mind, and to the organs of knowing. They *must* be outside what is known, so as not to interact in any way with the object to be known. If the word "interaction" be used, it cannot denote that overt production of change it signifies in its ordinary and practical use.

The theory of knowing is modeled after what was supposed to take place in the act of vision. The object refracts light to the eye and is seen; it makes a difference to the eye and to the person having an optical apparatus, but none to the thing seen. The real object is the object so fixed in its regal aloofness that it is a king to any beholding mind that may gaze upon it. A spectator theory of knowledge is the inevitable outcome. There have been theories which hold that mental activity intervenes, but they have retained the old premise. They have therefore concluded that it is impossible to know reality. Since mind intervenes, we know, according to them, only some modified semblance of the real object, some "appearance." It would be hard to find a more thoroughgoing confirmation than this conclusion provides of the complete hold possessed by the belief that the object of knowledge is a reality fixed and complete in itself, in isolation from an act of inquiry which has in it any element of production of change.

All of these notions about certainty and the fixed, about the nature of the real world, about the nature of the mind and its organs of knowing, are completely bound up with one another, and their consequences ramify into practically all important ideas entertained upon any philosophic question. They all flow—such is my basic thesis—from the separation (set up in the interest of the quest for absolute certainty) between theory and practice, knowledge and action. Consequently the latter problem cannot be attacked in isolation, by itself. It is too thoroughly entangled with fundamental beliefs and ideas in all sorts of fields.

In later chapters the theme will, therefore, be approached in relation to each of the above-mentioned points. We shall first take up the effect of the traditional separation upon the conception of the nature of philosophy, especially in connection with the question of the secure place of values in existence. We shall then pass on to an account of the way in which modern philosophies have been dominated by the problem of reconciling the conclusions of natural science with the objective validity of the values by which men live and regulate their conduct:—a problem which would have no existence were it not for the prior uncritical acceptance of the traditional notion that knowledge has a monopolistic claim to access to reality. The discussion will then take up various phases of the development of actual knowing as exemplified in scientific procedure, so as to show, by an analysis of experimental inquiry in its various phases, how completely the traditional assumptions, mentioned above, have been abandoned in concrete scientific procedure. For science in becoming experimental has itself become a mode of directed practical doing. There will then follow a brief statement of the effect of the destruction of the barriers which have divided theory and practice upon reconstruction of the basic ideas about mind and thought, and upon the solution of a number of long-standing problems as to the theory of knowledge. The consequences of substituting a search for security by practical means in place of quest of absolute certainty by cognitive means will then be considered in its bearing upon the problem of our judgments regarding the values which control conduct, especially its social phases.

2.   Philosophy's Search for the Immutable

In the previous chapter, we noted incidentally the distinction made in the classic tradition between knowledge and belief, or, as Locke put it, between knowledge and judgment. According to this distinction the certain and knowledge are coextensive. Disputes exist, but they are whether sensation or reason affords the basis of certainty; or whether existence or essence is its object. In contrast with this identification, the very word "belief" is eloquent on the topic of certainty. We *believe* in the absence of knowledge or complete assurance. Hence the quest for certainty has always been an effort to transcend belief. Now since, as we have already noted, all matters of practical action involve an element of uncertainty, we can ascend from belief to knowledge only by isolating the latter from practical doing and making.

In this chapter we are especially concerned with the effect of the ideal of certainty as something superior to belief upon the conception of the nature and function of philosophy. Greek thinkers saw clearly—and logically—that experience cannot furnish us, as respects cognition of existence, with anything more than contingent probability. Experience cannot deliver to us necessary truths; truths completely demonstrated by reason. Its conclusions are particular, not universal. Not being "exact" they come short of "science." Thus there arose the distinction between rational truths or, in modern terminology, truths relating to the relation of ideas, and "truths" about matters of existence, empirically ascertained. Thus not merely the arts of practice, industrial and social, were stamped matters of belief rather than of knowledge, but also all those sciences which are matters of inductive inference from observation.

One might indulge in the reflection that they are none the worse for all that, especially since the natural sciences have developed a technique for achieving a high degree of probability and for measuring, within assignable limits, the amount of probability which attaches in particular cases to conclusions. But historically the matter is not so simple as to permit of this retort. For empirical or observational sciences were placed in invidious contrast to rational sciences which dealt with eternal and universal objects and which therefore were possessed of necessary truth. Consequently all observational sciences as far as their material could not be subsumed under forms and principles supplied by rational science shared in the depreciatory view held about practical affairs. They are relatively low, secular and profane compared with the perfect realities of rational science.

And here is a justification for going back to something as remote in time as Greek philosophy. The whole classic tradition down to our day has continued to hold a slighting view of experience as such, and to hold up as the proper goal and ideal of true knowledge realities which even if they are located in empirical things cannot be known by experimental methods. The logical consequence for philosophy itself is evident. Upon the side of method, it has been compelled to claim for itself the possession of a method issuing from reason itself, and having the warrant of reason, independently of experience. As long as the view obtained that nature itself is truly known by the same rational method, the consequences—at least those which were evident— were not serious. There was no break between philosophy and genuine science—or what was conceived to be such. In fact, there was not even a distinction; there were simply various branches of philosophy, metaphysical, logical, natural, moral, etc., in a descending scale of demonstrative certainty. Since, according to the theory, the subject-matter of the lower sciences was inherently of a different character from that of true knowledge, there was no ground for rational dissatisfaction with the lower degree of knowledge called belief. Inferior knowledge or belief corresponded to the inferior state of subject-matter.

The scientific revolution of the seventeenth century effected a great modification. Science itself through the aid of mathematics carried the scheme of demonstrative knowledge over to natural objects. The "laws" of the natural world had that fixed character which in the older scheme had belonged only to rational and ideal forms. A mathematical science of nature couched in mechanistic terms claimed to be the only sound natural philosophy. Hence the older philosophies lost alliance with natural knowledge and the support that had been given to philosophy by them. Philosophy in maintaining its claim to be a superior form of knowledge was compelled to take an invidious and so to say malicious attitude toward the conclusions of natural science. The framework of the old tradition had in the meantime become embedded in Christian theology, and through religious teaching was made a part of the inherited culture of those innocent of any technical philosophy. Consequently, the rivalry between philosophy and the new science, with respect to the claim to know reality, was converted in effect into a rivalry between the spiritual values guaranteed by the older philosophic tradition and the conclusions of natural knowledge. The more science advanced the more it seemed to encroach upon the special province of the territory over which philosophy had claimed jurisdiction. Thus philosophy in its classic form became a species of apologetic justification for belief in an ultimate reality in which the values which should regulate life and control conduct are securely enstated.

There are undoubted disadvantages in the historic manner of approach to the problem which has been followed. It may readily be thought either that the Greek formulation which has been emphasized has no especial pertinency with respect to modern thought and especially to contemporary philosophy; or that no philosophical statement is of any great importance for the mass of non-philosophic persons. Those interested in philosophy may object that the criticisms passed are directed if not at a man of straw at least to positions that have long since lost their actuality. Those not friendly to any form of philosophy may inquire what import they have for any except professed philosophers.

The first type of objection will be dealt with somewhat *in extenso* in the succeeding chapter, in which I shall try to show how modern philosophies, in spite of their great diversity, have been concerned with problems of adjustment of the conclusions of modern science to the chief religious and moral tradition of the western world; together with the way in which these problems are connected with retention of the conception of the relation of knowledge to reality formulated in Greek thought. At the point in the discussion now reached, it suffices to point out that, in spite of great changes in detail, the notion of a separation be-

tween knowledge and action, theory and practice, has been perpetuated, and that the beliefs connected with action are taken to
be uncertain and inferior in value compared with those inherently connected with objects of knowledge, so that the former
are securely established only as they derived from the latter. Not
the specific content of Greek thought is pertinent to present
problems, but its insistence that security is measured by certainty
of knowledge, while the latter is measured by adhesion to fixed
and immutable objects, which therefore are independent of what
men do in practical activity.

The other objection is of a different sort. It comes from those
who feel that not merely Greek philosophy but philosophy in
any form is remote from all significant human concern. It is willing to admit or rather assert that it is presumptuous for philosophy to lay claim to knowledge of a higher order than that given
by natural science, but it also holds that this is no great matter in
any case except for professional philosophers.

There would be force in this latter objection were it not that
those who make it hold for the most part the same philosophy of
certainty and its proper object that is held by philosophers, save
in an inchoate form. They are not interested in the notion that
philosophic thought is a special means of attaining this object
and the certainty it affords, but they are far from holding, either
explicitly or implicitly, that the arts of intelligently directed action are the means by which security of values are to be attained.
With respect to certain ends and goods they accept this idea. But
in thinking of these ends and values as material, as related to
health, wealth, control of conditions for the sake of an inferior
order of consequences, they retain the same division between a
higher reality and a lower that is formulated in classic philosophy. They may be innocent of the vocabulary that speaks of reason, necessary truth, the universal, things in themselves and appearances. But they incline to believe that there is some other
road than that of action, directed by knowledge, to achieve ultimate security of higher ideals and purposes. They think of practical action as necessary for practical utilities, but they mark off
practical utilities from spiritual and ideal values. Philosophy did
not originate the underlying division. It only gave intellectual
formulation and justification to ideas that were operative in
men's minds generally. And the elements of these ideas are as ac-

tive in present culture as they ever were in the past. Indeed, through the diffusion of religious doctrines, the idea that ultimate values are a matter of special revelation and are to be embodied in life by special means radically different from the arts of action that deal with lower and lesser ends has been accentuated in the popular mind.

Here is the point which is of general human import instead of concern merely to professional philosophers. What about the security of values, of the things which are admirable, honorable, to be approved of and striven for? It is probably in consequence of the derogatory view held of practice that the question of the secure place of values in human experience is so seldom raised in connection with the problem of the relation of knowledge and practice. But upon any view concerning the status of action, the scope of the latter cannot be restricted to self-seeking acts, nor to those of a prudential aspect, nor in general to things of expediency and what are often termed "utilitarian" affairs. The maintenance and diffusion of intellectual values, of moral excellencies, the esthetically admirable, as well as the maintenance of order and decorum in human relations are dependent upon what men do.

Whether because of the emphasis of traditional religion upon salvation of the personal soul or for some other reason, there is a tendency to restrict the ultimate scope of morals to the reflex effect of conduct on one's self. Even utilitarianism, with all its seeming independence of traditional theology and its emphasis upon the general good as the criterion for judging conduct, insisted in its hedonistic psychology upon private pleasure as the motive for action. The idea that the stable and expanding institution of all things that make life worth while throughout all human relationships is the real object of *all* intelligent conduct is depressed from view by the current conception of morals as a special kind of action chiefly concerned with either the virtues or the enjoyments of individuals in their personal capacities. In changed form, we still retain the notion of a division of activity into two kinds having very different worths. The result is the depreciated meaning that has come to be attached to the very meaning of the "practical" and the useful. Instead of being extended to cover all forms of action by means of which all the values of life are extended and rendered more secure, including the diffusion of the fine arts and the cultivation of taste, the processes of education and all activities which are concerned with rendering human relationships more significant and worthy, the meaning of "practical" is limited to matters of ease, comfort, riches, bodily security and police order, possibly health, etc., things which in their isolation from other goods can only lay claim to restricted and narrow value. In consequence, these subjects are handed over to technical sciences and arts; they are no concern of "higher" interests which feel that no matter what happens to inferior goods in the vicissitudes of natural existence, the highest values are immutable characters of the ultimately real.

Our depreciatory attitude toward "practice" would be modified if we habitually thought of it in its most liberal sense, and if we surrendered our customary dualism between two separate kinds of value, one intrinsically higher and one inherently lower. We should regard practice as the only means (other than accident) by which whatever is judged to be honorable, admirable, approvable can be kept in concrete experienceable existence. In this connection the entire import of "morals" would be transformed. How much of the tendency to ignore permanent objective consequences in differences made in natural and social relations; and how much of the emphasis upon personal and internal motives and dispositions irrespective of what they objectively produce and sustain are products of the habitual depreciation of the worth of action in comparison with forms of mental processes, of thought and sentiment, which make no objective difference in things themselves?

It would be possible to argue (and, I think, with much justice) that failure to make action central in the search for such security as is humanly possible is a survival of the impotency of men in those stages of civilization when he had few means of regulating and utilizing the conditions upon which the occurrence of consequences depend. As long as man was unable by means of the arts of practice to direct the course of events, it was natural for him to seek an emotional substitute; in the absence of actual certainty in the midst of a precarious and hazardous world, men cultivated all sorts of things that would give them the *feeling* of certainty. And it is possible that, when not carried to an illusory point, the cultivation of the feeling gave man courage and confidence and enabled him to carry the burdens of life more successfully. But one could hardly seriously contend that this fact, if it be such, is one upon which to found a reasoned philosophy.

It is to the conception of philosophy that we come back. No mode of action can, as we have insisted, give anything approaching absolute certitude; it provides insurance but no assurance. Doing is always subject to peril, to the danger of frustration. When men began to reflect philosophically it seemed to them altogether too risky to leave the place of values at the mercy of acts the results of which are never sure. This precariousness might hold as far as empirical existence, existence in the sensible and phenomenal world, is concerned; but this very uncertainty seemed to render it the more needful that ideal goods should be shown to have, by means of knowledge of the most assured type, an indefeasible and inexpugnable position in the realm of the ultimately real. So at least we may imagine men to have reasoned. And to-day many persons find a peculiar consolation in the face of the unstable and dubious presence of values in actual experience by projecting a perfect form of good into a realm of essence, if not into a heaven beyond the earthly skies, wherein their authority, if not their existence, is wholly unshakeable.

Instead of asking how far this process is of that compensatory kind with which recent psychology has made us familiar, we are inquiring into the effect upon philosophy. It will not be denied, I suppose, that the chief aim of those philosophies which I have called classical, has been to show that the realities which are the objects of the highest and most necessary knowledge are also endowed with the values which correspond to our best aspirations, admirations and approvals. That, one may say, is the very heart of all traditional philosophic idealisms. There is a pathos, having its own nobility, in philosophies which think it their proper office to give an intellectual or cognitive certification to the ontological reality of the highest values. It is difficult for men to see desire and choice set earnestly upon the good and yet being frustrated, without their imagining a realm in which the good has come completely to its own, and is identified with a Reality in which resides all ultimate power. The failure and frustration of actual life is then attributed to the fact that this world is finite and phenomenal, sensible rather than real, or to the weakness of our finite apprehension, which cannot see that the discrepancy between existence and value is merely seeming, and that a fuller vision would behold partial evil an element in complete good. Thus the office of philosophy is to project by dialectic, resting supposedly upon self-evident premises, a realm in which the object of completest cognitive certitude is also one with the object of the heart's best aspiration. The fusion of the good and the true with unity and plenitude of Being thus becomes the goal of classic philosophy.

The situation would strike us as a curious one were it not so familiar. Practical activity is dismissed to a world of low grade reality. Desire is found only where something is lacking and hence its existence is a sign of imperfection of Being. Hence one must go to passionless reason to find perfect reality and complete certitude. But nevertheless the chief philosophic interest is to prove that the essential properties of the reality that is the object of pure knowledge are precisely those characteristics which have meaning in connection with affection, desire and choice. After degrading practical affairs in order to exalt knowledge, the chief task of knowledge turns out to be to demonstrate the absolutely assured and permanent reality of the values with which practical activity is concerned! Can we fail to see the irony in a situation wherein desire and emotion are relegated to a position inferior in every way to that of knowledge, while at the same time the chief problem of that which is termed the highest and most perfect knowledge is taken to be the existence of evil—that is, of desires errant and frustrated?

The contradiction involved, however, is much more than a purely intellectual one—which if purely theoretical would be innocuously lacking in practical consequences. The thing which concerns all of us as human beings is precisely the greatest attainable security of values in concrete existence. The thought that the values which are unstable and wavering in the world in which we live are eternally secure in a higher realm (which reason demonstrates but which we cannot experience), that all the goods which are defeated here are triumphant there, may give consolation to the depressed. But it does not change the existential situation in the least. The separation that has been instituted between theory and practice, with its consequent substitution of cognitive quest for absolute assurance for practical endeavor to make the existence of good more secure in experience, has had the effect of distracting attention and diverting energy from a task whose performance would yield definite results.

The chief consideration in achieving concrete security of values lies in the perfecting of *methods* of action. Mere activity, blind striving, gets nothing forward. Regulation of conditions upon which results depend is possible only by doing, yet only by doing which has intelligent direction, which takes cognizance of conditions, observes relations of sequence, and which plans and executes in the light of this knowledge. The notion that thought, apart from action, can warrant complete certitude as to the status of supreme good, makes no contribution to the central problem of development of intelligent methods of regulation. It rather depresses and deadens effort in that direction. That is the chief indictment to be brought against the classic philosophic tradition. Its import raises the question of the relation which action sustains to knowledge in fact, and whether the quest for certainty by other means than those of intelligent action does not mark a baneful diversion of thought from its proper office. It raises the question whether mankind has not now achieved a sufficient degree of control of methods of knowing and of the arts of practical action so that a radical change in our conceptions of knowledge and practice is rendered both possible and necessary.

That knowing, as judged from the actual procedures of scientific inquiry, has completely abandoned in fact the traditional separation of knowing and doing, that the experimental procedure is one that installs doing as the heart of knowing, is a theme that will occupy our attention in later chapters. What would happen to philosophy if it wholeheartedly made a similar surrender? What would be its office if it ceased to deal with the problem of reality and knowledge at large? In effect, its function would be to facilitate the fruitful interaction of our cognitive beliefs, our beliefs resting upon the most dependable methods of inquiry, with our practical beliefs about the values, the ends and purposes, that should control human action in the things of large and liberal human import.

Such a view renounces the traditional notion that action is inherently inferior to knowledge and preference for the fixed over the changing; it involves the conviction that security attained by active control is to be more prized than certainty in theory. But it does not imply that action is higher and better than knowledge, and practice inherently superior to thought. Constant and effective interaction of knowledge and practice is something quite different from an exaltation of activity for its own sake. Action, when directed by knowledge, is method and means, not an end. The aim and end is the securer, freer and more widely shared embodiment of values in experience by means of that active control of objects which knowledge alone makes possible.[1]

From this point of view, the problem of philosophy concerns the *interaction* of our judgments about ends to be sought with knowledge of the means for achieving them. Just as in science the question of the advance of knowledge is the question of *what to do*, what experiments to perform, what apparatus to invent and use, what calculations to engage in, what branches of mathematics to employ or to perfect, so *the* problem of practice is what do we need to *know*, how shall we obtain that knowledge and how shall we apply it?

It is an easy and altogether too common a habit to confuse a personal division of labor with an isolation of function and meaning. Human beings as individuals tend to devote themselves either to the practice of knowing or to the practice of a professional, business, social or esthetic art. Each takes the other half of the circle for granted. Theorists and practitioners, however, often indulge in unseemly wrangles as to the importance of their respective tasks. Then the personal difference of callings is hypostatized and made into an intrinsic difference between knowledge and practice.

If one looks at the history of knowledge, it is plain that at the beginning men tried to know because they had to do so in order to live. In the absence of that organic guidance given by their structure to other animals, man had to find out what he was about, and he could find out only by studying the environment which constituted the means, obstacles and results of his behavior. The desire for intellectual or cognitive understanding had no

---

1. In reaction against the age-long depreciation of practice in behalf of contemplative knowledge, there is a temptation simply to turn things upside down. But the essence of pragmatic instrumentalism is to conceive of *both* knowledge and practice as means of making goods—excellencies of all kinds—secure in experienced existence.

meaning except as a means of obtaining greater security as to the issues of action. Moreover, even when after the coming of leisure some men were enabled to adopt knowing as their special calling or profession, *merely* theoretical uncertainty continues to have no meaning.

This statement will arouse protest. But the reaction against the statement will turn out when examined to be due to the fact that it is so difficult to find a case of purely intellectual uncertainty, that is one upon which nothing hangs. Perhaps as near to it as we can come is in the familiar story of the Oriental potentate who declined to attend a horse race on the ground that it was already well known to him that one horse could run faster than another. His uncertainty as to which of several horses could outspeed the others may be said to have been purely intellectual. But also in the story nothing depended from it; no curiosity was aroused; no effort was put forth to satisfy the uncertainty. In other words, he did not care; it made no difference. And it is a strict truism that no one would care about *any* exclusively theoretical uncertainty or certainty. For by definition in being *exclusively* theoretical it is one which makes no difference anywhere.

Revulsion against this proposition is a tribute to the fact that actually the intellectual and the practical are so closely bound together. Hence when we imagine we are thinking of an exclusively theoretical doubt, we smuggle in unconsciously some consequence which hangs upon it. We think of uncertainty arising in the course of an inquiry; in this case, uncertainty until it is resolved blocks the progress of the inquiry—a distinctly practical affair, since it involves conclusions and the means of producing them. If we had no desires and no purposes, then, as sheer truism, one state of things would be as good as any other. Those who have set such store by the demonstration that Absolute Being already contains in eternal safety within itself all values, have had as their interest the fact that while the demonstration would make no difference in the concrete existence of these values—unless perhaps to weaken effort to generate and sustain them—it would make a difference in their own personal attitudes—in a feeling of comfort or of release from responsibility, the consciousness of a "moral holiday" in which some philosophers have found the distinction between morals and religion.

nature "of sake self-evident"

Such considerations point to the conclusion that the ultimate ground of the quest for cognitive certainty is the need for security in the results of action. Men readily persuade themselves that they are devoted to intellectual certainty for its own sake. Actually they want it because of its bearing on safeguarding what they desire and esteem. The need for protection and prosperity in action created the need for warranting the validity of intellectual beliefs.

After a distinctively intellectual class had arisen, a class having leisure and in a large degree protected against the more serious perils which afflict the mass of humanity, its members proceeded to glorify their own office. Since no amount of pains and care in action can ensure complete certainty, certainty in knowledge was worshipped as a substitute. In minor matters, those that are relatively technical, professional, "utilitarian," men continued to resort to improving their methods of operation in order to be surer of results. But in affairs of momentous value the requisite knowledge is hard to come by and the bettering of methods is a slow process to be realized only by the cooperative endeavor of many persons. The arts to be formed and developed are social arts; an individual by himself can do little to regulate the conditions which will render important values more secure, though with shrewdness and special knowledge he can do much to further his own peculiar aims—given a fair share of luck. So because of impatience and because, as Aristotle was given to pointing out, an individual is self-sufficient in that kind of thinking which involves no action, the ideal of a cognitive certainty and truth having no connection with practice, and prized because of its lack of connection, developed. The doctrine worked out practically so as to strengthen dependence upon authority and dogma in the things of highest value, while increase of specialized knowledge was relied upon in everyday, especially economic, affairs. Just as belief that a magical ceremony will regulate the growth of seeds to full harvest stifles the tendency to investigate natural causes and their workings, so acceptance of dogmatic rules as bases of conduct in education, morals and social matters, lessens the impetus to find out about the conditions which are involved in forming intelligent plans.

It is more or less of a commonplace to speak of the crisis which has been caused by the progress of the natural sciences in the last few centuries. The crisis is due, it is asserted, to the incompatibility between the conclusions of natural science about the world in which we live and the realm of higher values, of ideal and spiritual qualities, which get no support from natural science. The new science, it is said, has stripped the world of the qualities which made it beautiful and congenial to men; has deprived nature of all aspiration towards ends, all preference for accomplishing the good, and presented nature to us as a scene of indifferent physical particles acting according to mathematical and mechanical laws.

This effect of modern science has, it is notorious, set the main problems for modern philosophy. How is science to be accepted and yet the realm of values to be conserved? This question forms the philosophic version of the popular conflict of science and religion. Instead of being troubled about the inconsistency of astronomy with the older religious beliefs about heaven and the ascension of Christ, or the differences between the geological record and the account of creation in Genesis, philosophers have been troubled by the gap in kind which exists between the fundamental principles of the natural world and the reality of the values according to which mankind is to regulate its life.

Philosophers, therefore, set to work to mediate, to find some harmony behind the apparent discord. Everybody knows that the trend of modern philosophy has been to arrive at theories regarding the nature of the universe by means of theories regarding the nature of knowledge—a procedure which reverses the apparently more judicious method of the ancients in basing their conclusions about knowledge on the nature of the universe in which knowledge occurs. The "crisis" of which we have just been speaking accounts for the reversal.

Since science has made the trouble, the cure ought to be found in an examination of the nature of knowledge, of the conditions which make science possible. If the conditions of the possibility of knowledge can be shown to be of an ideal and rational character, then, so it has been thought, the loss of an idealistic cosmology in physics can be readily borne. The physical world can be surrendered to matter and mechanism, since we are assured that matter and mechanism have their foundation in immaterial mind. Such has been the characteristic course of modern spiritualistic philosophies since the time of Kant; indeed, since that of Descartes, who first felt the poignancy of the problem involved in reconciling the conclusions of science with traditional religious and moral beliefs.

It would presumably be taken as a sign of extreme naïveté, if not of callous insensitiveness, if one were to ask why all this ardor to reconcile the findings of natural science with the validity of values? Why should any increase of knowledge seem like a threat to what we prize, admire and approve? Why should we not proceed to employ our gains in science to improve our judgments about values, and to regulate our actions so as to make values more secure and more widely shared in existence?

I am willing to run the risk of charge of naïveté for the sake of making manifest the difference upon which we have been dwelling. If men had associated their ideas about values with practical activity instead of with cognition of antecedent Being, they would *not* have been troubled by the findings of science. They would have welcomed the latter. For anything ascertained about the structure of actually existing conditions would be a definite aid in making judgments about things to be prized and striven for more adequate, and would instruct us as to the means to be employed in realizing them. But according to the religious and philosophic tradition of Europe, the valid status of all the highest values, the good, true and beautiful, was bound up with their being properties of ultimate and supreme Being, namely, God. All went well as long as what passed for natural science gave no offence to this conception. Trouble began when science ceased to disclose in the objects of knowledge the possession of any such properties. Then some roundabout method had to be devised for substantiating them.

The point of the seemingly crass question which was asked is thus to elicit the radical difference made when the problem of values is seen to be connected with the problem of intelligent action. If the validity of beliefs and judgments about values is dependent upon the consequences of action undertaken in their behalf, if the assumed association of values with knowledge capable of being demonstrated apart from activity, is abandoned, then the problem of the intrinsic relation of science to value is wholly artificial. It is replaced by a group of practical problems: How shall we employ what we know to direct the formation of our beliefs about value and how shall we direct our practical behavior so as to test these beliefs and make possible better ones? The question is seen to be just what it has always been empirically: What shall we *do* to make objects having value more secure in existence? And we approach the answer to the problem with all the advantages given us by increase of knowledge of the conditions and relations under which this doing must proceed.

But for over two thousand years the weight of the most influential and authoritatively orthodox tradition of thought has been thrown into the opposite scale. It has been devoted to the problem of a purely cognitive certification (perhaps by revelation, perhaps by intuition, perhaps by reason) of the antecedent immutable reality of truth, beauty and goodness. As against such a doctrine, the conclusions of natural science constitute the materials of a serious problem. The appeal has been made to the Court of Knowledge and the verdict has been adverse. There are two rival systems that must have their respective claims adjusted. The crisis in contemporary culture, the confusions and conflicts in it, arise from a division of authority. Scientific inquiry seems to tell one thing, and traditional beliefs about ends and ideals that have authority over conduct tell us something quite different. The problem of reconciliation arises and persists for one reason only. As long as the notions persist that knowledge is a disclosure of reality, of reality prior to and independent of knowing, and that knowing is independent of a purpose to control the quality of experienced objects, the failure of natural science to disclose significant values in its objects will come as a shock. Those seriously concerned with the validity and authority of value will have a problem on their hands. As long as the notion persists that values are authentic and valid only on condition that they are properties of Being independent of human action, as long as it is supposed that their right to regulate action is dependent upon their being independent of action, so long there will be needed schemes to prove that values are, in spite of the findings of science, genuine and known qualifications of reality in itself. For men will not easily surrender all regulative guidance in action. If they are forbidden to find standards in the course of experience they will seek them somewhere else, if not in revelation, then in the deliverance of a reason that is above experience.

This then is the fundamental issue for present philosophy. Is the doctrine justified that knowledge is valid in the degree in which it is a revelation of antecedent existences or Being? Is the doctrine justified that regulative ends and purposes have validity only when they can be shown to be properties belonging to things, whether as existences or as essences, apart from human action? It is proposed to make another start. Desires, affections, preferences, needs and interests at least exist in human experience; they are characteristics of it. Knowledge about nature also exists. What does this knowledge imply and entail with respect to the guidance of our emotional and volitional life? How shall the latter lay hold of what is known in order to make it of service?

These latter questions do not seem to many thinkers to have the dignity that is attached to the traditional problems of philosophy. They are proximate questions, not ultimate. They do not concern Being and Knowledge "in themselves" and at large, but the state of existence at specified times and places and the state of affection, plans and purposes under concrete circumstances. They are not concerned with framing a general theory of reality, knowledge and value once for all, but with finding how authentic beliefs about existence as they currently exist can operate fruitfully and efficaciously in connection with the practical problems that are urgent in actual life.

In restricted and technical fields, men now proceed unhesitatingly along these lines. In technology and the arts of engineering and medicine, men do not think of operating in any other way. Increased knowledge of nature and its conditions does not raise the problem of validity of the value of health or of communication in general, although it may well make dubious the validity of certain conceptions men in the past have entertained about the nature of health and communication and the best ways of attaining these goods in fact.

In such matters, science has placed in our hands the means by which we can better judge our wants, and has aided in forming the instruments and operations by which to satisfy them. That the same sort of thing has not happened in the moral and distinctly humane arts is evident. Here is a problem which might well trouble philosophers.

Why have not the arts which deal with the wider, more generous, more distinctly humane values enjoyed the release and expansion which have accrued to the technical arts? Can it be seriously urged that it is because natural science has disclosed to us the kind of world which it has disclosed? It is easy to see that these disclosures are hostile to some beliefs about values which have been widely accepted, which have prestige, which have become deeply impregnated with sentiment, and which authoritative institutions as well as the emotion and inertia of men are slow to surrender. But this admission, which practically enforces itself, is far from excluding the formation of new beliefs about things to be honored and prized by men in their supreme loyalties of action. The difficulty in the road is a practical one, a social one, connected with institutions and the methods and aims of education, not with science nor with value. Under such circumstances the first problem for philosophy would seem to be to clear itself of further responsibility for the doctrine that the supreme issue is whether values have antecedent Being, while its further office is to make clear the revisions and reconstructions that have to be made in traditional judgments about values. Having done this, it would be in a position to undertake the more positive task of projecting ideas about values which might be the basis of a new integration of human conduct.

We come back to the fact that the genuine issue is not whether certain values, associated with traditions and institutions, have Being already (whether that of existence or of essence), but what concrete judgments we are to form about ends and means in the regulation of practical behavior. The emphasis which has been put upon the former question, the creation of dogmas about the way in which values are already real independently of what we do, dogmas which have appealed not in vain to philosophy for support, have naturally bred, in the face of the changed character of science, confusion, irresolution and numbness of will. If men had been educated to think about broader humane values as they have now learned to think about matters which fall within the scope of technical arts, our whole present situation would be very different. The attention which has gone to achieving a purely theoretical certainty with respect to them would have been devoted to perfecting the arts by which they are to be judged and striven for.

Indulge for a moment in an imaginative flight. Suppose that

men had been systematically educated in the belief that the existence of values can cease to be accidental, narrow and precarious only by human activity directed by the best available knowledge. Suppose also men had been systematically educated to believe that the important thing is not to get themselves personally "right" in relation to the antecedent author and guarantor of these values, but to form their judgments and carry on their activity on the basis of public, objective and shared consequences. Imagine these things and then imagine what the present situation might be.

The suppositions are speculative. But they serve to indicate the significance of the one point to which this chapter is devoted. The method and conclusions of science have without doubt invaded many cherished beliefs about the things held most dear. The resulting clash constitutes a genuine cultural crisis. But it is a crisis in culture, a social crisis, historical and temporal in character. It is not a problem in the adjustment of properties of reality to one another. And yet modern philosophy has chosen for the most part to treat it as a question of how the realities assumed to be the object of science can have the mathematical and mechanistic properties assigned to them in natural science, while nevertheless the realm of ultimate reality can be characterized by qualities termed ideal and spiritual. The cultural problem is one of definite criticisms to be made and of readjustments to be accomplished. Philosophy which is willing to abandon its supposed task of knowing ultimate reality and to devote itself to a proximate human office might be of great help in such a task. It may be doubted whether it can indefinitely pursue the task of trying to show that the results of science when they are *properly* interpreted do not mean what they seem to say, or of proving, by means of an examination of possibilities and limits of knowledge, that after all they rest upon a foundation congruous with traditional beliefs about values.

Since the root of the traditional conception of philosophy is the separation that has been made between knowledge and action, between theory and practice, it is to the problem of this separation that we are to give attention. Our main attempt will be to show how the actual procedures of knowledge, interpreted after the pattern formed by experimental inquiry, cancel the isolation of knowledge from overt action. Before engaging in this attempt, we shall in the next chapter show the extent to which modern philosophy has been dominated by effort to adjust to each other two systems of belief, one relating to the objects of knowledge and the other to objects of ideal value.

3.   Conflict of Authorities

It is the theme of the present chapter that modern philosophy, understanding by this term that which has been influenced by the rise of the newer natural science, has contained within itself an inner division. It has tried to combine acceptance of the conclusions of scientific inquiry as to the natural world with acceptance of doctrines about the nature of mind and knowledge which originated before there was such a thing as systematic experimental inquiry. Between the two there is an inherent incompatibility. Hence the best efforts of philosophy have been constantly frustrated by artificiality and by controversial conflicts. Of all the many artificial problems which philosophy has thereby inflicted upon itself, we are here concerned with but one, the one with which the last chapter was concerned in a general way. This is the supposed need of reconciling, of somehow adjusting, the findings of scientific knowledge with the validity of ideas concerning value.

For obvious reasons, Greek thought, from which stem the philosophic conceptions about the nature of knowledge as the sole valid grasp or vision of reality, did not have this problem. Its physics were in complete harmony with its metaphysics, and the latter were teleological and qualitative. Natural objects themselves tend, throughout their changes, toward ideal ends that are the final objects of highest knowledge. A science of natural changes is possible only because of this fact. The natural world is knowable in as far as its changes are dominated by forms or essences that are immutable, complete or perfect. In aspiring to actualize these prior and perfect forms, natural phenomena present characters in virtue of which they may be known, that is, defined and classified. Moreover, these ideal forms form reason in its full and perfect actuality of Being. To know them is to enjoy communion with perfect Being and thus to enjoy the highest happiness.

For man as a rational and yet natural being strives also to realize his end, and this realization is identical with apprehension of true and immutable Being. In this apprehension, man rises above the mutabilities of the natural world and comes into possession of a perfection which is incapable of lack and deprivation. Pure rationality is in its purity above physical nature. But in his essential being, his rationality, man is himself above nature. The reality which satisfies the quest for cognitive certitude thus also affords the unqualified possession of perfect good.

The need of adjustment of the results of knowledge and the apprehension and enjoyment of the highest good came when, in the seventeenth century, new methods of inquiry gave an entirely new turn to the conceptions which could be entertained about the natural world.

Very early in its history, modern science asserted that the teleology of Greek science was a futile and mischievous encumbrance, wholly mistaken in its idea of the goal and method of scientific inquiry, and putting mind on the wrong track. It repudiated the doctrine of ideal forms, rejecting them as "occult." As the new scientific method progressed, it became increasingly clear that the material of knowledge, provided one took science as the model form of knowledge, gave no justification for attributing to the objects of cognitive certainty those perfections which in Greek science had been their essential properties. At the same time, there was no disposition to break away from the tradition according to which the valid status of values must be determined by knowledge. Hence the crucial problem which modern philosophy found forced upon it, in as far as it accepted the conclusions of the new science while it also retained three significant elements of ancient thought: the first, that certainty, security, can be found only in the fixed and unchanging; the second, that knowledge is the only road to that which is intrinsically stable and certain; the third, that practical activity is an inferior sort of thing, necessary simply because of man's animal nature and the necessity for winning subsistence from the environment.

In one significant respect, moreover, modern thought started with accentuation of the gulf between the values which are intrinsic to the real and hence are not dependent upon action, and those goods which, being merely instrumental, are the objects of practical activity. For Greek thought never made a sharp separation between the rational and perfect realm and the natural world. The latter was indeed inferior and infected with non-being or privation. But it did not stand in any sharp dualism to the higher and perfect reality. Greek thinking accepted the senses, the body and nature with natural piety and found in nature a hierarchy of forms leading degree by degree to the divine. The soul was the realized actuality of the body, as reason was the transcendent realization of the intimation of ideal forms contained in the soul. The senses included within themselves forms which needed only to be stripped of their material accretions to be true stepping stones to higher knowledge.

Modern philosophy inherited the framework of Greek ideas about the nature of knowledge although rejecting its conclusions about natural objects. But it inherited them through the medium of Hebraic and Christian religion. The natural world in this tradition was fallen and corrupt. With the Greeks the element of rationality was supreme and the good came into human possession by the realized development of reason. The intervening religious development made the ethical more fundamental than the rational. The most significant issues concerned the relation of will, rather than intellect, to supreme and perfect Being. Thus there was effected a reversal of perspective as to the relations in perfect Being of the properties in virtue of which it is respectively an object of true knowledge and of perfect good and bliss. Righteousness, in accordance with the Hebraic factors adopted into Christian theology, was primary, and strictly intellectual properties were subordinate. The participation of the mind in perfect being could not be attained by intellect until the intellect was itself morally redeemed and purified. The difference between the pure Greek tradition and the Christian is brought out in some words of Cardinal Newman. "The Church holds that it were better for sun and moon to drop from heaven, for the earth to fail, and for all the many millions who are upon it to die of starvation in extremest agony rather than that one soul should commit one venial sin."

In saying that modern philosophy inherited the Greek tradition as passed through this intervening medium of Christian thought, I do not mean to say that all features of the Christian view of nature in relation to God and the fall of man were taken over. On the contrary, distinctively modern thought is marked by a revival of the Greek interest and delight in nature and natural observation. Thinkers deeply influenced by modern science often ceased to believe in divine revelation as supreme authority and adhered to natural reason in its place. But the supreme place of good as a defining property of the ultimately real remained the common premise of Jew, Catholic and Protestant. If not vouched for by revelation, it was warranted by the "natural light" of intellect. This phase of the religious tradition was so deeply ingrained in European culture that no philosopher except the thoroughgoing sceptics escaped its influence. In this sense modern philosophy began its career with an accentuation of the gap which exists between ultimate and eternal values and natural objects and goods.

Thinkers who remained within the framework of the classic tradition held that the moral perfection which is the inherent property of ultimate Being prescribes the law of human action. It constitutes the norm of all significant and enduring values. Reason is necessary to furnish the foundation of truths without which observations—or experience in general—cannot be constituted a science. But it is even more necessary to provide for the apprehension of the ultimate and immutable end and law of moral action. When the hierarchical ascent of nature to mind and to ideal forms was disturbed by the conviction that the subject-matter of natural science is exclusively physical and mechanistic, there arose the dualistic opposition of matter and spirit, of nature and ultimate ends and goods.

Qualities, excellencies and ends that were extruded from nature by the new science found their exclusive abode and warrant in the realm of the spiritual, which was above nature and yet which was its source and foundation. The function of reason in determination and enjoyment of the good no longer formed the consummation of nature. It had a distinct and separate office. The tension created by the opposition and yet necessary connection of nature and spirit gave rise to all the characteristic problems of modern philosophy. It could neither be frankly naturalistic, nor yet fully spiritualistic to the disregard of the conclusions of physical science. Since man was on one hand a part of nature and on the other hand a member of the realm of spirit, all problems came to a focus in his double nature.

The philosophy of Spinoza is noteworthy for its frank statement of this problem and for the uniquely thoroughgoing way in which, given its terms, it was solved. An unqualified naturalism in the sense in which he understood the new science was combined by a miracle of logic with an equally complete acceptance of the idea, derived from the religious tradition, that ultimate reality is the measure of perfection and the norm for human activity. The union thus effected is so complete as to afford a pattern of instruction regarding the problem of modern thought. In him, more than in any modern thinker, there are exhibited complete loyalty to the essential element in the Hebraic tradition—ultimate and self-sufficing Being as the standard of all human thought and action—with perpetuation of the Greek theory of knowledge and its exaltation of reason over experience, together with enthusiastic adherence to the new scientific view of nature. Thus he thought to obtain from the very heart of the new science a conclusive demonstration of the perfection of Being through which the human soul can alone obtain absolute security and peace. A scientific comprehension was to give, in full reality, by rational means, that assurance and regulation of life that nonrational religions had pretended to give.

In his unfinished essay on *The Improvement of the Understanding*, he frankly states his impelling motive. He had experienced, he says, that everything in the ordinary course of experience is empty and futile. In desperation he set himself to inquiring whether there is not a good capable of communicating itself, a good so assured and complete that the mind can adhere to it to the exclusion of all else: a good which when found and taken possession of would give him eternally a constant and supreme bliss. For he had discovered that the cause of the perturbations and vanities of life was that affection and desire were fixed upon things which perish. But "love directed toward that which is eternal and infinite feeds the mind wholly with joy unmixed with any sadness. . . . The true good of man is that he should attain, together with others if possible, to a knowledge of the union which the mind has with Nature as a whole." He concludes, "I wish to direct all the sciences to this one end and scope in order that we may attain to such perfection."

Certain, enduring and unalloyed Good through the union of mind with the whole of nature is the theme developed in detail in the *Ethics*. There results a philosophy which unites the Greek idea that man's highest good is demonstrative rational knowledge of immutable Being; the Hebrew and Christian conviction that the soul is capable of a way of life which secures constant and pure blessedness, and the premises and method of the new science, as he saw the latter. Nature was completely intelligible; it was at one with mind; to apprehend nature as a whole was to attain a cognitive certainty which also afforded a complete certainty of good for the purpose of control of appetite, desire and affection—this latter specification being one which Greek thought did not include and which it doubtless would have thought the height of presumption to lay claim to. Right ordering of human conduct, knowledge of the highest reality, the enjoyment of the most complete and unvarying value or good, were combined in one inclusive whole by means of adoption of the ideas of the complete interdependence of all things according to universal and necessary law—an idea which he found to be the basis of natural science.

There have been few attempts in modern philosophy as bold and as direct as is this one to effect a complete integration of scientific method with a good which is fixed and final, because based on the rock of absolute cognitive certainty. Few thinkers have been as willing to sacrifice details of the older tradition in order to save its substance as was Spinoza. The outcry from all quarters against him proved that, in the minds of his contemporaries and successors, he had made too many concessions to naturalistic science and necessary law. But this protest should not conceal from us two essential considerations about his work. The first of these is that Nature, as the object of knowledge, is capable of being the source of constant good and a rule of life, and thus has all the properties and the functions which the Jewish-Christian tradition attributed to God. He was hence entitled to confer upon it the name *Natura sive Deus*. For Nature, as he conceived it, carried with it all the emotional associations and all the moral force and authority found in the older religious view of God. It provided an immutable End and Law for conduct, and it was the source, when rationally known, of perfect peace and unqualified security. Nature was naturally—that is rationally—known, and knowledge of it was such a perfect good that when it takes possession of the human mind the lesser and otherwise disturbing objects of affection and passion are so included within it as to fall into their proper place of subordination: that is, of complete control.

The second consideration is that Spinoza exemplifies with extraordinary completeness the nature of the problem of all modern philosophies which have not deserted the classic tradition, and yet have made the conclusions of modern science their own. What makes Spinoza so admirably the exponent of this problem is that he adopted with ardor and without the reservations displayed by most modern thinkers the essential elements in the Greek tradition of intellectualism and naturalism, the Hebrew-Christian idea of the priority and primacy of the properties of ultimate Being which concern the control of human affection and endeavor, and the method and conclusions of the new natural science—as he saw them.

The reluctance of other thinkers to follow the model of solution of their common problems which he offered was not, however, wholly due to their desire to save portions of the older moral and religious tradition that he was willing to surrender for what seemed to him a greater and more enduring good—the unification of science with an ethico-religious control of the springs of human conduct. There were difficulties from the side of science itself. Its experimental trend, as distinct from its mathematical strain, was adverse to Spinoza's unquestioning faith that the logical order and connection of ideas is one with the order and connection of existence. For as the new science developed, the experimental necessity for sense data and verification by observation reduced the role of logical and mathematical conceptions from a primary to a secondary rank. Even his predecessor Descartes, also a devotee of rationalistic method, had seen that there had to be some warrant for the application of ideas to nature. Other philosophers felt that after all the perfections with which Spinoza had so richly dowered Nature as the object of knowledge, were, in spite of his professed denial of teleology, the fruit of emotion rather than of logic.

We do not need to trace these complications. They are important for our purpose because they induced so many variations in the treatment of a single underlying problem: the adjustment to each other of two unquestioned convictions: One, that knowledge in the form of science reveals the antecedent properties of reality; the other, that the ends and laws which should regulate human affection, desire and intent can be derived only from the properties possessed by ultimate Being. If the rest of the chapter is given to a brief survey of the diverse methods of adjustment which have been propounded, it is not for the sake of conveying information upon matters familiar to all students of philosophy. I am concerned only to set forth illustrations of the way in which unyielding adherence to traditional premises regarding the object of true knowledge and the source of moral authority have set the problem of modern thought, and to provide illustration of the diverse and incompatible ways in which "solutions" have been sought.

Before the rise of the new science of nature there was developed a method for adjusting the claims of natural reason and moral authority by means of a division of the field: the doctrine of "the two-fold nature of truth." The realm of the ends and values authoritative for conduct was that of the revealed will of God. The organ for its apprehension was faith. Nature is the object of knowledge and with respect to it the claims of reason are supreme. The two realms are so separate that no conflict can occur. The work of Kant may be regarded as a perpetuation of the method of adjustment by means of partition of territories. He did not of course demarcate the realm of moral authority on the ground of faith in revelation. He substituted the idea of faith grounded in practical reason. But he continued the older distinction of one realm where the intellect has sway and one in which the requirements of will are supreme. He retained also the notion of an isolation of the two fields so complete that there is no possible overlapping and hence no possibility of interference. If the kingdoms of science and of righteousness nowhere touch, there can be no strife between them. Indeed, Kant sought to arrange their relations or lack of relations in such a way that there should be not merely non-interference but a pact of at least benevolent neutrality.

Kant's system bristles with points of internal difficulty; many of these are objects of controversy. Ignoring these as irrelevant to our problem, it can fairly be asserted that the main characteristic of his system is precisely a division of territory between the objects of cognitive certitude and those of equally complete practical moral assurance. The titles of his two chief works, the *Cri-*

tiques of Pure Reason and of *Practical Reason* are memorials to this interpretation. The first aims to make secure, on rational *a priori* grounds, the foundations of natural knowledge; the second performs a like office for the foundations of moral and religious conceptions. Science is limited to phenomena in space and time in order that the world of higher and noumenal realities may be appropriated by ideals and spiritual values. Each has complete jurisdiction and undisputed sovereignty in its own realm.

Heine's view that the subject-matter of the practical critique was an afterthought, a concession to the needs and fears of the multitude represented by his manservant, is wittily expressed, but will not stand critical examination. Kant's argument for the justification of the certitude of the foundations of knowledge is couched at every point so as to indicate the necessity of a higher although intellectually unapproachable realm. There was nothing factitious, in Kant's own conception, in the way in which the two kingdoms excluded each other and yet made each other necessary. On the contrary, the neat way in which the elements of each dovetailed into those of the other was to him a convincing proof of the necessity of the system as a whole. If the dovetailing was the product of his own intellectual carpentry, he had no suspicion of the fact.

On the contrary, he thought he had disposed, once for all, of many of the most perplexing problems of prior philosophy. Upon the scientific side he was concerned to provide a final philosophical justification, beyond the reach of scepticism, for the Newtonian science. His conception of space and time as necessary forms of the possibility of perception was the justification of the application of mathematics to natural phenomena. Categories of thought necessary to understand perceived objects—an understanding necessary to science—supplied the foundation of permanent substances and uniform relations of sequence—or causation—demanded by the Newtonian theories of atoms and uniform laws. The tendency of the mind to pass beyond the limits of experience to the thought of unconditioned and self-sufficient totalities, "Ideas" of the universe, soul and God, was explained; and while cognitive validity was denied these Ideas, they were admitted as regulative ideals which directed inquiry and interpretation. Above all, the thought of these trans-phenomenal and super-empirical realities left room that practical reason with its imperative of duty and postulate of free choice could fill. Thus the supremacy of righteousness according to the Hebraic-Christian tradition was justified independently of revelation by purely rational means. Moral demand for the final and unquestionable authority of duty authorized and necessitated practical certainty as to the reality of objects beyond experience and incapable of cognitive verification. The quest for certainty was fulfilled; cognitive certainty in the region of phenomena, practical certainty in the realm of moral authority.

This outline of obvious points in Kant's system passes over points which have received much attention—such as the "subjectivity" of his view of space and time and the categories; the contrast of the *a priori* and the empirical, as well as, in the *Critique of Practical Reason*, the seemingly arbitrary way in which faith in God and immortality are introduced. But with reference to his ultimate aim of establishing a perfect and unshakeable adjustment of the certainty of intellectual beliefs and of moral beliefs, these matters are secondary. The point on the practical side that had to be protected at all hazards was that no concrete and empirical material be permitted to influence ultimate moral realities—since this would give natural science jurisdiction over them and bring them under the sway of mechanical causality. On the cognitive side, the corresponding point to be certified was restriction of natural science to a strictly phenomenal world. For then there could be no encroachment of specific scientific conclusions upon ultimate, that is ethico-religious, belief.

In its essential framework, the Kantian scheme thus agreed marvelously well with the needs of the historic crisis. It gave freedom—and a blessing—to both science and morals, with a guarantee that they could never interfere with each other. Granted the acceptance of the traditional belief that security of moral authority depends upon some source in Being apart from the experiences by which values are incarnated in concrete objects and institutions, the Kantian scheme has such merits that it is safe to predict that as long as that tradition continues to have vitality, the main elements of the Kantian system will have devoted disciples.

The Kantian method is of course but one of a number of the philosophic attempts at harmonization. There is one phase of it which may be said to continue the Cartesian attempt to find the locus of absolute certainty within the knowing mind itself, surrendering both the endeavor of the ancients to discover it in the world without, and of the medieval world to find it in an external revelation. In his search for forms and categories inherent in the very structure of knowing activity, Kant penetrated far below the superficial level of innate ideas in which his predecessors had tried to find the locus of certainty. Some of them were conditions of the possibility of there being such a thing as cognitive experience. Others were conditions of there being such a thing as moral experience. His idealistic successors pushed their way further on the road which Kant had broken:—even though he insisted that the doors were locked to traveling on it any further than he had gone.

Solution by the method of partition is always unsatisfactory to minds with an ambition for comprehensiveness, just as it commends itself to those of a more modest turn. Moreover, the very neatness with which the essential traits of Kant's two realms fitted each other suggested a single underlying and unifying principle. And Kant himself in various writings had suggested, particularly in his *Critique of Judgment*, considerations which softened the sharpness of their separation from each other. Fichte and Hegel saw in these things a challenge to complete a work which Kant had only confusedly undertaken and had not had the intellectual courage and clarity to execute.

The controlling purpose of the Post-Kantian idealistic systems was to accomplish by way of integration the task which Kant attempted by way of division. The contrast between the methods of Fichte and Hegel is worth a passing notice. Fichte was wholly in the Hebraic tradition of the supremacy of the moral. He accordingly attempted unification of the cognitive and the practical from the side of moral self, the self from which issues the imperative of duty. The "is" of knowledge is to be derived from the "ought to be" of morals. The effort does not seem promising; it appears to speak more for the ethical ardor of his personality than for the sobriety of his understanding. Yet given the premises as to the certainty and supremacy in Being of ideal values prior to all action, Fichte's method has a logic not to be impeached. If the moral ideal is the ultimate reality, it is proper to derive the structure and characteristics of the actual world from the necessities the ideal imposes and the demands it makes. Argument from the actual to the ideal is a precarious undertaking, since the actual is in so many respects so thoroughly un-ideal.

Hegel, on the other hand, is never weary of pouring contempt upon an Ideal that merely ought to be. "The actual is the rational and the rational is the actual." There is a definite relaxation of the stern Puritanism of Fichte. The moral task of man is not to create a world in accord with the ideal but to appropriate intellectually and in the substance of personality the meanings and values already incarnate in an actual world. Viewed historically, Hegel's system may be looked on as a triumph in material content of the modern secular and positivistic spirit. It is a glorification of the here and now, an indication of the solid meanings and values contained in actual institutions and arts. It is an invitation to the human subject to devote himself to the mastery of what is already contained in the here and now of life and the world, instead of hunting for some remote ideal and repining because it cannot be found in existence. In form, however, the old tradition remains intact. The validity of these meanings and values, their "absolute" character, is proved by their being shown to be manifestations of the absolute spirit according to a necessary and demonstrative logical development:—even though Hegel had to create a new logic to establish the identity of meaning and being.

The Hegelian system is somewhat too grandiose for present taste. Even his followers find it necessary to temper the claims made for his logical method. And yet if there be a synthesis in ultimate Being of the realities which can be cognitively substantiated and of the meanings which should command our highest admiration and approval, then concrete phenomena, barring a complete corruption due to some lapse, ought to be capable of being exhibited as definite manifestations of the eternal union of the real-ideal. Perhaps there is no system more repugnant to the admirers of Spinoza than the Hegelian; and yet Hegel himself felt, and with considerable reason, that he was simply doing in a specific and concrete way what Spinoza had undertaken in a formal and mathematical way. However, the point important for our purpose is that in both Fichte and Hegel there is expressed the animating spirit of modern idealism in dealing with the basic problem of all modern philosophies. They have sought by examination of the structure of the knowing function (psychological structure in the subjective idealisms and logical structure in the objective idealisms and usually with a union of both strains) to show that no matter what the detailed conclusions of the special sciences, the ideal authority of truth, goodness, and beauty are secure possessions of ultimate Being independently of experience and human action.

There have been attempts at adjustment of the results of knowledge and the demands of ethico-religious authority which have not been mindful of the classic tradition. Instead of bringing nature within the fold of value, the order has been reversed. The physical system has been treated as the supporter and carrier of all objects having the properties which confer authority over conduct. A word about the system of Herbert Spencer among the moderns is appropriate in this connection, as one about Lucretius would be if antiquity were the theme. The doctrine that universal evolution is the highest principle of the physical world, one in which all natural laws are brought to unity, is accompanied with the idea that the goal of evolution marks the ideal of moral and religious beliefs and endeavors. This conclusion is as surely an attempt to adjust the two elements of the problem as anything found in any idealistic system. Were there any doubt about this point, Spencer's insistence on the evanescence of evil in the ongoing evolutionary process would remove it. All evils are the fruits of transitional maladjustments in the movement of evolution. The perfect adjustment of man, personal and collective, to the environment is the evolutionary term, and is one which signifies the elimination of all evil, physical and moral. The ultimate triumph of justice and the union of the good of self with the good of others are identical with the working out of physical law. In objection to this or that phase of the Spencerian system it is easily forgotten that fundamentally he is occupied with the usual quest for a certainty in which a warrant of necessary knowledge is employed to establish the certainty of Good in reality.

Comprehensive systems are for the moment out of fashion; and yet if cognitive certainty is possible and if it is admitted that the justification of value lies in its being a property of the realities which are the objects of knowledge, comprehensiveness, whether of the Hegelian or the Spencerian type, would seem to be the proper ideal of philosophy. And if one believes that the conclusions of science exhaust the scope of the universe, then certainly all moral, social and political goods must fall within them; in that case such a task as that of Spencer's is not only legitimate but one which philosophy cannot evade without being subject to the charge of bad faith.

One more illustration awaits us. Contemporary philosophy in its realistic forms shows a tendency to revert to adjustment of the cognitive realm and the realm of values by means of the method of isolation. In detail, however, the method pursued is unlike that of Kant in that it does not start from the knowing mind but rather from the objects of knowing. These, it is argued, show a radical division into the existential and the non-existential. Physical science deals with the former; mathematics and logic with the latter. In the former, some things, namely sense-data, are objects of infallible apprehension; while certain essences or subsistences, immaterial in nature because non-existential and non-physical, are the subjects of an equally assured cognition by reason. Uncertainty appertains only to combinations of ultimate and simple objects, combinations formed in reflective thought. As long as we stick to the self-guaranteed objects, whether of sense or of pure intellect, there is no opening for any uncertainty or any risk.

In some of these realisms, intrinsic values are included among the immaterial essences of which we have infallible and immediate knowledge. Thus the scheme of cognitive certainty applies all the way through. Science, in its naturalistic sense, is true of existences; ultimate morals and logic are true of essences. Philosophy has to do with the just partitioning of the field, and with the problems that arise from the union of existences and essences.

Still another conception of philosophy of a more austere character has, however, been advanced. According to this view, values are hopelessly entangled with human affections and impulses, and are too variable to be the objects of any kind of sure knowledge—of anything but variable opinion and guesswork. The great mistake of historic philosophy has been to admit values in any shape within the sacred enclosure of perfect science. Philosophy is concerned only with propositions which are true in any possible world, existentially actual or not. Propositions about good and evil are too dependent upon a special form of existence, namely human beings with their peculiar traits, to find a place in the scheme of science. The only propositions which answer to the specification of pure universality are logical and mathematical. These by their nature transcend existence and apply in every conceivable realm. Owing to the recent developments of mathematics, a philosophy emancipated from the contingencies of existence is now for the first time possible.

This view of philosophy has been objected to on the ground that it rests on an arbitrary limitation of its subject-matter. But it may be questioned whether this restriction is not a logical development of that strain in historic philosophy which identifies its subject-matter with whatever is capable of taking on the form of cognitive certainty. Without committing one's self to the subjective view of values that seems to be implied, values are so intimately connected with human affections, choices and endeavors, that there *is* ground for holding that the insincere apologetic features of historic philosophies are connected with the attempt to combine a theory of the values having moral authority with a theory of ultimate Being. And a moderate amount of acquaintance with these philosophies discloses that they have been interested in justifying values drawn from current religious faiths and moral codes, not just eternal values as such:—that they have often used the concept of universal and intrinsic values to cover those which, if not parochial, were at least exponents of temporal social conditions.

The limitation of philosophy to propositions about what is logically possible eliminates all special physical propositions as well as all matters of morals, art and religion. In its chaste austerity it seems to fulfill the demand for cognitive certainty as no other conception of philosophy can do. Whether one accepts or rejects it, there is provided by it an explicit way in which to raise a question. Because of the sharpness of its delimitation of the office of philosophy, it elicits clearly the problem of the idea to be entertained of that office. For with the restriction that is made there remains over and untouched a problem of the greatest possible human significance. What is the bearing of our existential knowledge at any time, the most dependable knowledge afforded by inquiry, upon our judgments and beliefs about the ends and means which are to direct our conduct? What does knowledge indicate about the authoritative guidance of our desires and affections, our plans and policies? Unless knowledge gives some regulation, the only alternative is to fall back on custom, external pressure and the free play of impulse. There is then need of some theory on this matter. If we are forbidden to call this theory philosophy by the self-denying ordinance which restricts it to formal logic, need for the theory under some other name remains.

There is a fatal ambiguity in the conception of philosophy as a purely theoretical or intellectual subject. The ambiguity lies in the fact that the conception is used to cover both the attitude of the inquirer, the thinker, and the character of the subject-matter dealt with. The engineer, the physician, the moralist deal with a subject-matter which is practical; one, that is, which concerns things to be done and the way of doing them. But as far as personal disposition and purpose is concerned, their inquiries are intellectual and cognitive. These men set out to find out certain things; in order to find them out, there has to be a purgation of personal desire and preference, and a willingness to subordinate them to the lead of the subject-matter inquired into. The mind must be purified as far as is humanly possible of bias and of that favoritism for one kind of conclusion rather than another which distorts observation and introduces an extraneous factor into reflection.

Except, then, on the premise that the subject-matter of philosophy is fixed properties of antecedent Being, the fact that it is an intellectual pursuit signifies nothing beyond the fact that those who engage in it should respect the canons of fairness, impartiality, of internal consistency and external evidence. It carries no implication with it—except on the basis of a prior assumption— save that of intellectual honesty. Only upon the obverse of the adage that whoso drives fat oxen must himself be fat, can it be urged that logical austerity of personal attitude and procedure demands that the subject-matter dealt with must be made lean by stripping it of all that is human concern. To say that the object of philosophy is truth is to make a moral statement which applies to every inquiry. It implies nothing as to the kind of truth which is to be ascertained, whether it be of a purely theoretical nature, of a practical character, or whether it concerns the bearing of one upon the other. To assert that contemplation of truth for its own sake is the highest ideal is to make a judgment concerning authoritative value. To employ this judgment as a means of determining the office of philosophy is to violate the canon that inquiry should follow the lead of subject-matter.

It is fair, then, to conclude that the question of the relations of theory and practice to each other, and of philosophy to both of them, has often been compromised by failure to maintain the distinction between the theoretical interest which is another name for intellectual candor and the theoretical interest which defines the nature of subject-matter. Over and above this fact, there is reason to suppose that much of the impatience with the suggestion of the practical in connection with philosophy is due to the habit of associating "practical" with affairs of narrow personal concern. The significance of the idea cannot be thus sheared down without an elimination of intellectual regard for the values which are to have authority over our desires and purposes and thus over our entire conduct. It would seem as if only the cynical sceptic would willingly take such a stand.

The discussion has indulged in an excursion from the theme of the problem of modern philosophies. But it is relevant to our main topic if it serves to make clear the fundamental ground for the disparaging view held of practical activity. Depreciation is warranted on the basis of two premises: first, namely, that the object of knowledge is some form of ultimate Being which is antecedent to reflective inquiry and independent of it; secondly, that this antecedent Being has among its defining characteristics those properties which alone have authority over the formation of our judgments of value—that is, of the ends and purposes which should control conduct in all fields—intellectual, social, moral, religious, esthetic. Given these premises—and only if they are accepted—it follows that philosophy has for its sole office the cognition of this Being and its essential properties.

I can understand that the tenor of my discussion may have aroused a certain impatience among those familiar with current treatment of politics, morals and art. It will be asked: Where is there any evidence that this treatment is controlled by regard for antecedently fixed qualifications of what is taken to be ultimately real? It cannot be denied, and I have no interest in denying, that the vast bulk of critical discussion of such matters is conducted on quite different grounds, with hardly even a side glance at any standards which flow from any philosophy of ultimate grounds.

This admission causes two important considerations to stand out the clearer. Traditional religion *does* refer all ultimate authoritative norms to the highest reality, the nature of God; and failure on the part of those professedly accepting this religion to carry this reference over to concrete criticism and judgment in special fields of morals, politics and art, is only an evidence of the confusion in which modern thought is entangled. It is this fact which gives the strict adherents to old beliefs, such as those trained in the Catholic faith, an intellectual advantage over "liberals." For the latter have no philosophy adequate for their undertakings and commitments.

This consideration brings us to the second point. The failure to employ standards derived from true Being in the formation of beliefs and judgments in concrete fields is proof of an isolation from contemporary life that is forced upon philosophy by its adherence to the two principles which are basic in the classic tradition. In the Middle Ages there was no such isolation. Philosophy and the conduct of life were associated intimately with one another; there was genuine correspondence. The outcome is not fortunate for philosophy; it signifies that its subject-matter is more and more derived from the problems and conclusions of its own past history; that it is aloof from the problems of the culture in which philosophers live.

But the situation has a still more unfortunate phase. For it signifies intellectual confusion, practically chaos, in respect to the criteria and principles which are employed in framing judgments and reaching conclusions upon things of most vital importance. It signifies the absence of intellectual authority. Old beliefs have dissolved as far as definite operative hold upon the regulation of criticism and the formation of plans and policies, working ideals and ends, is concerned. And there is nothing else to take their place.

When I say "authority" I do not mean a fixed set of doctrines by which to settle mechanically problems as they arise. Such authority is dogmatic, not intellectual. I mean *methods* congruous with those used in scientific inquiry and adopting their conclusions; methods to be used in directing criticism and in forming the ends and purposes that are acted upon. We have obtained in constantly accelerated measure in the last few centuries a large amount of sound beliefs regarding the world in which we live;

we have ascertained much that is new and striking about life and man. On the other hand, men have desires and affections, hopes and fears, purposes and intentions which influence the most important actions performed. These need intellectual direction. Why has modern philosophy contributed so little to bring about an integration between what we know about the world and the intelligent direction of what we do? The purport of this chapter is to show that the cause resides in unwillingness to surrender two ideas formulated in conditions which both intellectually and practically were very different from those in which we now live. These two ideas, to repeat, are that knowledge is concerned with disclosure of the characteristics of antecedent existences and essences, and that the properties of value found therein provide the authoritative standards for the conduct of life.

Both of these traits are due to quest for certainty by cognitive means which exclude practical activity—namely, one which effects actual and concrete modifications in existence. Practical activity suffers from a double discrediting because of the perpetuation of these two features of tradition. It is a mere external follower upon knowledge, having no part in its determination. Instead of evolving its own standards and ends in its own developing processes, it is supposed to conform to what is fixed in the antecedent structure of things. Herein we locate the source of that internal division which was said to characterize modern philosophic thought. It accepts the conclusions of scientific inquiry without remaking the conceptions of mind, knowledge and the character of the object of knowledge that are involved in the methods by which these conclusions are reached.

The chapters of which this is the concluding portion are introductory. They have tried to make clear a problem and the reasons why it is a problem. If, as has been intimated, the problem arises from continued adherence to certain conceptions framed centuries ago and then embodied in the entire western tradition, the problem is artificial in as far as it would not arise from reflection upon actual conditions of science and life. The next task is accordingly to elucidate the reconstructions of tradition which are involved in the actual procedure and results of knowing, as this is exemplified in physical inquiry. The latter is taken as the type and pattern of knowing since it is the most perfected of all branches of intellectual inquiry. We shall see that for a long time it also was influenced by the survival of the traditional conceptions of knowledge and its supposed relationship to properties of antecedent existence, while in our own time it has finally emancipated itself and arrived at a consciousness of the principles contained in its own method. Having discovered what knowledge means in its own terms, that is, in those of the conduct of knowing as a going concern, we shall be ready to appreciate the great transformation that is demanded in the older notions of mind and knowledge. Particularly we shall see how completely the separation of knowing and doing from one another has broken down. The conclusion of this part of the discussion will be that standards and tests of validity are found in the consequences of overt activity, not in what is fixed prior to it and independently of it. This conclusion will lead us to the final point, the transformation that is required in the conception of the values which have authority over conduct.

4. The Art of Acceptance and the Art of Control

There was a time when "art" and "science" were virtually equivalent terms. There is a reminiscence of this period in university organization in the phrase "faculty of arts and sciences." A distinction was drawn between the "mechanical" and the "liberal" arts. In part, this distinction was between industrial arts and social arts, those concerned with things and those concerned directly with persons. Grammar and rhetoric, for example, in dealing with speech, the interpretation of literature and the arts of persuasion, were higher than blacksmithing and carpentry. The mechanical arts dealt with things which were merely means; the liberal arts dealt with affairs that were ends, things having a final and intrinsic worth. The obviousness of the distinction was reenforced by social causes. Mechanics were concerned with mechanical arts; they were lower in the social scale. The school in which their arts were learned was the school of practice: apprenticeship to those who had already mastered the craft and mystery. Apprentices literally "learned by doing," and "doing" was routine repetition and imitation of the acts of others, until personal skill was acquired. The liberal arts were studied by those who were to be in some position of authority, occupied with some exercise of social rule. Such persons had the material means that afforded leisure, and were to engage in callings that had especial honor and prestige. Moreover, they learned not by mechanical repetition and bodily practice in manipulation of materials and tools, but "intellectually," through a kind of study which involved mind, not body.

The situation is not recalled as if it had a merely historical significance. It describes in large measure a state of affairs that exists to-day. The distinction between "learned professions" and the occupations of the shop and factory, with corresponding differences of social status, of educational preparation, of concern chiefly with material things or with persons and social relations, is too familiar to call for recourse to past history. The chief difference in the present situation is due to the rise of technological industry and of a pecuniary economy, at the expense of the inherited status of the "gentleman," the owner of large estates in land. So our allusion is pertinent not to history, but to still existing conditions that are influential in creating and maintaining the division between theory and practice, mind and body, ends and instrumentalities.

In addition to this distinction between higher and lower arts, there always hovered in the background a distinction between all arts and "science" in the true and ultimate sense of the words. The liberal arts involved much more of knowledge and of theoretical study, of use of "mind," than did the mechanical. But in their ultimate import they were still connected with art, with doing, although with a mode of practice held in higher esteem. They remained within the limits of experience, although of an experience having a kind of value not found in the baser arts. The philosophic tradition, as for example it is formulated by Aristotle, ranked social arts lower than pure intellectual inquiry, than knowledge as something not to be put to any use, even a social and moral one. It is conceivable that historically this point of view might have remained a mere laudation of its own calling on the part of a small intellectual class. But, as we have already noted, in the expansion of the Church as a dominant power in Europe, religion affiliated this philosophic conception to itself. Theology was regarded as "science" in a peculiar, a unique, sense, for it alone was knowledge of supreme and ultimate Being. And the Church had a direct influence over the hearts and conduct, the beliefs and judgments, of men that a secluded intellectual class could never win. As the guardians and dispensers of the truths and sacraments that determined the eternal destiny, the eternal happiness or misery of the soul, they effected the embodiment of ideas originating in philosophy in the culture of Christendom.

In consequence, differences and distinctions characteristic of actual social life received the sanction not merely of the rational formulation of a few philosophic thinkers but of that power which had the highest authority and influence in the lives of men. For this reason, the survey that has been made of the classic philosophic statement of the dualism between theory and practice, between mind and body, between reason and experience (always thought of in terms of sense and the body) is much more than a piece of historic information. For in spite of enormous extension of secular interests and of natural science, of expansion of practical arts and occupations, of the almost frantic domination of present life by concern for definite material interests and the organization of society by forces fundamentally economic, there is no widely held philosophy of life which replaces the traditional classic one as that was absorbed and modified by the Christian faith.

Traditional philosophy thus has a treble advantage. It has behind it the multitude of imaginative and emotional associations and appeals that cluster about any tradition which has for long centuries been embodied in a dominant institution; they continue to influence, unconsciously, the minds of those who no longer give intellectual assent to the tenets on which the tradition intellectually rests. It has, secondly, the backing of the persistence of the social conditions out of which the formulation of the dualism between theory and practice originally grew—the familiar grading of activities from the servile and mechanical to the liberal, the free and socially esteemed. In addition, there is the enforced recognition of the peril and frustration in the actual world of meanings and goods most prized, a matter which makes men ready to listen to the story of a higher realm in which these values are eternally safe.

In the third place, and finally, there is the negative counterpart of these positive facts. Conditions and forces that dominate in actual fact the modern world have not attained any coherent intellectual expression of themselves. We live, as is so often remarked, in a state of divided allegiance. In outward activities and current enjoyments, we are frenetically absorbed in mundane affairs in ways which, if they were formulated for intellectual acceptance, would be repudiated as low and unworthy. We give our emotional and theoretical assent to principles and creeds which are no longer actively operative in life. We have retained enough of the older tradition to recognize that a philosophy which formulated what, on the whole and in the mass, we are most concerned with, would be intolerably materialistic in character. On the other hand, we are not prepared, either intellectually or morally, to frame such a philosophy of the interests and activities that actually dominate our lives as would elevate *them* to a plane of truly liberal and humane significance. We are unable to show that the ideals, values and meanings which the philosophy we nominally hold places in another world, are capable of characterizing in a concrete form, with some measure of security, the world in which we live, that of our actual experience.

On this account any sincere empirical philosophy that holds to the possibility of the latter alternative must be prophetic rather than descriptive. It can offer hypotheses rather than report of facts adequately in existence. It must support these hypotheses by argument, rather than by appeal to matters clearly within the range of easy observation. It is speculative in that it deals with "futures." Candor demands that these considerations be frankly set forth. But there is also another side to the matter. There is a distinction between hypotheses generated in that seclusion from observable fact which renders them fantasies, and hypotheses that are projections of the possibilities of facts already in existence and capable of report. There is a difference between the imaginative speculations that recognize no law except their own dialectic consistency, and those which rest on an observable movement of events, and which foresee these events carried to a limit by the force of their own movement. There is a difference between support by argument from arbitrarily assumed premises, and an argument which sets forth the implications of propositions resting upon facts already vitally significant.

The groundwork of fact that is selected for especial examination and description in the hypothesis which is to be set forth is the procedure of present scientific inquiry, in those matters that are most fully subject to intellectual control—namely, the physical sciences. The state of inquiry in them is an observable fact, not a speculation nor a matter of opinion and argument. The selection of this field of fact rather than some other as that from which to project a hypothesis regarding a future possible experience in which experience will itself provide the values, meanings and standards now sought in some transcendent world, has both theoretical and practical justification. From the point of view of technical philosophy, the nature of knowledge has always been the foundation and point of departure for philosophies that have separated knowing from doing and making, and that in consequence have elevated the objects of knowledge, as measures of genuine reality, above experiences of objects had by the way of affection and practical action. If, accordingly, it can be shown that the actual procedures by which the most authentic and dependable knowledge is attained have completely surrendered the separation of knowing and doing; if it can be shown that overtly executed operations of interaction are requisite to obtain the knowledge called scientific, the chief fortress of the classic philosophical tradition crumbles into dust. With this destruction disappears also the reason for which some objects, as fixed in themselves, out of and above the course of human experience and its consequences, have been set in opposition to the temporal and concrete world in which we live.

The *practical* reason for selecting such a technical matter as the method of physical science is the fact that the application of natural science, through the medium of inventions and technologies, is the finally controlling and characteristic fact of modern life. That western civilization is increasingly industrial in character is a commonplace; it should be an equally familiar fact that this industrialization is the direct fruit of the growth of the experimental method of knowing. The effects of this industrialization in politics, social arrangements, communication and intercourse, in work and play, in the determination of the locus of influence, power and prestige, are characteristic marks of present experience in the concrete. They are the ultimate source of that waning of the effective influence of older beliefs that has been alluded to. They also provide the reason why a philosophy which merely reflected and reported the chief features of the existing situation as if they were final, without regard to what they may become, would be so repulsively materialistic. Both the positive fact that our actual life is more and more determined by the results of physical science, and the negative fact that these results are so largely an obstacle to framing a philosophy consonant with present experience—so influential in inducing men to hold on to elements of the older tradition—are reasons for selecting the procedure of natural science as the main theme of our examination.

There will be little time and opportunity for discussion of the problem in its immediately practical form—the potential significance of that industrial society which has emerged in consequence of the conclusions and methods of physical knowledge. But it may be pointed out that, in principle, it signifies simply that the results of intelligence, instead of remaining aloof and secluded from practice, are embodied in influential ways in the activities and experience which actually obtains. Say what we please in derogation of "applied science," in principle this is what the latter signifies. And there are few persons, I imagine, who would wittingly proclaim that incarnation of knowledge and understanding in the concrete experiences of life is anything but a good. Derogation on principle of application of knowledge is, in itself, merely an expression of the old tradition of the inherent superiority of knowledge to practice, of reason to experience.

There is a genuine and extremely serious problem in connection with the application of science in life. But it is a practical, not theoretical, one. That is to say, it concerns the economic and legal organization of society in consequence of which the knowledge which regulates activity is so much the monopoly of the few, and is used by them in behalf of private and class interests and not for general and shared use. The problem concerns the possible transformation of social conditions with respect to their economic and pecuniary basis. This problem time and space will not permit me to consider. But the pecuniarily economic phase of society is something radically different from industrialization, and from the inherent consequences of technology in current life. To identify the two affairs breeds only confusion. It must also be noted that this is a question which has of itself nothing to do with the matter of the relations of theory and practice, of knowledge and its application in doing and making. The practical and social problem is one of effecting a more general equitable distribution of the elements of understanding and knowledge in connection with work done, activities undertaken, and a consequent freer and more generously shared participation in their results.

Before engaging in consideration of the significance of the method of science for formation of the theory of knowledge and of mind, we shall take up some general points. These are all connected, at bottom, with the contrast between the idea of experience framed when arts were mainly routine, skills acquired by *mere* exercise and practice, and the idea of experience appropriate when arts have become experimental: or, put briefly, between experience as *empirical* and as *experimental*. "Experience" once meant the results accumulated in memory of a variety of past doings and undergoings that were had without control by insight, when the net accumulation was found to be practically available in dealing with present situations. Both the original perceptions and uses and the application of their outcome in present doings were accidental—that is, neither was determined by an understanding of the relations of cause and effect, of means and consequences, involved. In that sense they were non-rational, non-scientific. A typical illustration is a bridge builder who constructs simply on the basis of what has been done and what happened in the past, without reference to knowledge of strains and stresses, or in general of physical relationships actually involved; or the art of medicine, as far as it rests simply upon the accidents of remedial measures used in the past without knowledge of *why* some worked and others did not. A measure of skill results, but it is the fruit of cut and dried methods, of trial and error—in short it is "empirical."

The disparaging notion of experience framed under such conditions is an honest report of actual conditions; philosophers in setting experience down as inherently inferior to rational science were truthful. What they added was another matter. It was a statement that this inferiority was inherently connected with the body, with the senses, with material things, with the uncertainly changing as over against the certain because immutable. Unfortunately their theories in explanation of the defects of experience persisted and became classic after experience itself, in some of its forms, had become experimental in the sense of being directed by understanding of conditions and their consequences. Two points are especially significant with reference to the split thus produced between the traditional theory of experience and that which results from noting its experimental character.

In the traditional theory, which still is the prevailing one, there were alleged to exist inherent defects in perception and observation as means of knowledge, in reference to the subject-matter they furnish. This material, in the older notion, is inherently so particular, so contingent and variable, that by no possible means can it contribute to *knowledge*; it can result only in opinion, mere belief. But in modern science, there are only *practical* defects in the senses, certain limitations of vision, for example, that have to be corrected and supplemented by various devices, such as the use of the lens. Every insufficiency of observation is an instigation to invent some new instrument which will make good the defect, or it is a stimulus to devising indirect means, such as mathematical calculations, by which the limitations of sense will be circumvented. The counterpart of this change is one in the conception of thought and its relation to knowing. It was earlier assumed that higher knowledge must be supplied by pure thought; pure because apart from experience, since the latter involves the senses. Now, it is taken for granted that thought, while indispensable to knowledge of natural existence, can never in itself provide that knowledge. Observation is indispensable both to provide authentic materials to work upon and to test and verify the conclusions reached by theoretical considerations. A specified kind of experience is indispensable to science instead of all experience setting a limit to the possibility of true science.

There is an objective counterpart of this shift. In the older theory, sense and experience were barriers to true science because they are implicated in natural change. Their appropriate and inevitable subject-matter was variable and changing things. Knowledge in its full and valid sense is possible only of the immutable, the fixed; that alone answers the quest for certainty. With regard to changing things, only surmise and opinion are possible, just as practically these are the source of peril. To a scientific man, in terms of what he does in inquiry, the notion of a natural science which should turn its back upon the changes of things, upon events, is simply incomprehensible. What he is interested in knowing, in understanding, are precisely the changes that go on; they set his problems, and problems are solved when changes are interconnected with one another. Constants and relative invariants figure, but they are relations between changes, not the constituents of a higher realm of Being. With this modification with respect to the object comes one in the structure and content of "experience." Instead of there being a fixed difference between it and something higher—rational thought—there is a difference between two kinds of experience; one which is occupied with uncontrolled change and one concerned with directed and regulated change. And this difference, while fundamentally important, does not mark a fixed division. Changes of the first type are something *to be brought under control* by means of action directed by understanding of relationships.

In the old scheme, knowledge, as science, signified precisely and exclusively turning away from change to the changeless. In the new experimental science, knowledge is obtained in exactly the opposite way, namely, through deliberate institution of a definite and specified course of change. *The* method of physical inquiry is to introduce some change in order to see what other change ensues; the correlation between these changes, when measured by a series of operations, constitutes the definite and desired object of knowledge. There are two degrees of control of change which differ practically but are alike in principle. In astronomy, for example, we cannot introduce variation into remote heavenly bodies. But we can deliberately alter the conditions under which we observe them, which is the same thing in principle of logical procedure. By special instruments, the use of lens and prism, by telescopes, spectroscopes, interferometers, etc., we modify observed data. Observations are taken from widely different points in space and at successive times. By such means interconnected variations are observed. In physical and chemical matters closer at hand and capable of more direct manipulation, changes introduced affect the things under inquiry. Appliances and re-agents for bringing about variations in the things studied are employed. The progress of inquiry is identical with advance in the invention and construction of physical instrumentalities for producing, registering and measuring changes.

Moreover, there is no difference in logical principle between the method of science and the method pursued in technologies. The difference is practical; in the scale of operations conducted; in the lesser degree of control through isolation of conditions operative, and especially in the purpose for the sake of which regulated control of modifications of natural existences and energies is undertaken; especially, since the dominant motive of large scale regulation of the course of change is material comfort or pecuniary gain. But the technique of modern industry, in commerce, communication, transportation and all the appliances of light, heat and electricity, is the fruit of the modern application of science. And this so-called "application" signifies that the same kind of intentional introduction and management of changes which takes place in the laboratory is induced in the factory, the railway and the power house.

The central and outstanding fact is that the change in the

method of knowing, due to the scientific revolution begun in the sixteenth and seventeenth centuries, has been accompanied by a revolution in the attitude of man toward natural occurrences and their interactions. This transformation means, as was intimated earlier, a complete reversal in the traditional relationship of knowledge and action. Science advances by adopting the instruments and doings of directed practice, and the knowledge thus gained becomes a means of the development of arts which bring nature still further into actual and potential service of human purposes and valuations. The astonishing thing is that in the face of this change wrought in civilization, there still persist the notions about mind and its organs of knowing, together with the inferiority of practice to intellect, which developed in antiquity as the report of a totally different situation.

The hold which older conceptions have gained over the minds of thinkers, the sway of inertia in habits of philosophic thought, can be most readily judged by turning to books on epistemology and to discussions of problems connected with the theory of knowledge published in the philosophical periodicals. Articles on logical method will be found which reflect the procedures of actual knowing, that is of the practice of scientific inquiry. But logic is then usually treated as "mere" methodology, having little (probably nothing would be nearer the mark) to do with the theory of knowledge. The latter is discussed in terms of conceptions about mind and its organs; these conceptions are supposed to be capable of adequate formation apart from observation of what goes on when men engage in successful inquiry. Of late, the main problem in such discussions is to frame a theory of "consciousness" which shall explain knowing, as if consciousness were either a fact whose meaning is self-evident, or something less obscure in content and more observable than are the objective and public procedures of scientific investigation. This type of discussion persists; it is, in current conception, *the* theory of knowledge, the natural and inevitable way in which to discuss its basic problems! Volumes could not say more for the persistence of traditional ideas. The import of even a rudimentary discussion of actual experimental method can hardly be gathered, then, without bearing in mind its significance as a contrast effect.

While the traits of experimental inquiry are familiar, so little use has been made of them in formulating a theory of knowledge

and of mind in relation to nature that a somewhat explicit statement of well known facts is excusable. They exhibit three outstanding characteristics. The first is the obvious one that all
experimentation involves *overt* doing, the making of definite
changes in the environment or in our relation to it. The second is
that experiment is not a random activity but is directed by ideas
which have to meet the conditions set by the need of the problem
inducing the active inquiry. The third and concluding feature, in
which the other two receive their full measure of meaning, is that
the outcome of the directed activity is the construction of a new
empirical situation in which objects are differently related to one
another, and such that the *consequences* of directed operations
form the objects that have the property of being *known*.

The rudimentary prototype of experimental doing for the sake
of knowing is found in ordinary procedures. When we are trying
to make out the nature of a confused and unfamiliar object, we
perform various acts with a view to establishing a new relationship to it, such as will bring to light qualities which will aid in
understanding it. We turn it over, bring it into a better light, rat-
tle and shake it, thump, push and press it, and so on. The object
as it is experienced prior to the introduction of these changes
baffles us; the intent of these acts is to make changes which will
elicit some previously unperceived qualities, and by varying conditions of perception shake loose some property which as it
stands blinds or misleads us.

While such experimentations, together with a kind of experimental playing with things just to see what will happen, are the
chief source of the everyday non-scientific store of information
about things around us, forming the bulk of "common-sense"
knowledge, the limitations of the mode of procedure are so evident as to require no exposition. The important thing in the history of modern knowing is the reinforcement of these active doings by means of instruments, appliances and apparatus devised
for the purposes of disclosing relations not otherwise apparent,
together with, as far as overt action is concerned, the development of elaborate techniques for the introduction of a much
greater range of variations—that is, a systematic variation of
conditions so as to produce a corresponding series of changes in
the thing under investigation. Among these operations should be
included, of course, those which give a permanent register of

what is observed and the instrumentalities of exact measurement by means of which changes are correlated with one another.

These matters are so familiar that their full import for the theory of knowing readily escapes notice. Hence the need of comparing this kind of knowledge of natural existences with that obtaining before the rise of the experimental method. The striking difference is, of course, the dependence placed upon doing, doing of a physical and overt sort. Ancient science, that is, what passed as science, would have thought it a kind of treason to reason as the organ of knowing to subordinate it to bodily activity on material things, helped out with tools which are also material. It would have seemed like admitting the superiority of matter to rational mind, an admission which from its standpoint was contradictory to the possibility of knowledge.

With this fundamental change goes another, that in the attitude taken toward the material of direct sense-perception. No notion could be further away from the fact than the somewhat sedulously cultivated idea that the difference between ancient and modern science is that the former had no respect for perception and relied exclusively upon speculation. In fact, the Greeks were keenly sensitive to natural objects and were keen observers. The trouble lay not in substitution of theorizing from the outset for the material of perception, but in that they took the latter "as is"; they made no attempt to modify it radically before undertaking thinking and theorizing about it. As far as observation unaided by artificial appliances and means for deliberate variation of observed material went, the Greeks went far.

Their disrespect for sensibly observed material concerned only its form. For it had to be brought under logical forms supplied by rational thought. The fact that the material was not exclusively logical, or such as to satisfy the requirements of rational form, made the resulting knowledge less scientific than that of pure mathematics, logic and metaphysics occupied with eternal Being. But as far as science extended, it dealt with the material of sense-perception as it directly offered itself to a keen and alert observer. In consequence, the material of Greek natural science is much closer to "common sense" material than are the results of contemporary science. One can read the surviving statements of it without any more technical preparation than say a knowledge of Euclidean geometry, while no one can follow understandingly the reports of most modern investigations in physics without a highly technical preparatory education. One reason the atomic theory propounded in antiquity made so little headway is that it did not agree with the results of ordinary observation. For this presented objects clothed with rich qualities and falling into kinds or species that were themselves marked by qualitative, rather than by merely quantitative and spatial, differences. In antiquity it was the atomic theory which was purely speculative and "deductive" in character.

These statements would be misunderstood if they were taken to imply an allegation that in ancient science sense gives knowledge, while modern science excludes the material of sense; such an idea inverts the facts. But ancient science accepted the *material* of sense-perception on its face, and then organized it, as it naturally and originally stood, by operations of logical definition, classification into species and syllogistic subsumption. Men either had no instruments and appliances for modifying the ordinary objects of observation, for analyzing them into their elements and giving them new forms and arrangements, or they failed to use those which they had. Thus in *content*, or subject-matter, the conclusions of Greek science (which persisted till the scientific revolution of the seventeenth century), were much closer to the objects of everyday experience than are the objects of present scientific thought. It is not meant that the Greeks had more respect for the *function* of perception through the senses than has modern science, but that, judged from present practice, they had altogether too much respect for the *material* of direct, unanalyzed sense-perception.

They were aware of its defects from the standpoint of knowledge. But they supposed that they could correct these defects and supplement their lack by purely logical or "rational" means. They supposed that thought could take the material supplied by ordinary perception, eliminate varying and hence contingent qualities, and thus finally reach the fixed and immutable form which makes particulars have the character they have; define this form as the essence or true reality of the particular things in question, and then gather a group of perceived objects into a species which is as eternal as its particular exemplifications are perishable. The passage from ordinary perception to scientific knowledge did not therefore demand the introduction of actual,

overt and observed changes into the *material* of sense perception. Modern science, with its changes in the subject-matter of
direct perception effected by the use of apparatus, gets away not
from observed material as such, but from the qualitative characteristics of things as they are originally and "naturally" observed.

It may thus be fairly asserted that the "categories" of Greek
description and explanation of natural phenomena were esthetic
in character; for perception of the esthetic sort is interested in
things in their immediate qualitative traits. The logical features
they depended upon to confer scientific form upon the material
of observation were harmony, proportion or measure, symmetry: these constitute the "logos" that renders phenomena capable of report in rational discourse. In virtue of these properties,
superimposed upon phenomena but thought to be elicited from
them, natural objects are knowable. Thus the Greeks employed
thinking not as a means of changing given objects of observation
so as to get at the conditions and effects of their occurrence, but
to impose upon them certain static properties not found in them
in their changeable occurrence. The essence of the static properties conferred upon them was harmony of form and pattern.
Craftsmen, architects, sculptors, gymnasts, poets had taken raw
material and converted it into finished forms marked by symmetry and proportion; they accomplished this task without the
prior disintegrative reduction which characterizes modern making in the factory. Greek thinkers performed a like task for nature as a whole. Instead, however, of employing the material
tools of the crafts, they depended upon thought alone. They borrowed the *form* provided them in Greek art in abstraction from
its material appliances. They aimed at constructing out of nature, as observed, an artistic whole for the eye of the soul to behold. Thus for science nature was a cosmos. It was composed,
but it was not a composite of elements. That is, it was a qualitative whole, a whole as is a drama, a statue or a temple, in virtue
of a pervading and dominant qualitative unity; it was not an ag-
gregate of homogenous units externally arranged in different
modes. Design was the form and pattern intrinsically characteristic of things in their fixed kinds, not something first formed
in a designing mind and then imposed from without.

In his *Creative Evolution*, Bergson remarks that to the Greek
mind that reality which is the object of the truest knowledge is

found in some privileged moment when a process of change attains its climactic apogee. The Ideas of Plato and the Forms of Aristotle, as he says, may be compared in their relation to particular things to the horses of the Parthenon frieze in relation to the casual movements of horses. The essential movement which gives and defines the character of the horse is summed up in the eternal moment of a static position and form. To see, to grasp, that culminating and defining form, and by grasping to possess and enjoy it, is to know.

This *aperçu* of Bergson illustrates the conception of the essentially artistic character possessed for Greek science by the object of knowledge. It is borne out by the details of Greek science. I know of no one thing more significant for an understanding of Greek science than Aristotle's treatment of quantity as an accident, that is, as something which can vary within limits (set by the inherent essence and measure, *logos*) of a thing without affecting its nature. When we think of the Cartesian definition of quantity as the essence of matter, we appreciate that an intellectual revolution has taken place: a radical change in point of view and not just the product of more, and more accurately stated, information, but a change involving surrender of the esthetic character of the object. Contrast the place occupied in modern science by relations with the Aristotelian illustrations of their nature—namely, distinctions of more and less, greater and smaller, etc. For the point of Aristotle's treatment is that relations, like quantity, are indifferent to the essence or nature of the object, and hence are of no final account for scientific knowledge. This conception is thoroughly appropriate to an esthetic point of view, wherein that which is internally complete and self-sufficing is the all-important consideration.

The addiction of Pythagorean-Platonism to number and geometry might seem to contradict what has been said. But it is one of the exceptions that proves the rule. For geometry and number in this scheme were means of ordering natural phenomena as they are directly observed. They were principles of measure, symmetry and allotment that satisfied canons essentially esthetic. Science had to wait almost two thousand years for mathematics to become an instrument of analysis, of resolution into elements for the sake of recomposition, through equations and other functions.

I pass by the evidence of the qualitative character of Greek science afforded by the central position of kinds or species in Peripatetic science. The instance is too obvious. More instructive is the purely qualitative treatment of movements, especially as this is the matter that gives the clue to the revolution wrought by Galileo. Movement was a term covering all sorts of qualitative alterations, such as warm things becoming cold, growth from embryo to adult form, etc. It was never conceived of as merely motion, i.e., change of position in a homogeneous space. When we speak of a musical movement, or a political movement, we come close to the sense attached to the idea in ancient science: a series of changes tending to complete or perfect a qualitative whole and fulfill an end.

Movement instead of continuing indefinitely spent itself; it tended inherently toward its own cessation, toward rest. The problem was not what external forces bring the arrow to a state of relative rest but what external forces, currents of air, etc., keep it moving and prevent its speedier attainment of its own natural goal, rest. Cessation of movement is either exhaustion, a kind of fatigue, or it marks the culmination of intrinsic proper being or essence. The heavenly bodies, just because they are heavenly, and therefore quasi-divine, are unwearied, never tiring, and so keep up their ceaseless round. For rest when it meant fulfillment was not dead quiescence but complete and therefore *unchanging* movement. Only thought is completely possessed of this perfect self-activity; but the constant round of heavenly bodies is the nearest physical manifestation of the self-enclosed changeless activity of thought, which discovers nothing, learns nothing, effects nothing, but eternally revolves upon itself.

The treatment of place—or rather places—is the counterpart of this qualitative diversification of movements. There is movement up from the earth, in the measure of their lightness, of those things which belong in the upper spaces; a downward movement to the earth of those things which because of their grossness attain their end and arrive at their home only in the gross and relatively cold earth. To the intermediate regions is appropriate neither upward nor downward movement but the back and forth and wavering movement characteristic of winds and the (apparent) motions of the planets. As the cold and heavy moves down, the light and fiery, the finest material moves upward. The stars of the firmament being the most nearly divine, the most purged of the irregular and merely potential, pursue that undeviating circular course which is the nearest approach in nature to the eternal self-activity of thought, which is at once beyond nature and its culmination or "final cause."

These details are mentioned to make clear the completely qualitative character of antique science. There was no conflict with ideas about values, because the qualities belonging to objects of science *are* values; they are the things we enjoy and prize. Throughout nature as a qualitative whole there is a hierarchy of forms from those of lower value to those of higher. The revolution in science effectively initiated by Galileo consisted precisely in the abolition of qualities as traits of scientific objects *as such*. From this elimination proceeded just that conflict and need of reconciliation between the scientific properties of the real and those which give moral authority. Therefore to apprehend what the new astronomy and physics did for human beliefs, we have to place it in its contrast with the older natural science in which the qualities possessed by objects of scientific knowledge were precisely the same as those possessed by works of art, the properties which are one with beauty and with all that is admirable.

The work of Galileo was not a development, but a revolution. It marked a change from the qualitative to the quantitative or metric; from the heterogeneous to the homogeneous; from intrinsic forms to relations; from esthetic harmonies to mathematical formulae; from contemplative enjoyment to active manipulation and control; from rest to change; from eternal objects to temporal sequence. The idea of a two-realm scheme persisted for moral and religious purposes; it vanished for purposes of natural science. The higher realm which had been the object of true science became the exclusive habitat of objects connected with values that in their relation to man furnish the norm and end of human destiny. The lower realm of change which had been the subject of opinion and practice became the sole and only object of natural science. The realm in which opinion held sway was no longer a genuine although inferior portion of objective being. It was a strictly human product, due to ignorance and error. Such was the philosophy which, because of the new science, replaced the old metaphysics. But—and this "but" is of fundamental importance—in spite of the revolution, the old conceptions of knowledge as related to an antecedent reality and of moral regulation as derived from properties of this reality, persisted.

Neither the scientific nor the philosophic change came at once, even after experimental inquiry was initiated. In fact as we shall see later, philosophy proceeded conservatively by compromise and accommodation, and was read into the new science, so that not till our own generation did science free itself from some basic factors of the older conception of nature. Much of the scientific revolution was implicit, however, in the conclusions which Galileo drew from his two most famous experiments. The one with falling bodies at the tower of Pisa destroyed the old distinction of intrinsic qualitative differences of gravity and levity, and thus gave an enormous shock to the qualitative explanatory principles of science. It thus tended to undermine the description and explanation of natural phenomena in terms of heterogeneous qualities. For it showed that the immanent motion of bodies was connected with a common homogeneous property, one measured by their resistance to being set in motion and to having their motion arrested or deflected when once set in operation. This property, called inertia, was finally identified by Newton with mass, so that mass or inertia became the scientific definition or stable co-efficient of matter, in complete indifference to the qualitative differentiations of wet-dry, hot-cold, which were henceforth things to be explained by means of mass and motion, not fundamental explanatory principles.

Taken in isolation, it is conceivable that this result would have been only a shock, or at most a ferment. Not so, however, when it was connected with his experiment of balls rolling down a smooth inclined plane (of which his experiment with the pendulum was a variation), the nearest approximation he could make to observation of freely falling bodies. His purpose was to determine the relation of the measured time of falling to the measured space passed through. Observed results confirmed the hypothesis he had previously formed, namely, that the space traversed is proportional to the square of the elapsed time. If we forget the background of Peripatetic science against which this conclusion was projected, it appears as a mathematical determination of acceleration, and in connection with the concept of mass, as affording a new and accurate definition of force. This result is highly important. But apart from the classic background of beliefs about nature, it would have been of the same type as important discoveries in physics to-day. In its opposition to the basic ideas of Peripatetic science, it ushered in the scientific revolution. Galileo's conclusions were absolutely fatal to the traditional conception that all bodies in motion come naturally to rest because of their own intrinsic tendency to fulfill an inherent nature. The ingenious mind of Galileo used his results to show that if a body moving on a horizontal plane, not subjected to the independent force of uniform gravity, were substituted for the body on an inclined plane, it would when once set in motion continue in motion indefinitely—the idea later formulated in Newton's first law of motion.

The revolution opened the way to description and explanation of natural phenomena on the basis of homogeneous space, time, mass and motion. Our discussion is not an account of the historic development, and details are passed over. But some of the generic results which followed must be summarily mentioned. Galileo's conclusion did not at first affect the tradition that bodies at rest remained at rest. But his logic and the further use of his methods revealed that when a gross body is brought to rest, motion is transferred to its own particles and to those of the body which checked its movement. Thus heat became subject to mechanical treatment, and in the end the conversion of mechanical motion, heat, light, electricity into one another without loss of energy was established. Then it was shown by Newton, following Copernicus and Huygens, that the movements of the planets obey the same mechanical laws of mass and acceleration as mundane bodies. Heavenly bodies and movements were brought under the same laws as are found in terrestrial phenomena. The idea of the difference in kind between phenomena in different parts of space was abolished. All that counted for science became mechanical properties formulated in mathematical terms:—the significance of mathematical formulation marking the possibility of complete equivalence or homogeneity of translation of different phenomena into one another's terms.

From the standpoint of the doctrine that the purpose of knowledge is to grasp reality and that the object of cognition and real objects are synonymous terms, there was but one conclusion possible. This, in the words of a recent writer, was that "the Newtonian astronomy revealed the whole heavenly realm as a dark and limitless emptiness wherein dead matter moved under the impulse of insensate forces, and thus finally destroyed the poetic dream of ages." [1]

The conclusion holds good, however, only under condition that the premise be held to. If and as far as the qualitative world was taken to be an object of knowledge, and not of experience in some other form than knowing, and as far as knowing was held to be the standard or sole valid mode of experiencing, the substitution of Newtonian for Greek science (the latter being but a rationalized arrangement of the qualitatively enjoyed world of direct experience) signified that the properties that render the world one of delight, admiration and esteem, have been done away with. There is, however, another interpretation possible. A philosophy which holds that we experience things as they really are apart from knowing, and that knowledge is a mode of experiencing things which facilitates control of objects for purposes of non-cognitive experiences, will come to another conclusion.

To go into this matter at this point would, however, anticipate later discussion. Consequently we confine comment here to the one question: Just what did the new experimental method do to the qualitative objects of ordinary experience? Forget the conclusions of Greek philosophy, put out of the mind all theories about knowledge and about reality. Take the simple direct facts: Here are the colored, resounding, fragrant, lovable, attractive, beautiful things of nature which we enjoy, and which we suffer when they are hateful, ugly, disgusting. Just what is the effect upon them wrought by physical science?

If we consent for the time being to denude the mind of philosophical and metaphysical presuppositions, and take the matter in the most simple and naïve way possible, I think our answer, stated in technical terms, will be that it *substitutes data for objects*. (It is not meant that this outcome is the whole effect of the experimental method; that as we saw at the outset is complex; but that the first effect as far as stripping away qualities is concerned is of this nature.) That Greek science operated with *objects* in the sense of the stars, rocks, trees, rain, warm and cold days of ordinary experience is evident enough. What is signified

---

1. Barry, *The Scientific Habit of Thought*, New York, 1927, p. 249. I owe much more to this volume than this particular quotation.

by saying that the first effect of experimentation was to reduce these things from the status of objects to that of data may not be so clear.[2] By data is signified subject-matter for *further* interpretation; something to be thought about. *Objects* are finalities; they are complete, finished; they call for thought only in the way of definition, classification, logical arrangement, subsumption in syllogisms, etc. But data signify "material to serve"; they are indications, evidence, signs, clues to and of something still to be reached; they are intermediate, not ultimate; means, not finalities.

In a less technical way the matter may be stated as follows: The subject-matter which had been taken as satisfying the demands of knowledge, as the material with which to frame solutions, became something which set *problems*. Hot and cold, wet and dry, light and heavy, instead of being self-evident matters with which to explain phenomena, were things to be investigated; they were "effects," not causal principles; they set question marks instead of supplying answers. The differences between the earth, the region of the planets, and the heavenly ether, instead of supplying ultimate principles which could be used to mark off and classify things, were something to be explained and to bring under identical principles. Greek and medieval science formed an art of accepting things as they are enjoyed and suffered. Modern experimental science is an art of control.

The remarkable difference between the attitude which accepts the objects of ordinary perception, use and enjoyment as final, as culminations of natural processes and that which takes them as starting points for reflection and investigation, is one which reaches far beyond the technicalities of science. It marks a revolution in the whole spirit of life, in the entire attitude taken toward whatever is found in existence. When the things which exist around us, which we touch, see, hear and taste are regarded as interrogations for which an answer must be sought (and must be sought by means of deliberate introduction of changes till they are reshaped into something different), nature as it already exists ceases to be something which must be accepted and submitted to, endured or enjoyed, just as it is. It is now something to be

---

2. For this shift from objects to data see G. H. Mead's essay in the volume entitled *Creative Intelligence*, New York, 1917.

modified, to be intentionally controlled. It is material to act upon so as to transform it into new objects which better answer our needs. Nature as it exists at any particular time is a challenge, rather than a completion; it provides possible starting points and opportunities rather than final ends.

In short, there is a change from knowing as an esthetic enjoyment of the properties of nature regarded as a work of divine art, to knowing as a means of secular control—that is, a method of purposefully introducing changes which will alter the direction of the course of events. Nature as it exists at a given time is material for arts to be brought to bear upon it to reshape it, rather than already a finished work of art. Thus the changed attitude toward change to which reference was made has a much wider meaning than that which the new science offered as a technical pursuit. When correlations of changes are made the goal of knowledge, the fulfillment of its aim in discovery of these correlations is equivalent to placing in our hands an instrument of control. When one change is given, and we know with measured accuracy its connection with another change, we have the potential means of producing or averting that other event. The esthetic attitude is of necessity directed to what is already there; to what is finished, complete. The attitude of control looks to the future, to production.

The same point is stated in another way in saying that the reduction of given objects to data for a knowing or an investigation still to be undertaken liberates man from subjection to the past. The scientific attitude, as an attitude of interest in change instead of interest in isolated and complete fixities, is necessarily alert for problems; every new question is an opportunity for further experimental inquiries—for effecting more directed change. There is nothing which a scientific mind would more regret than reaching a condition in which there were no more problems. That state would be the death of science, not its perfected life. We have only to contrast this disposition with that which prevails in morals and politics to realize the difference which has already been made, as well as to appreciate how limited its development still is. For in higher practical matters we still live in dread of change and of problems. Like men of olden time—with respect to natural phenomena—we prefer to accept and endure or to enjoy—as the case may happen to be—what is, what we find in possession of the field, and at most, to arrange it under concepts, and thus give it the form of rationality.

Before the rise of experimental method, change was simply an inevitable evil; the world of phenomenal existence, that is of change, while an inferior realm compared with the changeless, was nevertheless there and had to be accepted practically as it happened to occur. The wise man if he were sufficiently endowed by fortune would have as little to do with such things as possible, turning away from them to the rational realm. Qualitative forms and complete ends determined by nature are not amenable to human control. They are grateful when they happen to be enjoyed, but for human purposes nature means fortune, and fortune is the contrary of art. A good that happens is welcome. Goods, however, can be made secure in existence only through regulation of processes of change, a regulation dependent upon knowledge of their relations. While the abolition of fixed tendencies toward definite ends has been mourned by many as if it involved a despiritualization of nature, it is in fact a precondition of the projection of new ends and of the possibility of realizing them through intentional activity. Objects which are not fixed goals of nature and which have no inherent defining forms become candidates for receiving new qualities; means for serving new purposes. Until natural objects were denuded of determinate ends which were regarded as the proper outcome of the intrinsic tendency of nature's own operations, nature could not become a plastic material of human desires and purposes.

Such considerations as these are implicit in that changed attitude which by experimental analysis reduces objects to data: the aim of science becomes discovery of constant relations among changes in place of definition of objects immutable beyond the possibility of alteration. It is interested in the mechanism of occurrences instead of in final causes. In dealing with the proximate instead of with the ultimate, knowledge deals with the world in which we live, the world which is experienced, instead of attempting through the intellect to escape to a higher realm. Experimental knowledge is a mode of doing, and like all doing takes place at a time, in a place, and under specifiable conditions in connection with a definite problem.

The notion that the findings of science are a disclosure of the inherent properties of the ultimate real, of existence at large, is a survival of the older metaphysics. It is because of injection of an irrelevant philosophy into interpretation of the conclusions of science that the latter are thought to eliminate qualities and values from nature. Thus is created the standing problem of modern philosophy:—the relation of science to the things we prize and love and which have authority in the direction of conduct. The same injection, in treating the results of mathematical-mechanistic science as a definition of natural reality in its own intrinsic nature, accounts for the antagonism shown to naturalism, and for the feeling that it is the business of philosophy to demonstrate the being of a realm beyond nature, one not subject to the conditions which mark all natural objects. Drop the conception that knowledge is knowledge only when it is a disclosure and definition of the properties of fixed and antecedent reality; interpret the aim and test of knowing by what happens in the actual procedures of scientific inquiry, and the supposed need and problem vanish.

For scientific inquiry always starts from things of the environment experienced in our everyday life, with things we see, handle, use, enjoy and suffer from. This is the ordinary qualitative world. But instead of accepting the qualities and values—the ends and forms—of this world as providing the objects of knowledge, subject to their being given a certain logical arrangement, experimental inquiry treats them as offering a challenge to thought. They are the materials of problems not of solutions. They are *to be* known, rather than objects of knowledge. The first step in knowing is to locate the problems which need solution. This step is performed by altering obvious and given qualities. These are effects; they are things *to be* understood, and they are understood in terms of their generation. The search for "efficient causes" instead of for final causes, for extrinsic relations instead of intrinsic forms, constitutes the aim of science. But the search does not signify a quest for reality in contrast with experience of the unreal and phenomenal. It signifies a search for those relations upon which the *occurrence* of real qualities and values depends, by means of which we can regulate their occurrence. To call existences as they are directly and qualitatively experienced "phenomena" is not to assign to them a metaphysical status. It is to indicate that they set the problem of ascertaining the relations of interaction upon which their occurrence depends.

It is unnecessary that knowledge should be concerned with existence as it is directly experienced in its concrete qualities. Direct experiencing itself takes care of that matter. What science is concerned with is the *happening* of these experienced things. For its purpose, therefore, they *are* happenings, events. Its aim is to discover the conditions and consequences of their happening. And this discovery can take place only by modifying the given qualities in such ways that *relations* become manifest. We shall see later that these relations constitute the proper objects of science as such. We are here concerned to emphasize the fact that elimination of the qualities of experienced existence is merely an intermediate step necessary to the discovery of relations, and that when it is accomplished the scientific object becomes the means of control of occurrence of experienced things having a richer and more secure equipment of values and qualities.

Only when the older theory of knowledge and metaphysics is retained, is science thought to inform us that nature in its true reality is but an interplay of masses in motion, without sound, color, or any quality of enjoyment and use. What science actually does is to show that any natural object we please may be treated in terms of relations upon which its occurrence depends, or as an event, and that by so treating it we are enabled to get behind, as it were, the immediate qualities the object of direct experience presents, and to regulate their happening, instead of having to wait for conditions beyond our control to bring it about. Reduction of experienced objects to the form of relations, which are neutral as respects qualitative traits, is a prerequisite of ability to regulate the course of change, so that it may terminate in the occurrence of an object having desired qualities.

As long, for example, as water is taken to be just the thing which we directly experience it to be, we can put it to a few direct uses, such as drinking, washing, etc. Beyond heating it there was little that could be done purposefully to change its properties. When, however, water is treated not as the glistening, rippling object with the variety of qualities that delight the eye, ear, and palate, but as something symbolized by H_2O, something from which these qualities are completely absent, it becomes amenable to all sorts of other modes of control and adapted to other uses. Similarly, when steam and ice are no longer treated as what they are in their qualitative differences from one another in direct experience, but as homogeneous molecules moving at measured velocities through specified distances, differential qualities that were barriers to effective regulations, as long as they were taken as finalities, are done away with. A single way of acting with respect to them in spite of their differences is indicated. This mode of action is capable of extension to other bodies, in principle to any bodies irrespective of qualitative differences of solid, liquid and gaseous, provided they are given a like mathematical formulation. Thus all sorts of modes of expansion and contraction, of refrigeration and evaporation, of production and regulation of explosive power, become possible. From the practical standpoint, bodies become aggregates of energies to be used in all kinds of ways, involving all sorts of substitutions, transformations, combinations and separations. But the object of direct or perceptible experience remains the same qualitative object, enjoyable and usable, it always was. Water as an object of science, as H_2O with all the other scientific propositions which can be made about it, is not a rival for position in real being with the water we see and use. It is, because of experimental operations, an added instrumentality of multiplied controls and uses of the real things of everyday experience.

I am aware that this method of dealing with the great problem of modern philosophy will be regarded by many as too cavalier a disposition of a great issue; the solution if there be any (and many thinkers would perhaps feel any solution to be a real deprivation) is too simple and easy to be satisfactory. But I shall be content if the account leads anyone to reconsider the traditional beliefs which stand in the way of acceptance of the solution that is proposed. These preconceptions are the assumption that knowledge has a uniquely privileged position as a mode of access to reality in comparison with other modes of experience, and that as such it is superior to practical activity. Both of these ideas were formulated in a period when knowing was regarded as something which could be effected exclusively by means of the rational powers of mind. The development of scientific inquiry with its complete dependence upon experimentation has proved the profound error of the latter position. Is it not time to revise the philosophical conceptions which are founded on a belief now proved to be false? The sum and substance of the present argument is that if we frame our conception of knowledge on the experimental model, we find that it is a way of operating upon and with the things of ordinary experience so that we can frame our ideas of them in terms of their interactions with one another, instead of in terms of the qualities they directly present, and that thereby our control of them, our ability to change them and direct their changes as we desire, is indefinitely increased. Knowing is itself a mode of practical action and is *the* way of interaction by which other natural interactions become subject to direction. Such is the significance of the experimental method as far as we have as yet traced its course.

As was stated at the beginning of this part of the discussion, the examination of scientific knowing is undertaken not so much for its own sake as in order to supply material for projecting a hypothesis about something less technical and of wider and more liberal application. The ulterior issue is the possibility that actual experience in its concrete content and movement may furnish those ideals, meanings and values whose lack and uncertainty in experience as actually lived by most persons has supplied the motive force for recourse to some reality beyond experience: a lack and uncertainty that account for the continued hold of traditional philosophical and religious notions which are not consonant with the main tenor of modern life. The pattern supplied by scientific knowing shows that in this one field at least it is possible for experience, in becoming genuinely experimental, to develop its own regulative ideas and standards. Not only this, but in addition the progress of knowledge of nature has become secure and steady only because of this transformation. The conclusion is a good omen for the possibility of achieving in larger, more humane and liberal fields a similar transformation, so that a philosophy of experience may be empirical without either being false to actual experience or being compelled to explain away the values dearest to the heart of man.

Ideas at Work

Of all philosophical problems that which concerns the nature and worth of ideas is probably the one that most readily appeals to any cultivated mind. The eulogistic flavor which hangs about the word Idealism is a tribute to the respect men pay to thought and its power. The obnoxious quality of materialism is due to its depression of thought, which is treated as an illusion or at most an accidental by-product; materialism leaves no place where ideas have creative or regulative effect. In some sense the cause of ideas, of thought, is felt to be that of the distinctive dignity of man himself. Serious minds have always desired a world in which experiences would be productive of ideas, of meanings, and in which these ideas in turn would regulate conduct. Take away ideas and what follows from them and man seems no better than the beasts of the field.

It is, however, an old story that philosophers have divided into opposed schools as to the nature of ideas and their power. To the extreme right are those who, under the banner of Idealism, have asserted that thought is the creator of the universe and that rational ideas constitute its structure. This constitutive work, however, is something done once for all by thought in a transcendental aboriginal work. The empirical world in which we live from day by day is crass and obdurate, stubbornly un-ideal in character because it is only an appearance of the reality of which thought is the author. This philosophic mode of paying reverence to ideas is thus compensatory rather than vital. It has nothing to do with rendering the natural and social environment of our experience a more ideal abode, namely, one characterized by meanings which are the fruits of thought. There are those who would be willing to exchange the thought which constitutes reality once for all for that thinking which by continued particular acts renders our experienced world here and now more charged with coherent and luminous meanings.

At the other pole is the school of sensational empiricists who hold that the doctrine that thought in any mode of operation is originative is an illusion. It proclaims the necessity of direct, first-hand contact with things as the source of all knowledge. Ideas are pale ghosts of flesh and blood impressions; they are images, pallid reflections, dying echoes of first hand intercourse with reality which takes place in sensation alone.

In spite of the polar opposition between the two schools, they depend upon a common premise. According to both systems of philosophy, *reflective* thought, thinking that involves inference and judgment, is not originative. It has its test in antecedent reality as that is disclosed in some non-reflective immediate knowledge. Its validity depends upon the possibility of checking its conclusions by identification with the terms of such prior immediate knowledge. The controversy between the schools is simply as to the organ and nature of previous direct knowledge. To both schools, reflection, thought involving inference, is *re*productive; the "proof" of its results is found in comparison with what is known without any inference. In traditional empiricism the test is found in sensory impressions. For objective idealism, reflective inquiry is valid only as it reproduces the work previously effected by constitutive thought. The goal of human thinking is approximation to the reality already instituted by absolute reason. The basic premise is also shared by realists. The essence of their position is that reflective inquiry is valid as it terminates in apprehension of that which already exists. When thinking introduces any modification into antecedent reality it falls into error; in fact, productive origination on the part of mind defines error.

The issue is connected with the analysis of experimental knowing which was begun in the preceding chapter. For the common premise of these philosophical schools, so opposed to one another in most ways, goes back to adoption of the idea about knowledge in relation to what is independently real which, originating in Greek thought, has become engrained in tradition. In our summary of the characteristics of experimental thinking, its second trait was said to be the direction of experiment by ideas, the fact that experiment is not random, aimless action, but always includes, along with groping and relatively blind doing, an element of deliberate foresight and intent, which determines that one operation rather than another be tried. In this chapter we shall, accordingly, consider the implications for the theory of ideas that follow from experimental method. Let us suppose, for the time being, that all that we can know about ideas is derived from the way in which they figure in the reflective inquiries of science. What conception of their nature and office shall we then be led to form?

We shall begin, somewhat abruptly, with a statement of the nature of conceptions which has been framed on the basis of recent conclusions in physical science. We shall then compare this idea about ideas with that which was embodied in the Newtonian philosophy of nature and science, and take up the reasons which compelled the abandonment of the latter. Finally we shall recur to a comparison of the result reached with the doctrine embodied in traditional philosophies—one that is identical with that found in the now discredited Newtonian natural philosophy.

The position of present science on this matter has been stated as follows: "To find the length of an object, we have to perform certain physical operations. The concept of length is therefore fixed when the operations by which length is measured are fixed; that is, the concept of length involves as much as and nothing more than the set of operations by which length is determined. In general, we mean by any concept nothing more than a set of operations; *the concept is synonymous with the corresponding set of operations.*"[1] The same idea is repeated by Eddington in his Gifford Lectures. His statement is as follows: "The vocabulary of the physicist comprises a number of words such as length, angle, velocity, force, potential, current, etc., which we call 'physical quantities.' It is now recognised that these should be *defined* according to the way in which we recognise them when actually confronted with them, and not according to the metaphysical significance which we may have anticipated for them. In the old textbooks mass was defined as 'quantity of matter'; but when it came to an actual determination of mass, an experimental

1. Bridgman, *The Logic of Modern Physics*, New York, 1927, p. 5. The italics are in the text.

method was prescribed which had no bearing on this definition."[2] The adoption of this point of view with respect to the
meaning and content of thinking, and as to the validity or soundness of the ideas by means of which we understand natural
events, makes possible what has been lacking throughout the
history of thought, a genuinely experimental empiricism. The
phrase "experimental empiricism" sounds redundant. It ought to
be so in fact, since the adjective and the noun should have the
same significance, so that nothing is gained by using the two
terms. But historically such is not the case. For, historically, empirical philosophies have been framed in terms of sensations or
sense data. These have been said to be the material out of which
ideas are framed and by agreement with which they are to be
tested. Sensory qualities are the antecedent models with which
ideas must agree if they are to be sound or "proved."[3] These doctrines have always evoked an abundance of criticisms. But the
criticisms have taken the form of depreciating the capacity of
"experience" to provide the source and test of our fundamentally important ideas in either knowledge or morals. They have
used the weaknesses of sensational empiricism to reinforce the
notion that ideas are framed by reason apart from any experi-

2. *The Nature of the Physical World*, Cambridge and New York, 1928, pp. 254–
255. It is implied in the quotation that concepts are recognized by means of
the experimental operations by which they are determined; that is, operations
define and test the validity of the meanings by which we state natural happenings. This implication is made explicit a few sentences further along when in
speaking of Einstein Mr. Eddington says his theory "insists that each physical
quantity should be defined as the result of certain operations of measurement
and calculation." The principle is anticipated in Peirce's essay on "How to
Make Our Ideas Clear" published as far back as 1878—now reprinted in a
volume of essays, edited by Morris R. Cohen, and entitled *Chance, Love, and
Logic*, New York, 1923. Peirce states that the sole meaning of the idea of an
object consists of the consequences which result when the object is acted upon
in a particular way. The principle is one element in the pragmatism of James.
The idea is also akin to the "instrumental" theory of conceptions, according
to which they are intellectual instruments for directing our activities in relation to existence. The principle of "extensive abstraction" as a mode of defining things is similar in import. On account of ambiguities in the notion of
pragmatism—although its *logical* import is identical—I shall follow Bridgman in speaking of "operational thinking."
3. The whole empirical logic of Mill professedly, and as far as consistent with
itself, is an endeavor to show that all propositions involving reflection and
ideas must be proved, or demonstrated to be true, by reduction to propositions consisting only of material directly given in sensation.

ence whatsoever; to support what is known in the vocabulary of philosophical systems as an *a priori* rationalism.

From the standpoint of the operational definition and tests of ideas, ideas have an empirical origin and status. But it is that of *acts* performed, acts in the literal and existential sense of the word, deeds done, not reception of sensations forced on us from without. Sensory qualities are important. But they are intellectually significant only as consequences of acts intentionally performed. A color seen at a particular locus in a spectral band is, for example, of immense intellectual importance in chemistry and in astro-physics. But *merely* as seen, as a bare sensory quality, it is the same for the clodhopper and the scientist; in either case, it is the product of a direct sensory excitation; it is just and only another color the eye has happened upon. To suppose that its cognitive value can be eked out or supplied by associating it with other sensory qualities of the same nature as itself, is like supposing that by putting a pile of sand in the eye we can get rid of the irritation caused by a single grain. To suppose, on the other hand, that we must appeal to a synthetic activity of an independent thought to give the quality meaning in and for knowledge, is like supposing that by thinking in our heads we can convert a pile of bricks into a building. Thinking, carried on inside the head, can make some headway in forming the *plan* of a building. But it takes actual operations to which the plan, as the fruit of thought, gives instrumental guidance to make a building out of separate bricks, or to transform an isolated sensory quality into a significant clew to knowledge of nature.

Sensory qualities experienced through vision have their cognitive status and office, not (as sensational empiricism holds) in and of themselves in isolation, or as merely forced upon attention, but because they are the consequences of definite and intentionally performed operations. Only in connection with the intent, or idea, of these operations do they amount to anything, either as disclosing any fact or giving test and proof of any theory. The rationalist school was right in as far as it insisted that sensory qualities are significant for knowledge only when connected by means of ideas. But they were wrong in locating the connecting ideas in intellect apart from experience. Connection is instituted through operations which define ideas, and operations are as much matters of experience as are sensory qualities.

It is not too much to say, therefore, that for the first time there is made possible an empirical theory of ideas free from the burdens imposed alike by sensationalism and *a priori* rationalism. This accomplishment is, I make bold to say, one of three or four outstanding feats of intellectual history. For it emancipates us from the supposed need of always harking back to what has already been given, something had by alleged direct or immediate knowledge in the past, for the test of the value of ideas. A definition of the nature of ideas in terms of operations to be performed and the test of the validity of the ideas by the *consequences* of these operations establishes connectivity within concrete experience. At the same time, by emancipation of thinking from the necessity of testing its conclusions solely by reference to antecedent existence it makes clear the originative possibilities of thinking.

John Locke has always been the central figure in the empirical school. With extraordinary thoroughness he laid the foundations of that empirical logic which tests the validity of every belief about natural existence by the possibility of resolving the content of the belief into simple ideas originally received through the senses. If we want to know what "solidity" or any other idea is, we are, in his own words, "sent to the senses." In developing this theory of the origin and test of our natural knowledge (for he excepted mathematical and moral ideas) he found himself building upon the foundation laid by his illustrious contemporary, Sir Isaac Newton. The latter was convinced of the unsoundness of the rationalistic philosophy of science represented by Descartes, for a time the great rival of Newton for supremacy in the scientific world. Newton's own use of mathematics and also his conception of gravitation (with some other of his physical ideas) exposed him, however, to the charge of reviving the "occult essences" of scholasticism. Accordingly, he was very emphatic upon the point that he was thoroughly empirical in premises, method and conclusions; empirical in that he had gone to his senses and taken what he found there as the origin and justification of his primary scientific ideas about nature. As we shall see, certain assumptions of Newton were in fact far from empirical in any experimental sense of that word, but were introduced by him into the philosophical foundations of natural science and were thence taken over into the whole philosophic theory of science to be questioned only in our own day.

No saying of Newton's is more widely known than that "I do not invent hypotheses." This is only his negative way of asserting complete reliance upon a subject-matter guaranteed by the senses—which in turn signifies, as we have just said, that all scientific ideas go *back* to sense perceptions previously had for both their origin and their warrant. We shall consider first the effect of Newton's procedure upon the supposed foundations of natural science, and then consider how the recognition of an operational—and relational—definition of scientific conceptions instead of a discrete and sensory one has destroyed those foundations.

While Newton employed mathematical conceptions with a freedom equal to that of Descartes and with a heuristic power far exceeding Descartes, he differentiated his own method from that of the latter by insisting that the objects to which his mathematical calculations applied were not products of thought, but were given, as far as the properties which figured in his science were concerned, in sense. That is, he did not claim that he could sensibly observe the ultimate particles or atoms which were the foundation of his system, but he did claim that he had sensible grounds for assuming their existence, and especially he insisted that all the properties with which his scientific theory endowed these particles were derived from and were verifiable in direct sense-perception. In his own words: "Whatever is not derived from phaenomena is to be called a hypothesis; and hypotheses . . . have no place in experimental philosophy." The positive counterpart of this negative statement is as follows: "The qualities of bodies which admit of neither intension nor remission of degree and which are found to belong to all bodies within the reach of experiments, are to be assumed the universal qualities of all bodies whatsoever."

Newton's assumption that he was only extending to the ultimate proper objects of physical science those qualities of experienced objects that are disclosed in direct perception is made evident by such passages as the following: "We no other way know the extension of bodies than by our senses, nor do these reach it in all bodies. But because we perceive extension in all bodies that are sensible, therefore we ascribe it universally to all others also.

That abundance of bodies are hard, we learn by experience; and because the hardness of the whole arises from the hardness of the parts, we therefore justly infer the hardness of the undivided particles not only of the bodies we feel but of all others. That all bodies are impenetrable we gather not from reason but from sensation. . . . That all bodies are moveable and are endued with certain powers (which we call the *vires inertiae*) of persevering in their motion or in their rest we only infer from like properties observ'd in the bodies that we have seen." Or as Newton says of his "principles," summing it all up: "I consider them not as occult Qualities but as general Laws of Nature . . . their Truth *appearing to us by Phaenomena*." The principles in question were mass, gravity, hardness, impenetrability, extension, motion, inertia, etc.

The essential point of his argument is that non-sensible bodies, namely, the ultimate particles to which mathematical reasoning applies, are endowed with no properties save those which are found by experience to belong to all bodies of which we do have sensible experience. The static (spatial extension, volume) qualities, and the dynamic properties (resistance, perseverance in motion) of ultimate physical realities, are homogeneous with the common qualities of sensibly perceived things. Color, sound, heat, odor, etc., go out, since they permit of absence, and of remission and increase of degrees—or are not universally present. Volume, mass, inertia, motion and moveability, remain as universal qualities. What would happen if the objection were raised that the existence of the ultimate particles is hypothetical, since they are not observed? What becomes of his empiricism even if the properties ascribed to particles are all sensibly verified, provided the bearers of these properties are not observed? It can hardly be said that Newton explicitly discusses this question. It seemed to him practically self-evident that since sensible bodies were divisible without losing the properties that form his "principles," we are entitled to assume the existence of certain last particles of the same kind incapable of further division. And while, in logical consistency, he could hardly have admitted the argument, the fact that he found that he could "explain" actual occurrences on the basis of this assumption seemed to give him ample confirmation of their existence. Perhaps in the following passage he comes as near as anywhere to dealing explicitly with the point: After saying that if *all* particles, all bodies whatever, were capable of being broken, they would then wear away, he goes on to say that in that case the "Nature of Things depending on them would be changed," and adds "and therefore that *Nature may be lasting*, the Changes of corporeal Things are to be placed only in the various Separations and new Associations and Motions of these permanent Particles." "So that nature may be lasting!" It would be hard to find a franker statement of the motive which controlled Newton's doctrine. There was needed some guarantee that Nature would not go to pieces and be dissipated or revert to chaos. How could the unity of anything be secure unless there was something persistent and unchanging behind all change? Without such fixed indissoluble unities, no final certainty was possible. Everything was put in peril of dissolution. These metaphysical fears rather than any experimental evidence determined the nature of the fundamental assumptions of Newton regarding atoms. They furnished the premises which he regarded as scientific and as the very foundations of the possibility of science. "All changes are to be placed in only the separations and new associations of permanent particles." In this statement there is contained a professedly scientific restatement of the old human desire for something fixed as the warrant and object of absolute certainty. Without this fixity knowledge was impossible. Changes are to be known by treating them as indifferent spatial approaches and withdrawals taking place between things that are themselves eternally the same. Thus to establish certainty in existence and in knowledge, "God in the Beginning form'd Matter in solid, massy, hard, impenetrable Particles."

It was logically inevitable that as science proceeded on its experimental path it would sooner or later become clear that all conceptions, all intellectual descriptions, must be formulated in terms of operations, actual or imaginatively possible. There are no conceivable ways in which the existence of ultimate unchangeable substances which interact without undergoing change in themselves can be reached by means of experimental operations. Hence they have no empirical, no experimental standing; they are pure dialectic inventions. They were not even necessary for application of the mathematical method of Newton. Most of his analytic work in his *Principles* would remain unchanged, if his physical particles were dropped out and geometrical points were substituted. What reason can be assigned for Newton's desertion of an experimental method and for the adoption in its stead of an obviously dialectical conception—since the conception that the permanence of nature depends upon the assumption of a plurality of discrete immutable substances is clearly dialectical? Doubtless in part the reason was that the scheme worked or seemed to work. Without developing or acknowledging the consequences of this mode of justification, objections based on theory could always be met by pointing to the marvelous conclusions of physical inquiry.

But a more fundamental reason was that the minds of men, including physical inquirers, were still possessed by the old notion that reality in order to be solid and firm must consist of those fixed immutable things which philosophy calls substances. Changes could be *known* only if they could be somehow reduced to recombinations of original unchanging things. For these alone can be objects of certainty—the changing is as such the uncertain—and only the certain and exact is knowledge. Thus a popular metaphysics, given rational formulation by the Greeks, and taken over into the intellectual tradition of the western world, controlled at first the interpretations placed upon the procedures and conclusions of experimental knowing.

This hypothesis as to the origin of the non-experimental factor in the Newtonian philosophy is confirmed by his own use of the metaphysics of the ideas of substance and essential properties. The fact that Newton adopted the Democritean rather than the Aristotelian conception of substance is of course of immense importance scientifically. But philosophically speaking it is of slight import compared with the fact that he followed the supposed necessities of dialectic reasoning rather than the lead of experienced subject-matter in accepting without question the notion that there must be at the foundation of all existence certain things which are intrinsically unchangeable, and that such immutable entities are the objects of any true knowledge because they give the warrant of fixed certitude.

With his acceptance of the old doctrines of substances goes that of the doctrine of essence. If fixed unchangeable things exist, they must have certain inherent, unchangeable properties. Changes are accidental and external; they occur *between* substances and do not affect their inner nature. If they did, substances would not be substances; they would change and rot away. Hence, in spite of starting upon the experimental and mathematical path, Newtonian science kept the idea that atoms are characterized by eternal properties or qualities, that is by essences. Substances are "solid, hard, massy, impenetrable, moveable particles." Their essence is precisely these unchangeable, fixed qualities of solidity, mass, motion, inertia.

It thus appears that Newton retained a part of the qualitative equipment of the objects of Greek science, in spite of their irrelevance to both mathematics and experiment. When one searches through philosophical commentary and discussion (based mainly on Locke's version of Newton's results), one finds a great deal of discussion about the fact that the so-called secondary qualities, color, sound, odor, taste, were eliminated from "reality." But not a word as far as I can discover is said about the fact that *other* sensible qualities under the name of primary were retained in defining the object of science. And yet this retention is the *fons et origo malorum*. The actual fact was that science by means of its operational conceptions was instituting as its objects of thought things in a dimension different from *any* of the direct *qualities* of objects. It was not a question of getting rid of some immediate sense qualities; but of a treatment indifferent to any and all qualities. Newton could not realize this fact, because he insisted that the existence of hard and fixed unchanging substances was the basis of science. Given such substances they had to have some qualities as their inherent properties.

Hence Newton generously endowed them with those properties which he insisted were directly taken from sense experience itself. Consider the consequences for subsequent thought. Getting rid of some qualities which had been regarded as essential to natural things while retaining others, did not forward in the least the actual work of science, while it did work inevitably to establish a fixed gulf and opposition between the things of ordinary perception, use and enjoyment and the objects of science which, according to tradition, were the only ultimately "real" objects. The story of the extent to which this opposition became the underlying problem of modern philosophy need not be retold. Nor are we called upon here to consider the way in which it generated an "epistemological" problem of knowledge in the general terms of relation of subject and object, as distinct from the logical

problem of the methods by which inquiry shall attain understanding. For qualities expelled from scientific objects were given
an asylum "in the mind"; they became mental and psychical in
nature, and the problem arose how mind composed of such elements, having nothing in common with objects of science—by
doctrinal definition the real things of nature—could possibly
reach out and know their own opposites. In another connection,
that result would provide a theme most important to discuss:—
from its origin in Berkeley's contention that since "secondary"
qualities are avowedly mental and since primary qualities cannot
be disassociated from them, the latter must be mental also,
through all the sinuosities of modern thought in dealing with the
"problem." But the first of these points, the rivalry of scientific
objects and empirical objects for position in natural existence,
has already been dealt with and the latter problem is not immediately relevant.

We are here concerned with the Newtonian assumption that
we must carry over into the conception and definition of physical objects some of the qualities directly experienced in sense-
perception, while their presence in such sense-experience is the
warrant or "proof" of their validity as ideas. There was no direct
experience of the ultimate massy, hard, impenetrable and indi-
visible and hence unchangeable particles—since indeed their
eternal permanence obviously was a thing incapable of any
experience except by some equally eternal mind. Hence these
qualities must be *thought*, they must be inferred. In themselves
they exist by themselves. But for us, they exist as objects of
thought only. Hence as ideas they need a warrant and justification which primary qualities of immediate perception do not
need, since these are self-warranting—according to the doctrine.

Now so deeply engrained are the conclusions of the old tradition of rationalism versus (sensationalistic) empiricism, that the
question will still be raised: What other certification could be
given or can now be given for the properties of scientific physical
objects save by inferential extension of the universally found
properties of all objects of sense perception? Is there any alternative unless we are prepared to fall back upon *a priori* rational
conceptions supposed to bring their own sufficient authority
with them?

It is at this point that the recent recognition that the conceptions by which we think scientific objects are derived neither from sense nor from *a priori* conceptions has its logical and philosophical force. Sense qualities, as we saw in the previous chapter, are something *to be* known, they are challenges to knowing, setting problems for investigation. Our scientific knowledge is something *about* them, resolving the problems they propose. Inquiry proceeds by reflection, by thinking; but *not*, most decidedly, by thinking as conceived in the old tradition, as something cooped up within "mind." For experimental inquiry or thinking signifies *directed activity*, doing something which varies the conditions under which objects are observed and directly had and by instituting new arrangements among them. Things perceived suggest to us (originally just evoke or stimulate) certain ways of responding to them, of treating them. These operations have been continuously refined and elaborated during the history of man on earth, although it is only during the last few centuries that the whole affair of controlled thinking and of its issue in genuine knowledge, has been seen to be bound up with their selection and determination.

The central question thus arises: What determines the selection of operations to be performed? There is but one answer:—the nature of the problem to be dealt with—an answer which links the phase of experiment now under discussion with that considered in the last chapter. The first effect of experimental analysis is, as we saw, to reduce objects directly experienced to data. This resolution is required because the objects in their first mode of experience are perplexing, obscure, fragmentary; in some way they fail to answer a need. Given data which locate the nature of the problem, there is evoked a thought of an operation which if put into execution may eventuate in a situation in which the trouble or doubt which evoked inquiry will be resolved. If one were to trace the history of science far enough, one would reach a time in which the acts which dealt with a troublesome situation would be organic responses of a structural type together with a few acquired habits. The most elaborate technique of present inquiry in the laboratory is an extension and refinement of these simple original operations. Its development has for the most part depended upon the utilization of physical instruments, which when inquiry was developed to a certain point were purposely invented. In principle, the history of the construction of suitable operations in the scientific field is not different from that of their evolution in industry. Something needed to be done to accomplish an end; various devices and methods of operation were tried. Experiences of success and failure gradually improved the means used. More economical and effective ways of acting were found—that is, operations which gave the desired kind of result with greater ease, less irrelevancy and less ambiguity, greater security. Each forward step was attended with making better tools. Often the invention of a tool suggested operations not in mind when it was invented and thus carried the perfecting of operations still further. There is thus no *a priori* test or rule for the determination of the operations which define ideas. They are themselves experimentally developed in the course of actual inquiries. They originated in what men naturally do and are tested and improved in the course of doing.

This is as far as the answer to the query can be carried in a formal way. Consequences that successfully solve the problems set by the conditions which give rise to the need of action supply the basis by means of which acts, originally "naturally" performed, become the operations of the art of scientific experimentation. In content, a much more detailed answer can be given. For this answer, one would turn to the historical development of science, in which is recorded what kind of operations have definitely been found to effect the transformation of the obscure and perplexing situations of experience into clear and resolved situations. To go into this matter would be to expound the character of the concepts actually employed in the best developed branches of reflection or inquiry.

While such a discussion is apart from our purpose, there is one common character of all such scientific operations which it is necessary to note. *They are such as disclose relationships.* A simple case is the operation by which length is defined by one object placed end upon end upon another object so many times. This type of operation, repeated under conditions themselves defined by specified operations, not merely fixes the relation of two things to each other called *their* length, but defines a generalized concept of length. This conception in connection with other operations, such as those which define mass and time, become instruments by means of which a multitude of relations between bodies can be established. Thus the conceptions which define units of measurement of space, time and motion become the intellectual instrumentalities by which all sorts of things with no qualitative similarity with one another can be compared and brought within the same system. To the original gross experience of things there is superadded another type of experience, the product of deliberate art, of which *relations* rather than qualities are the significant subject-matter. These connections are as much experienced as are the qualitatively diverse and irreducible objects of original natural experiences.

Qualities present themselves as just what they are, statically demarcated from one another. Moreover, they rarely change, when left to themselves, in such ways as to indicate the interactions or relations upon which their occurrence depends. No one ever observed the production of the thing having the properties of water, nor the mode of generation of a flash of lightning. In sensory perception the qualities are either too static or too abruptly discrete to manifest the specific connections that are involved in their coming into existence. Intentional variation of conditions gives an idea of these connections. Through thought of them the things are understood or truly known. Only slowly, however, did there dawn the full import of the scientific method. For a long time the definitions were supposed to be made not in terms of relations but through certain properties of antecedent things. The space, time and motion of physics were treated as inherent properties of Being, instead of as abstracted relations. In fact, two phases of inquiry accompany each other and correspond to each other. In one of these phases, everything in qualitative objects except their happening is ignored, attention being paid to qualities only as signs of the nature of the particular happening in question: that is, objects are treated as *events*. In the other phase, the aim of inquiry is to correlate events with one another. Scientific conceptions of space, time and motion constitute the generalized system of these correlations of events. Thus they are doubly dependent upon operations of experimental art: upon those which treat qualitative objects as events, and upon those which connect events thus determined with one another.

In these statements we have, however, anticipated the actual movement of scientific thought. This took a long time to arrive at recognition of its own import. Till our own day, scientific conceptions were interpreted in the light of the old belief that con-

ceptions to be valid must correspond to antecedent intrinsic
properties resident in objects dealt with. Certain properties regarded by Newton as inherent in substances and essential to
them, in independence of connectivity, were indeed speedily seen
to be relations. This conversion happened first as to hardness
and impenetrability, which were seen to be reducible to mass. *Vis
inertiae* was a measure of mass. By careful thinkers "force" was
treated as a measure of acceleration and so a name for a relation,
not as an inherent property of an isolated thing by virtue of
which one thing could compel another to change. Nevertheless,
until the promulgation of Einstein's restricted theory of relativity, mass, time and motion were regarded as intrinsic properties of ultimate fixed and independent substances.

We shall postpone till later consideration of the circumstances
attending the change. We are here concerned with the fact that
when it took place it was, in spite of its upsetting effects upon the
foundation of the Newtonian philosophy of science and of nature, from the logical point of view only a clear acknowledgment
of what had all the time been the moving principle of the development of scientific method. To say this is not to disparage the
scientific importance of the discovery that mass varies with velocity and of the result of the Michelson-Morley experiment on
the velocity of light. Such discoveries were doubtless necessary in
order to force recognition of the operational or relational character of scientific conceptions. And yet, logically, the way in
which space, time and motion, with their various functions,
appear in mathematical equations and are translated into equivalent formulations with respect to one another—something which
is impossible for qualities as such—indicates that a relational
treatment had always been involved. But the imagination of men
had become used to ideas framed on the pattern of large masses
and relatively slow velocities. It required observation of changes
of high velocity, as of light over great distances, and of minute
changes occurring at infinitesimal distances to emancipate imagination from its acquired habitudes. The discovery that mass varies with velocity did away with the possibility of continuing to
suppose that mass is the defining characteristic of things in isolation from one another—such isolation being the sole condition
under which mass could be regarded as immutable or fixed.

The difference made in the actual content of scientific theory is of course enormous. Yet it is not so great as the difference made in the logic of scientific knowledge, nor as in philosophy. With the surrender of unchangeable substances having properties fixed in isolation and unaffected by interactions, must go the notion that certainty is attained by attachment to fixed objects with fixed characters. For not only are no such objects found to exist, but the very nature of experimental method, namely, definition by operations that are interactions, implies that such things are not capable of being known. Henceforth the quest for certainty becomes the search for methods of control; that is, regulation of conditions of change with respect to their consequences.

Theoretical certitude is assimilated to practical certainty; to *security*, trustworthiness of instrumental operations. "Real" things may be as transitory as you please or as lasting in time as you please; these are specific differences like that between a flash of lightning and the history of a mountain range. In any case they are for knowledge "events" not substances. What knowledge is interested in is the correlation among these changes or events—which means in effect that the event called the mountain range must be placed within a system consisting of a vast multitude of included events. When these correlations are discovered, the possibility of control is in our hands. Scientific objects as statements of these inter-relations are instrumentalities of control. They are objects of the *thought* of reality, not disclosures of immanent properties of real substances. They are in particular the thought of reality from a particular point of view: the most highly generalized view of nature as a system of interconnected changes.

Certain important conclusions follow. The test of the validity of ideas undergoes a radical transformation. In the Newtonian scheme, as in the classic tradition, this test resided in properties belonging to ultimate real objects in isolation from one another, and hence fixed or unchanging. According to experimental inquiry, the validity of the object of thought depends upon the *consequences* of the operations which define the object of thought. For example, colors are conceived in terms of certain numbers. The conceptions are valid in the degree in which, by means of these numbers, we can predict future events, and can regulate the interactions of colored bodies as signs of changes that take place. The numbers are signs or clues of intensity and direction of changes going on. The only things relevant to the question of their validity is whether they are dependable signs. That heat is a mode of motion does not signify that heat and cold as qualitatively experienced are "unreal," but that the qualitative experience can be treated as an event measured in terms of units of velocity of movement, involving units of position and time, so that it can be connected with other events or changes similarly formulated. The test of the validity of any particular intellectual conception, measurement or enumeration is functional, its use in making possible the institution of interactions which yield results in control of actual experiences of observed objects.

In contrast with this fact, in the Newtonian philosophy measurements are important because they were supposed to disclose just how much of a certain property belonged to some body as its own isolated and intrinsic property. Philosophically, the effect of this view was to reduce the "reality" of objects to just such mathematical and mechanical properties—hence the philosophical "problem" of the relation of real physical objects to the objects of experience with their qualities and immediate values of enjoyment and use. Mr. Eddington has said that "the whole of our physical knowledge is based on measures," and that "whenever we state the properties of a body in terms of physical quantities, we are imparting the responses of various metrical indicators to its presence, *and nothing more.*" [4] His graphic illustration of the physical formulation of what happens when an elephant slides downhill comes to mind. The mass of the elephant is the reading of a pointer on a weighing scale; the slope of the hill, the reading of a plumb line against the divisions of a protractor; bulk, a series of readings on the scale of a pair of calipers; color, readings of a photometer for light; the duration of the slide, a series of readings on a watch dial, etc.

It seems almost too obvious for mention that a scientific object consisting of a set of measurements of relations between two qualitative objects, and itself accordingly non-qualitative, cannot possibly be taken, or even mis-taken, for a new kind of "real" object which is a rival to the "reality" of the ordinary object. But so loath are we to surrender traditional conceptions and unwilling as philosophers to surrender as unreal problems which

4. *The Nature of the Physical World*, pp. 152 and 257.

have long engaged attention, that even Mr. Eddington feels called upon to reclothe these scientific measured relations with qualities as something which "mind" mysteriously introduced! Prisoners in jails are often given numbers and are "known" by the numbers assigned. It has not yet occurred to any one that these numbers are the real prisoners, and that there is always a duplicate real object; one a number, and the other a flesh and blood person, and that these two editions of reality have to be reconciled. It is true that the numbers which constitute by means of measurements the object of scientific thought are not assigned so arbitrarily as those of prisoners, but there is no difference in philosophical principle.

Incidentally, Mr. Eddington remarks in his discussion of the metric properties of the object of thought that a knowledge of all possible responses of a concrete thing as measured by suitable devices "would completely determine *its relation to its environment.*" The relations a thing sustains are hardly a competitor to the thing itself. Put positively, the physical object, as scientifically defined, is not a duplicated real object, but is a statement, as numerically definite as is possible, of the relations between sets of changes the qualitative object sustains with changes in other things—ideally of all things with which interaction might under any circumstances take place.

Since these correlations are what physical inquiry *does* know, it is fair to conclude that they are what it intends or means to know: on analogy with the legal maxim that any reasonable person intends the reasonably probable consequences of what he does. We come back again to the frequently repeated statement that the problem which has given so much trouble to modern philosophy—that of reconciling the reality of the physical object of science with the richly qualitative object of ordinary experience, is a factitious one. All that is required in order to apprehend that scientific knowledge as a mode of active operation is a potential ally of the modes of action which sustain values in existence, is to surrender the traditional notion that knowledge is possession of the inner nature of things and is the only way in which they may be experienced as they "really" are.

For if one change is correlated definitely with others it can be employed as an indication of their occurrence. Seeing one thing happen we can promptly infer upon what it depends, and what needs to be reinforced or to be weakened if its presence is to be made more secure or is to be done away with. In itself, the object is just what it is experienced as being, hard, heavy, sweet, sonorous, agreeable or tedious and so on. But in being "there" these traits are effects, not causes. They cannot as such be used as means, and when they are set up as ends in view, we are at a loss how to secure them. For just as qualities there are no constant and definite relations which can be ascertained between them and other things. If we wish to regard them not as fixed properties but as things to be attained, we must be able to look upon them as dependent events. If we wish to be able to judge *how* they may be attained, we must connect them as changes with other changes more nearly in our power, until by means of a transitive series of connected changes we arrive at that which we can initiate by our own acts. If one with understanding of the whole situation were to set out to devise means of control of the experience of qualitative values, he would plot a course which would be identical with that followed by experimental science; one in which the results of knowledge would bear the same relation to acts to be performed as do those of actual physical knowledge.

Ability, through a definite or measured correlation of changes, to connect one with another as sign or evidence is the precondition of control. It does not of itself provide direct control; reading the index hand of a barometer as a sign of probable rain does not enable us to stop the coming of the rain. But it does enable us to change our relations to it: to plant a garden, to carry an umbrella on going out, to direct the course of a vessel at sea, etc. It enables *preparatory* acts to be undertaken which make values less insecure. If it does not enable us to regulate just what is to take place, it enables us to direct some phase of it in a way which influences the stability of purposes and results. In other cases, as in the arts proper, we can not only modify our own attitude so as to effect useful preparation for what is to happen, but we can modify the happening itself. This use of one change or perceptible occurrence as a sign of others and as a means of preparing ourselves, did not wait for the development of modern science. It is as old as man himself, being the heart of all intelligence. But accuracy and scope of such judgments, which are the only means with power to direct the course of events and to effect the security of values, depends upon the use of methods such as modern physics has made available.

Extent of control is dependent, as was suggested a moment ago, upon capacity to find a connected series of correlated changes, such that each linked pair leads on to another in the direction of a terminal one which can be brought about by our own action. It is this latter condition which is especially fulfilled by the objects of scientific thought. Physical science disregards the qualitative heterogeneity of experienced objects so as to make them all members in one comprehensive homogeneous scheme, and hence capable of translation or conversion one into another. This homogeneity of subject-matter over a broad range of things which are as disparate from each other in direct experience as sound and color, heat and light, friction and electricity, is the source of the wide and free control of events found in modern technology. Common sense knowledge can connect things as sign and thing indicated here and there by isolated couples. But it cannot possibly join them all up together so that we can pass from any one to any other. The homogeneity of scientific objects, through formulation in terms of relations of space, time and motion, is precisely the device which makes this indefinitely broad and flexible scheme of transitions possible. The meaning which one event has is translatable into the meanings which others possess. Ideas of objects, formulated in terms of the relations which changes bear to one another, having common measures, institute broad, smooth highways by means of which we can travel from the thought of one part of nature to that of any other. In ideal at least, we can travel from any meaning—or relation—found anywhere in nature to the meaning to be expected anywhere else.

We have only to compare thinking and judging objects in terms of these measured interactions with the classic scheme of a hierarchy of species and genera to see the great gain that has been effected. It is the very nature of fixed kinds to be as exclusive with respect to those of a different order as it is to be inclusive with respect to those which fall within the class. Instead of a thoroughfare from one order to another, there was a sign: No passage. The work of emancipation which was initiated by experimentation, setting objects free from limitation by old habits and customs, reducing them to a collection of data forming a problem for inquiry, is perfected by the method of conceiving and defining objects through operations which have as their consequence accurate metric statements of changes correlated with changes going on elsewhere.

The resolution of objects and nature as a whole into facts stated exclusively in terms of quantities which may be handled in calculation, such as saying that red *is* such a number of changes while green is another, seems strange and puzzling only when we fail to appreciate what it signifies. In reality, it is a declaration that this is the effective way to *think* things; the effective mode in which to frame ideas of them, to formulate their meanings. The procedure does not vary in principle from that by which it is stated that an article is worth so many dollars and cents. The latter statement does not say that the article is literally or in its ultimate "reality" so many dollars and cents; it says that for purpose of exchange that is the way to *think* of it, to judge it. It has many other meanings and these others are usually more important inherently. But *with respect to trade*, it *is* what it is worth, what it will sell for, and the price value put upon it expresses the relation it bears to other things in exchange. The advantage in stating its worth in terms of an abstract measure of exchange such as money, instead of in terms of the amount of corn, potatoes or some other special thing it will exchange for, is that the latter method is restricted and the former generalized. Development of the systems of units by which to measure sensible objects (or form ideas of them) has come along with discovery of the ways in which the greatest amount of free movement from one conception to another is possible.

The formulation of ideas of experienced objects in terms of measured quantities, as these are established by an intentional art or technique, does not say that this is the way they *must* be thought, the *only* valid way of thinking them. It states that for the purpose of generalized, indefinitely extensive translation from one idea to another, this is the way to think them. The statement is like any other statement about instruments, such as that so-and-so is the best way of sending a number of telegraphic dispatches simultaneously. As far as it is actually the best instrumentality, the statement is correct. It has to be proved by *working* better than any other agency; it is in process of continuous revision and improvement. For purposes except that of general and extensive translation of one conception into another, it does not follow that the "scientific" way is the best way of thinking an affair. The nearer we come to an action that is to have an individualized unique object of experience for its conclusion, the less do we think the things in question in these exclusively metric terms. The physician in practice will not think in terms as general and abstract as those of the physiologist in the laboratory, nor the engineer in the field in those as free from special application as will the physicist in his work-shop. There are many ways of thinking things in relation to one another; they are, as conceptions, instruments. The value of an instrument depends upon what is to be done with it. The fine scale micrometer which is indispensable in the successful performance of one operation would be a hindrance in some other needed act; and a watch spring is useless to give elasticity to a mattress.

There is something both ridiculous and disconcerting in the way in which men have let themselves be imposed upon, so as to infer that scientific ways of thinking of objects give the inner reality of things, and that they put a mark of spuriousness upon all other ways of thinking of them, and of perceiving and enjoying them. It is ludicrous because these scientific conceptions, like other instruments, are hand-made by man in pursuit of realization of a certain interest—that of the maximum convertibility of every object of thought into any and every other. It is a wonderful ideal; the ingenuity which man has shown in devising means of realizing the interest is even more marvelous. But these ways of thinking are no more rivals of or substitutes for objects as directly perceived and enjoyed than the power-loom, which is a more effective instrument for weaving cloth than was the old hand-loom, is a substitute and rival for cloth. The man who is disappointed and tragic because he cannot wear a loom is in reality no more ridiculous than are the persons who feel troubled because the objects of scientific conception of natural things have not the same uses and values as the things of direct experience.

The disconcerting aspect of the situation resides in the difficulty with which mankind throws off beliefs that have become habitual. The test of ideas, of thinking generally, is found in the consequences of the acts to which the ideas lead, that is in the new arrangements of things which are brought into existence. Such is the unequivocal evidence as to the worth of ideas which is derived from observing their position and role in experimental knowing. But tradition makes the tests of ideas to be their agreement with some *antecedent* state of things. This change of outlook and standard from what precedes to what comes after, from the retrospective to the prospective, from antecedents to consequences, is extremely hard to accomplish. Hence when the physical sciences describe objects and the world as being such and such, it is thought that the description is of reality as it exists in itself. Since all value-traits are lacking in objects as science presents them to us, it is assumed that *Reality* has not such characteristics.

In the previous chapter, we saw that experimental method, in reducing objects to data, divests experienced things of their qualities, but that this removal, judged from the standpoint of the whole operation of which it is one part, is a condition of the control which enables us to endow the objects of experience with other qualities which we want them to have. In like fashion, thought, our conceptions and ideas, are designations of operations to be performed or already performed. Consequently their value is determined by the outcome of these operations. They are sound if the operations they direct give us the results which are required. The authority of thought depends upon what it leads us to through directing the performance of operations. The business of thought is not to conform to or reproduce the characters already possessed by objects but to judge them as potentialities of what they become through an indicated operation. This principle holds from the simplest case to the most elaborate. To judge that this object is sweet, that is, to refer the idea or meaning "sweet" to it without actually experiencing sweetness, is to predict that when it is tasted—that is, subjected to a specified operation—a certain consequence will ensue. Similarly, to think of the world in terms of mathematical formulae of space, time and motion is not to have a picture of the independent and fixed essence of the universe. It is to describe experienceable objects as material upon which certain operations are performed.

The bearing of this conclusion upon the relation of knowledge and action speaks for itself. Knowledge which is merely a reduplication in ideas of what exists already in the world may afford us the satisfaction of a photograph, but that is all. To form ideas whose worth is to be judged by what exists independently of them is not a function that (even if the test could be applied, which seems impossible) goes on within nature or makes any difference there. Ideas that are plans of operations to be performed are integral factors in actions which change the face of the world. Idealistic philosophies have not been wrong in attaching vast importance and power to ideas. But in isolating their function and their test from action, they failed to grasp the point and place where ideas have a constructive office. A genuine idealism and one compatible with science will emerge as soon as philosophy accepts the teaching of science that ideas are statements not of what is or has been but of acts to be performed. For then mankind will learn that, intellectually (that is, save for the esthetic enjoyment they afford, which is of course a true value), ideas are worthless except as they pass into actions which rearrange and reconstruct in some way, be it little or large, the world in which we live. To magnify thought and ideas for their own sake apart from what they do (except, once more, esthetically) is to refuse to learn the lesson of the most authentic kind of knowledge—the experimental—and it is to reject the idealism which involves responsibility. To praise thinking above action because there is so much ill-considered action in the world is to help maintain the kind of a world in which action occurs for narrow and transient purposes. To seek after ideas and to cling to them as means of conducting operations, as factors in practical arts, is to participate in creating a world in which the springs of thinking will be clear and ever-flowing. We recur to our general issue. When we take the instance of scientific experience in its own field, we find that experience when it is experimental does not signify the absence of large and far-reaching ideas and purposes. It is dependent upon them at every point. But it generates them within its own procedures and tests them by its own operations. In so far, we have the earnest of a possibility of human experience, in all its phases, in which ideas and meanings will be prized and will be continuously generated and used. But they will be integral with the course of experience itself, not imported from the external source of a reality beyond.

6. The Play of Ideas

The problem of the nature, office and test of ideas is not exhausted in the matter of physical conceptions we have discussed in the preceding chapter. Mathematical ideas are indispensable instruments of physical research, and no account of the method of the latter is complete that does not take into account the applicability of mathematical conceptions to natural existence. Such ideas have always seemed to be the very type of pure conceptions, of thought in its own nature unadulterated with material derived from experience. To a constant succession of philosophers, the role of mathematics in physical analysis and formulation has seemed to be a proof of the presence of an invariant rational element within physical existence, which is on that account something more than physical; this role of conceptions has been the stumbling block of empiricists in trying to account for science on an empirical basis.

The significance of mathematics for philosophy is not confined to this seemingly superphysical phase of the physical world, and a superempirical factor in knowledge of it. Mathematical conceptions as expressions of pure thought have also seemed to provide the open gateway to a realm of essence that is independent of existence, physical or mental—a self-subsisting realm of ideal and eternal objects which are the objects of the highest—that is, the most assured—knowledge. As was earlier noted, the Euclidean geometry was undoubtedly the pattern for the development of a formally rational logic; it was also a marked factor in leading Plato to his doctrine of a world of supersensible and superphysical ideal objects. The procedure of mathematics has, moreover, always been the chief reliance of those who have asserted that the demonstrated validity of all reflective thinking depends upon rational truths immediately known without any element of inference entering in. For mathematics was supposed to rest upon a basis of first truths or axioms, self-evident in nature, and needing only that the eye of reason should fall upon them to be recognized for what they are. The function of indemonstrables, of axioms and definitions, in mathematical deduction has been the ground for the distinction between intuitive and discursive reason, just as deductions have been taken to be the convincing proof that there is a realm of pure essences logically connected with one another:—universals having internal bonds with one another.

The theory that conceptions are definitions of consequences of operations needs therefore to be developed with reference to mathematical ideas both for its own sake, and for its bearing upon the philosophic issues which are basic to the logic of rationalism and to the metaphysics of essences and universals or invariants. We shall begin with mathematical concepts in their physical sense, and then consider them as they are developed apart from existential application. Although Descartes defined natural existence as extension, the classic tradition that only sense and imagination, among the organs of mind, refer to physical existence caused him to feel bound to offer justification for the doctrine that natural phenomena can be scientifically stated by purely mathematical reasoning without need of recourse to experimentation. His proof of the existence of God served the purpose of justifying this application of mathematical conceptions in physics. With Spinoza, the correspondence between physical existence and ideas did not need to be substantiated by God because it *was* God. This correspondence when modified to give thought such a priority as to include existence within itself became the animating motif of Post-Kantian idealistic systems.

Newton, being a man of science rather than a professed philosopher, made such assumptions as he thought scientific procedure demanded and its conclusions warranted. The skepticism of Hume (anticipated, however, by Berkeley as far as the Newtonian metaphysics of mathematical space and time were concerned) was, as is notorious, the chief factor in leading Kant to regard space and time as *a priori* forms of all perceptual experience. One of the grounds for Kant's conviction that his doctrine was incontrovertible was that he thought it had the support of Newtonian physics and was necessary to give that physics a firm foundation.

The consideration important for our special purpose is, however, the fact that Newton with respect to the doctrine of space, time and motion (involved in all conception of things dealt with in the universal physics of nature) frankly deserted the empirical method he professed to use in respect to the properties of the ultimate fixed substances. At the same time, he regarded the physical and the mathematical as complementary conceptions of two sets of properties of fixed forms of immutable Being. He assumed, in addition to atoms having mass, inertia and extension, the existence of empty immaterial space and time in which these substances lived, moved and had their being. The combination of the properties of these two kinds of Being provided the union of the empirically observed properties of phenomena with those that were rational and mathematical:—a union so complete and so intimate that it conferred upon the Newtonian system that massive solidity and comprehensiveness which seemed to render his system in its essential framework the last word possible of the science of nature.

Definition of space, time and motion from "the relation they bear to sense" is according to him "a vulgar prejudice." As well as any contemporary physicist, he knew that phenomena of space, time and motion in their perceived forms are found in a frame of reference which is relative to an observer. In escape from the relativity of *observable* traits of the spatial and temporal motions of bodies, he assumed the existence of a fixed container of empty space in which bodies are located and an equably flowing time, empty in itself, in which changes take place. From this assumption, it followed that atoms have an intrinsically measurable motion of their own, independent of any connection with an observer. Absolute space, time and motion were thus the immutable frame within which all particular phenomena take place.

The assumption of these rational absolutes was also required by his basic metaphysics of fixed substances having their own inherent and unchangeable (or essential) properties of mass, extension and inertia. The sole ground of assurance that ultimate hard and massy particles persist without internal change, that all changes are merely matters of their external "separations and associations," was the existence of something empty and fixed within which the latter occur. Without such an intervening medium, interaction with one another would be equivalent to internal changes in atoms. Space provided the condition under which changes would be external and indifferent to ultimate physical substances. Since, then, changes have nothing to do directly with the relations of atoms to one another, the temporal order of changes cannot be connected with the atoms themselves. There must be some evenly flowing external change—in reality no change at all—in reference to which they have fixed positions of before and after and of simultaneity. Since velocity and acceleration of observed motions would be disjoined from absolute position and date if they were relative to an observer—to the disruption of the whole physical scheme—motion must also be absolute.

While professing empiricism, Newton thus got the benefit of the rationalistic system of strict deductive necessity. Invariant time, space and motion furnished phenomena those properties to which mathematical reasoning could be attached as a disclosure of inherent properties. The positions of bodies could be treated as an assemblage of geometrical points and the temporal properties of their motions be considered as if they were mere instants. Everything observed had, in its scientific treatment, to conform mathematically to specifications laid down by the mathematics of space and time. Until our own day, until the conception of the determination of simultaneity of occurrence was challenged by Einstein, the system continued to receive at least Pickwickian assent from scientists.

There is no trouble of course about the determination of simultaneity when two events occur within one and the same region of observation. Newton, because of his assumption of absolute time, assumed that the measurement of simultaneity had precise meaning for events not occurring within the same observed field. Einstein saw that this assumption was the Achilles heel of the entire scheme. He demanded an experimental method of determining simultaneity—without which events cannot be dated with respect to one another. He made the demand not on purely general principles, but because of a definite problem with relation to the velocity of light. For the existing state of the doctrine of light presented a discrepancy not to be resolved on the basis of the received scheme. The observed constancy of light with reference to the place from which its direction was observed and its velocity measured, did not agree with a fundamental principle of dynamics; with its postulate concerning frames of reference for coordinate systems having uniform movements of translation. Instead of maintaining the old theory and denying the validity of the observed result of the Michelson-Morley experiment, Einstein asked what change in conceptions was demanded by the experimental result. He saw that the measurement of time relations, centering in the concept of simultaneity, was the crucial point.

So he said, "We require a definition of simultaneity such that this definition supplies us with a method *by which in particular cases* the physicist *can decide by experiment* whether or not two events occurred simultaneously."[1] He suggested an arrangement by which two flashes of light, not in themselves capable of inclusion in one region of observation, be reflected to a mirror placed midway between the origin of the two flashes. They are simultaneous if they are then included within one and the same act of observation. To a layman, the suggestion might seem innocuous. But taken in its context, it signified that the temporal relation of events was to be measured by means of the consequences of an operation which constitutes as its outcome a single field of observed phenomena. It signified, in connection with the fact regarding the constancy of velocity of light, that events occurring at different times according to two watches keeping exactly the same time, placed at the points of the origin of the flashes, may be simultaneous. In scientific content, this was equivalent to doing away with Newton's absolutes; it was the source of the doctrine of restricted relativity. It signified that local or individualized times are not the same as a generic common time of physics: in short, it signified that physical time designates a *relation* of events, not the inherent property of objects.

What is significant for our purpose is that it marked the end, as far as natural science is concerned, of the attempt to frame scientific conceptions of objects in terms of properties assigned to those objects independently of the observed consequences of an experimental operation. Since the former doctrine about the proper way to form conceptions, to the effect that agreement with antecedent properties determines the value or validity of

1. Einstein, *Relativity*, New York, 1920, p. 26. Italics not in original.

ideas, was the doctrine common to all philosophic schools—except the pragmatic one of Peirce—the logical and philosophical transformation thus effected may be said to be more far-reaching than even the extraordinary development in the content of natural science which resulted. It is not too much to say that whatever should be future developments in discoveries about light, or that even if the details of the Einstein theory of relativity should be some time discredited, a genuine revolution, and one which will not go backward, has been effected in the theory of the origin, nature and test of scientific ideas.

In respect to the special theme of the nature of mathematico-physical conceptions, the pertinent conclusion is evident. For the conclusion of Einstein, in eliminating absolute space, time and motion as physical existences, does away with the doctrine that statements of space, time and motion as they appear in physics concern inherent properties. For that notion, it compels the substitution of the notion that they designate *relations of events*. As such relations, they secure, in their generality, the possibility of linking together objects viewed as events in a general system of linkage and translation. They are the means of correlating observations made at different times and places, whether by one observer or by many, so that translations may be effected from one to another. In short, they do the business that all thinking and objects of thought have to effect: they connect, through relevant operations, the discontinuities of individualized observations and experiences into continuity with one another. Their validity is a matter of their efficacy in performance of this function; it is tested by results and not by correspondence with antecedent properties of existence.

It is possible to extend this conclusion to logical forms in general. The fact that there are certain formal conditions of the validity of inference has been used as the ultimate warrant of a realm of invariant Being. But in analogy with the conclusion regarding mathematical conceptions, logical forms are statements of the means by which it is discovered that various inferences may be translated into one another, or made available with respect to one another, in the widest and most secure way. Fundamentally, the needs satisfied by inference are not fully met as long as special instances are isolated from one another.

The difference between the operational conception of conceptions and the traditional orthodox one may be indicated by an illustrative analogy.[2] A visitor to a country finds certain articles used for various purposes, rugs, baskets, spears, etc. He may be struck by the beauty, elegance and order of their designs, and, assuming a purely esthetic attitude toward them, conclude that they are put to use only incidentally. He may even suppose that their instrumental use marks a degradation of their inherent nature, a concession to utilitarian needs and conveniences. A "tough-minded" observer may be convinced that they were intended to be put to use, and had been constructed for that purpose. He would, indeed, recognize that there must have been raw materials which were inherently adapted for conversion to such appliances. But he would not on that account believe the things to be original instead of being made articles; still less would he conceive them to be the original "realities" of which crude or raw material were imitations or inadequate phenomenal exemplifications. As he traced the history of these instrumentalities and found them beginning in forms which were nearer to raw materials, gradually being perfected in economy and efficiency, he would conclude that the perfecting had been an accompaniment of use for ends, changes being introduced to remedy deficiencies in prior operations and results. His tender-minded companion might, on the other hand, infer that the progressive development showed that there was some original and transcendental pattern which had been gradually approximated empirically, an archetype laid up in the heavens.

One person might argue that, while the development of designs had been a temporal process, it had been wholly determined by patterns of order, harmony and symmetry that have an independent subsistence, and that the historic movement was simply a piecemeal approximation to eternal patterns. He might elaborate a theory of formal coherence of relations having nothing to do with particular objects except that of being exemplified in them. His tough-minded companion might retort that any object made to serve a purpose must have a definite structure of its own

2. The phrase "conception of conceptions" is used to suggest that the interpretation is self-applying:—that is, the conception advanced is also a designation of a method to be pursued. One may lead a horse to water but cannot compel him to drink. If one is unable to perform an indicated operation or declines to do so, he will not of course get its meaning.

which demands an internal consistency of parts in connection with one another, and that man-made machines are typical examples; that while these cannot be made except by taking advantage of conditions and relations previously existing, machines and tools are adequate to their function in the degree in which they produce rearrangement of antecedent things so that they may work better for the need in question. If speculatively inclined, he might wonder whether our very ideals of internal order and harmony had not themselves been formed under the pressure of constant need of redisposing of things so that they would serve as means for consequences. If not too tough-minded, he would be willing to admit that after a certain amount of internal rearrangement and organization had been effected under the more direct pressure of demand for effective instrumentalities, an enjoyed perception of internal harmony on its own account would result, and that study of formal relations might well give a clew to methods which would result in improvement of internal design for its own sake with no reference whatever to special further use.

Apart from metaphor, the existence of works of fine art, of interest in making them and of enjoyment of them, affords sufficient evidence that objects exist which are wholly "real" and yet are man-made; that making them must observe or pay heed to antecedent conditions, and yet the objects intrinsically be redispositions of prior existence; that things as they casually offer themselves *suggest* ends and enjoyments they do not adequately realize; that these suggestions become definite in the degree they take the form of ideas, of indications of operations to be performed in order to effect a desired eventual rearrangement. These objects, when once in existence, have their own characters and relations, and as such suggest standards and ends for further production of works of art, with less need for recourse to original "natural" objects; they become as it were a "realm" having its own purposes and regulative principles. At the same time, the objects of this "realm" tend to become over-formal, stereotyped and "academic" if the internal development of an art is too much isolated, so that there is recurrent need for attention to original "natural" objects in order to initiate new significant movements.

The notion that there are no alternatives with respect to mathematical objects save that they form an independent realm of essences; or are relations inherent in some antecedent physical structure—denominated space and time; or else are mere psychological, "mental" things, has no support in fact. The supposition that these alternatives are exhaustive is a survival of the traditional notion that identifies thought and ideas with *merely* mental acts—that is, those *inside* mind. Products of intentional operations are objectively real and are valid if they meet the conditions involved in the intent for the sake of which they are constructed. But human interaction is a contributing factor in their production, and they have worth in the human use made of them.

The discussion so far does not, however, directly touch the question of "pure" mathematics, mathematical ideas in themselves. Newton's mathematics was professedly a mathematics of physical although non-material existence: of existential absolute space, time and motion. Mathematicians, however, often regard their distinctive conceptions as non-existential in any sense. The whole tendency of later developments, which it is unnecessary for our purposes to specify (but of which the doctrine of n-dimensional "spaces" is typical), is to identify pure mathematics with pure logic. Some philosophers employ therefore the entities of pure mathematics so as to rehabilitate the Platonic notion of a realm of essence wholly independent of all existence whatever.

Does the doctrine of the operational and experimentally empirical nature of conceptions break down when applied to "pure" mathematical objects? The key to the answer is to be found in a distinction between operations overtly performed (or imagined to be performed) and operations *symbolically* executed. When we act overtly, consequences ensue; if we do not like them, they are nevertheless there in existence. We are entangled in the outcome of what we do; we have to stand its consequences. We shall put a question that is so elementary that it may seem silly. How can we have an end *in view* without having an end, an existential result, in fact? With the answer to this question is bound up the whole problem of intentional regulation of what occurs. For unless we can have ends-in-view without experiencing them in concrete fact, no regulation of action is possible. The question might be put thus: How can we act without acting, without doing something?

If, by a contradiction in terms, it had been possible for men to think of this question before they had found how to answer it, it would have been given up as insoluble. How can man make an anticipatory projection of the outcome of an activity in such a way as to direct the performance of an act which shall secure or avert that outcome? The solution must have been hit upon accidentally as a by-product, and then employed intentionally. It is natural to suppose that it came as a product of social life by way of communication; say, of cries that having once directed activities usefully without intent were afterwards used expressly for that purpose. But whatever the origin, a solution was found when *symbols* came into existence. By means of symbols, whether gestures, words or more elaborate constructions, we act without acting. That is, we perform experiments by means of symbols which have results which are themselves only symbolized, and which do not therefore commit us to actual or existential consequences. If a man starts a fire or insults a rival, effects follow; the die is cast. But if he rehearses the act in symbols in privacy, he can anticipate and appreciate its result. Then he can act or not act overtly on the basis of what is anticipated and is not there in fact. The invention or discovery of symbols is doubtless by far the single greatest event in the history of man. Without them, no intellectual advance is possible; with them, there is no limit set to intellectual development except inherent stupidity.

For long ages, symbols were doubtless used to regulate activity only *ad hoc*; they were employed incidentally and for some fairly immediate end. Moreover, the symbols used at first were not examined nor settled upon with respect to the office they performed. They were picked up in a casual manner from what was conveniently at hand. They carried all sorts of irrelevant associations that hampered their efficacy in their own special work. They were neither whittled down to accomplish a single function nor were they of a character to direct acts to meet a variety of situations:—they were neither definite nor comprehensive. Definition and generalization are incompetent without invention of proper symbols. The loose and restricted character of popular thinking has its origin in these facts; its progress is encumbered by the vague and vacillating nature of ordinary words. Thus the second great step forward was made when special symbols were devised that were emancipated from the load of irrelevancy carried by words developed for social rather than for intellectual purposes, their meaning being helped out by their immediate local context. This liberation from accidental accretions changed clumsy and ambiguous instruments of thought into sharp and precise tools. Even more important was the fact that instead of being adapted to local and directly present situations, they were framed in detachment from direct overt use and *with respect to one another*. One has only to look at mathematical symbols to note that the operations they designate are others of the same kind as themselves, that is, symbolic not actual. The invention of technical symbols marked the possibility of an advance of thinking from the common sense level to the scientific.

The formation of geometry by the Greeks is probably that which historically best illustrates the transition. Before this episode, counting and measuring had been employed for "practical" ends, that is, for uses directly involved in nearby situations. They were restricted to particular purposes. Yet having been invented and having found expression in definite symbols, they formed, as far as they went, a subject-matter capable of independent examination. New operations could be performed upon them. They could, and in no disrespectful sense, be played with; they could be treated from the standpoint of a fine art rather than from that of an immediately useful economic craft. The Greeks with their dominant esthetic interest were the ones who took this step. Of the creation by the Greeks of geometry it has been said that it was stimulated "by the art of designing, guided by an aesthetic appreciation of symmetrical figures. The study of such figures, and the experimental construction of tile figures, decorative borders, conventional sculptures, moldings and the like had made the early Greeks acquainted not only with a great variety of regular geometrical forms, but with techniques by which they could be constructed, compounded and divided exactly, in various ways. Unlike their predecessors, the Greeks made an intellectual diversion of all they undertook." Having discovered by trial and error a large number of interrelated properties of figures, they proceeded to correlate these with one another and with new ones. They effected this work in ways which "gradually eliminated from their thought about them all guess work, all accidental experiences such as errors of actual drawing and measurement, and all ideas except those which were absolutely essential. Their science thus became a science of ideas exclusively." [3]

The importance of the intellectual transition from concrete to abstract is generally recognized. But it is often misconceived. It is not infrequently regarded as if it signified simply the selection by discriminative attention of some one quality or relation from a total object already sensibly present or present in memory. In fact it marks a change in dimensions. Things are concrete to us in the degree in which they are either means directly used or are ends directly appropriated and enjoyed. Mathematical ideas were "concrete" when they were employed exclusively for building bins for grain or measuring land, selling goods, or aiding a pilot in guiding his ship. They became abstract when they were freed from connection with any particular existential application and use. This happened when operations made possible by symbols were performed exclusively with reference to facilitating and directing other operations *also symbolic in nature*. It is one kind of thing, a concrete one, to measure the area of a triangle so as to measure a piece of land, and another kind—an abstract one—to measure it simply as a means of measuring other areas symbolically designated. The latter type of operation makes possible a system of conceptions related together *as* conceptions; it thus prepares the way for formal logic.

Abstraction from use in special and direct situations was coincident with the formation of a science of ideas, of meanings, whose relations to one another rather than to things was the goal of thought. It is a process, however, which is subject to interpretation by a fallacy. Independence from any specified application is readily taken to be equivalent to independence from application as such; it is as if specialists, engaged in perfecting tools and having no concern with their use and so interested in the operation of perfecting that they carry results beyond any existing possibilities of use, were to argue that therefore they are dealing with an independent realm having no connection with tools or utilities. This fallacy is especially easy to fall into on the part of intellectual specialists. It played its part in the generation of *a priori* rationalism. It is the origin of that idolatrous attitude to-

3. Barry, *The Scientific Habit of Thought*, New York, 1927, pp. 212–213.

ward universals so often recurring in the history of thought. Those who handle ideas through symbols as if they were things —for ideas *are* objects of thought—and trace their mutual relations in all kinds of intricate and unexpected relationships, are ready victims to thinking of these objects as if they had no sort of reference to things, to existence.

In fact, the distinction is one between operations to be actually performed and possible operations as such, as merely possible. Shift of reflection to development of possible operations in their logical relations *to one another* opens up opportunities for operations that would never be directly suggested. But its origin and eventual meaning lie in acts that deal with concrete situations. As to origin in overt operations there can be no doubt. Operations of keeping tally and scoring are found in both work and games. No complex development of the latter is possible without such acts and their appropriate symbols. These acts are the originals of number and of all developments of number. There are many arts in which the operations of enumeration characteristic of keeping tally are explicitly used for measuring. Carpentry and masonry for example cannot go far without some device, however rude, for estimating size and bulk. If we generalize what happens in such instances, we see that the indispensable need is that of *adjusting things as means, as resources, to other things as ends.*

The origin of counting and measuring is in economy and efficiency of such adjustments. Their results are expressed by physical means, at first notches, scratches, tying knots; later by figures and diagrams. It is easy to find at least three types of situations in which this adjustment of means to ends are practical necessities. There is the case of allotment or distribution of materials; of accumulation of stores against anticipated days of need; of exchange of things in which there is a surplus for things in which there is a deficit. The fundamental mathematical conceptions of equivalence, serial order, sum and unitary parts, of correspondence and substitution, are all implicit in the operations that deal with such situations, although they become explicit and generalized only when operations are conducted symbolically in reference to one another.

The failure of empiricism to account for mathematical ideas is due to its failure to connect them with acts performed. In accord with its sensationalistic character, traditional empiricism sought their origin in sensory impressions, or at most in supposed abstraction from properties antecedently characterizing physical things. Experimental empiricism has none of the difficulties of Hume and Mill in explaining the origin of mathematical truths. It recognizes that experience, the actual experience of men, is one of doing acts, performing operations, cutting, marking off, dividing up, extending, piecing together, joining, assembling and mixing, hoarding and dealing out; in general, selecting and adjusting things as means for reaching consequences. Only the peculiar hypnotic effect exercised by exclusive preoccupation with knowledge could have led thinkers to identify experience with reception of sensations, when five minutes' observation of a child would have disclosed that sensations count only as stimuli and registers of motor activity expended in doing things.

All that was required for the development of mathematics as a science and for the growth of a logic of ideas, that is, of implications of operations with respect one to another, was that some men should appear upon the scene who were interested in the operations on their own account, as operations, and not as means to specified particular uses. When symbols were devised for operations cut off from concrete application, as happened under the influence of the esthetic interest of the Greeks, the rest followed naturally. Physical means, the straightedge, the compass and the marker remained, and so did physical diagrams. But the latter were only "figures," images in the Platonic sense. Intellectual force was carried by the operations they symbolized, ruler and compass were only means for linking up with one another a series of operations represented by symbols. Diagrams, etc., were particular and variable, but the operations were uniform and general in their intellectual force:—that is, in their relation to other operations.

When once the way was opened to thinking in terms of possible operations irrespective of actual performance, there was no limit to development save human ingenuity. In general, it proceeded along two lines. On the one hand, for the execution of tasks of physical inquiry, special intellectual instrumentalities were needed, and this need led to the invention of new operations and symbolic systems. The Cartesian analytics and the calculuses of Leibniz and Newton are cases in point. Such developments have created a definite body of subject-matter that, historically, is as empirical as is the historic sequence of, say, spinning-machines. Such a body of material arouses need for examination on its own account. It is subjected to careful inspection with reference to the relations found within its own content. Indications of superfluous operations are eliminated; ambiguities are detected and analyzed; massed operations are broken up into definite constituents; gaps and unexplained jumps are made good by insertion of connecting operations. In short, certain canons of rigorous interrelation of operations are developed and the old material is correspondingly revised and extended.

Nor is the work merely one of analytic revision. The detection, for example, of the logical looseness of the Euclidean postulate regarding parallels suggested operations previously unthought of, and opened up new fields—those of the hyper-geometries. Moreover, the possibility of combining various existing branches of geometry as special cases of more comprehensive operations (illustrated by the same instance) led to creation of mathematics of a higher order of generality.

I am not interested in tracing the history of mathematics. What is wanted is to indicate that once the idea of possible operations, indicated by symbols and performed *only* by means of symbols, is discovered, the road is opened to operations of ever increasing definiteness and comprehensiveness. Any group of symbolic operations suggests further operations that may be performed. *Technical* symbols are framed with precisely this end in view. They have three traits that distinguish them from casual terms and ideas. They are selected with a view to designating unambiguously one mode of interaction and one only. They are linked up with symbols of other operations forming a system such that transition is possible with the utmost economy of energy from one to another. And the aim is that these transitions may occur as far as possible in *any* direction. 1. "Water" for example suggests an indefinite number of acts; seeing, tasting, drinking, washing without specification of one in preference to another. It also marks off water from other colorless liquids only in a vague way. 2. At the same time, it is restricted; it does not connect the liquid with solid and gaseous forms, and still less does it indicate operations which link the production of water to other things into which its constituents, oxygen and hydrogen, enter. It is isolated instead of being a transitive concept. 3. The chemical conception, symbolized by H_2O, not only meets these two requirements which "water" fails to meet, but oxygen and hydrogen are in turn connected with the whole system of chemical elements and specified combinations among them in a systematic way. Starting from the elements and the relation defined in H_2O one can, so to speak, travel through all the whole scope and range of complex and varied phenomena. Thus the scientific conception carries thought and action away from qualities which are finalities as they are found in direct perception and use, to the mode of production of these qualities, and it performs this task in a way which links this mode of generation to a multitude of other "efficient" causal conditions in the most economical and effective manner.

Mathematical conceptions, by means of symbols of operations that are irrespective of actual performance, carry abstraction much further; one has only to contrast "2" as attached physically to H, to "2" as pure number. The latter designates an operative relation applic*able* to anything whatsoever, though not actually applied to any specified object. And, of course, it stands in defined relations to all other numbers, and by a system of correspondences with continuous quantities as well. That numbers disregard all qualitative distinctions is a familiar fact. This disregard is the consequence of construction of symbols dealing with possible operations in abstraction from the actuality of performance. If time and knowledge permitted, it could be shown that the difficulties and paradoxes which have been found to attend the logic of number disappear when instead of their being treated as either essences or as properties of things in existence, they are viewed as designations of potential operations. Mathematical space is not a kind of space distinct from so-called physical and empirical space, but is a name given to operations ideally or formally possible with respect to things having spacious qualities: it is not a mode of Being, but a way of thinking things so that connections among them are liberated from fixity in experience and implication from one to another is made possible.

The distinction between physical and mathematical conception may be brought out by noting an ambiguity in the term "possible" operations. Its primary meaning is actually, existentially, possible. Any idea as such designates an operation that *may* be performed, not something in actual existence. The *idea* of the sweetness of, say, sugar, is an indication of the consequences of a possible operation of tasting as distinct from a directly experienced quality. Mathematical ideas are designations of possible operations in another and secondary sense, previously expressed in speaking of the possibility of symbolic operations with respect *to one another*. This sense of possibility is *com*possibility of operations, not possibility of performance with respect to existence. Its test is non-incompatibility. The statement of this test as consistency hardly carries the full meaning. For consistency is readily interpreted to signify the conformity of one meaning with others already had, and is in so far restrictive. "Non-incompatibility" indicates that all developments are welcome as long as they do not conflict with one another, or as long as restatement of an operation prevents actual conflict. It is a canon of liberation rather than of restriction. It may be compared with natural selection, which is a principle of elimination but not one controlling positive development.

Mathematics and formal logic thus mark highly specialized branches of intellectual industry, whose working principles are very similar to those of works of fine art. The trait that strikingly characterizes them is combination of freedom with rigor—freedom with respect to development of new operations and ideas; rigor with respect to formal compossibilities. The combination of these qualities, characteristic also of works of great art, gives the subject great fascination for some minds. But the belief that these qualifications remove mathematical objects from all connection with existence expresses a religious mood rather than a scientific discovery.[4]

The significant difference is that of two types of possibility of operation, material and symbolic. This distinction when frozen into the dogma of two orders of Being, existence and essence, gives rise to the notion that there are two types of logic and two

4. "The long-continued and infrequently interrupted study of absolutely invariant existences exercises a powerful hypnotic influence on the mind. . . . The world which it separates from the rest of experience and makes into the whole of being is a world of unchanging and apparently eternal order, the only Absolute cold intellect need not reject. A conviction thus establishes itself which finally affects the whole of waking thought: that in this experience one has at last discovered the eternal and ultimate Truth." Barry, Op. cit., pp. 182–183.

criteria of truth, the formal and the material, of which the formal is higher and more fundamental. In truth, the formal development is a specialized offshoot of material thinking. It is derived ultimately from acts performed, and constitutes an extension of such acts, made possible by symbols, on the basis of congruity with one another. Consequently formal logic represents an analysis of exclusively symbolic operations; it is, in a pregnant and not external sense, symbolic logic. This interpretation of mathematical and (formal) logical ideas is not a disparagement of them except from a mystical point of view. Symbols, as has already been noted, afford the only way of escape from submergence in existence. The liberation afforded by the free symbolism of mathematics is often a means of ulterior return to existential operations that have a scope and penetrating power not otherwise attainable. The history of science is full of illustrations of cases in which mathematical ideas for which no physical application was known suggested in time new existential relations.

The theory which has been advanced of the nature of essences (universals, invariants) may be tested by comparing the conditions which symbolic operations fulfill with the attributes traditionally imputed to the former. These attributes are ideality, universality, immutability, formality, and the subsistence of relations of implication that make deduction possible. There is a one to one correspondence between these characters and those of objects of thought which are defined in terms of operations that are compossible with respect to one another.

The correspondence will be approached by pointing out the traits of a machine which marks its structure in view of the function it fulfills. It is obvious that this structure can be understood not by sense but only by *thought* of the relations which the parts of the machine sustain to one another, in connection with the work the machine as a whole performs (the consequences it effects). Sensibly, one is merely overwhelmed in the presence of a machine by noises and forms. Clarity and order of perceived objects are introduced when forms are judged in relation to operations, and these in turn in relation to work done. Movements may be seen in isolation, and products, goods turned out, may be perceived in isolation. The machine is *known* only when these are *thought* in connection with one another. In this thought, motions and parts are judged as *means*; they are referred intellectually to something else; to think of anything as means is to apprehend an object in *relation*. Correlatively, the physical effect is judged as *consequence*—something related. The relation of means-consequence may thus justifiably be termed ideal in the sense of ideational.

Operations as such, that is, as connective interactions, are uniform. Physically and sensibly, a machine changes through friction, exposure to weather, etc., while products vary in quality. Processes are local and temporal, particular. But the relation of means and consequence which defines an operation remains one and the same in spite of these variations. It is a universal. A machine turns out a succession of steel spheres, like ball-bearings. These closely resemble one another, because they are products of like process. But there is no absolute exactitude among them. Each process is individual and not exactly identical with others. But the *function* for which the machine is designed does not alter with these changes; an operation, being a relation, is not a process. An operation determines any number of processes and products all differing from one another; but *being* a telephone or a cutting tool is a self-identical universal, irrespective of the multiplicity of special objects which manifest the function.

The relation is thus invariant. It is eternal, not in the sense of enduring throughout all time, or being everlasting like an Aristotelian species or a Newtonian substance, but in the sense that an operation as a relation which is grasped in thought is independent of the instances in which it is overtly exemplified, although its meaning is found only in the *possibility* of these actualizations.

The relation, between things as means and things as consequences, which defines a machine is ideal in another sense. It is the standard by which the value of existential processes are estimated. The deterioration or improvement in use of a concrete machine and the worth of an invention are judged by reference to efficiency in accomplishment of a function. The more adequately the functional relation can be apprehended in the abstract, the better can the engineer detect defects in an existent machine and project improvements in it. Thus the thought of it operates as a model; it has an archetypal character with respect to particular machines.

Thought of an object as an ideal therefore determines a characteristic internal structure or form. This formal structure is only approximated by existing things. One may conceive of a steam engine which has a one hundred per cent efficiency, although no such ideal is even remotely approached in actuality. Or, one may like Helmholtz conceive an ideal optical apparatus in which the defects of the existing human eye are not found. The ideal relationship of means to ends exists as a formal possibility determined by the nature of the case even though it be not thought of, much less realized in fact. It subsists as a possibility, and as a possibility it is in its formal structure necessary. That is to say, the conditions which have to be met and fulfilled in the idea of a machine having an efficiency of one hundred per cent are set by the necessities of the case; they do not alter with defects in our apprehension of them. Hence essences may be regarded as having Being independent of and logically prior to our thought of them. There is, however, in this fact nothing of the mystery or transcendental character which is often associated with it. It signifies that *if* one is to attain a specified result one must conform to the conditions which are means of securing this result; *if* one is to get the result with the maximum of efficiency, there are conditions having a necessary relationship to that intent.

This necessity of a structure marked by formal relationships which fulfill the conditions of serving as means for an end, accounts for the relations of implication which make deduction possible. One goes into a factory and finds that the operation of reaching an end, say, making in quantity shoes of a uniform standard, is subdivided into a number of processes, each of which is adapted to the one which precedes, and, until the final one, to that which follows. One does not make a miracle or mystery of the fact that while each machine and each process is physically separate, nevertheless all are adapted to one another. For he knows that they have been designed, through a "rationalization" of the undertaking, to effect this end.

The act of knowing is also highly complex. Experience shows that it also may be best effected by analysis into a number of distinct processes, which bear a serial relation to one another. Terms and propositions which symbolize the possible operations that are to control these processes are designed so that they will lead one to another with the maximum of definiteness, flexibility and fertility. In other words, they are constructed with reference to the function of implication. Deduction or dialectic is the operation of developing these implications, which may be novel and unexpected just as a tool often gives unexpected results when working under new conditions. One is entitled to marvel at the constructive power with which symbols have been devised having far-reaching and fruitful implications. But the wonder is misdirected when it is made the ground for hypostatizing the objects of thought into a realm of transcendent Being.

This phase of the discussion is not complete till it has been explicitly noted that all general conceptions (ideas, theories, thought) are hypothetical. Ability to frame hypotheses is the means by which man is liberated from submergence in the existences that surround him and that play upon him physically and sensibly. It is the positive phase of abstraction. But hypotheses are conditional; they have to be tested by the consequences of the operations they define and direct. The discovery of the value of hypothetical ideas when employed to suggest and direct concrete processes, and the vast extension of this operation in the modern history of science, mark a great emancipation and correspondent increase of intellectual control. But their final value is not determined by their internal elaboration and consistency, but by the consequences they effect in existence as that is perceptibly experienced. Scientific conceptions are not a revelation of prior and independent reality. They are a system of hypotheses, worked out under conditions of definite test, by means of which our intellectual and practical traffic with nature is rendered freer, more secure and more significant.

Our discussion has been one-sided in that it has dealt with the matter of conceptions mainly in reference to the "rationalistic" tradition of interpretation. The reasons for this emphasis are too patent to need exposition. But before leaving the topic, it should be noted that traditional empiricism has also misread the significance of conceptions or general ideas. It has steadily opposed the doctrine of their *a priori* character; it has connected them with experience of the actual world. But even more obviously than the rationalism it has opposed, empiricism has connected the origin, content and measure of validity of general ideas with antecedent existence. According to it, concepts are formed by comparing particular objects, already perceived, with one another, and then eliminating the elements in which they disagree and retaining that which they have in common. Concepts are thus simply memoranda of identical features in objects already perceived; they are conveniences, bunching together a variety of things scattered about in concrete experience. But they have to be *proved* by agreement with the material of particular antecedent experiences; their value and function is essentially retrospective. Such ideas are dead, incapable of performing a regulative office in new situations. They are "empirical" in the sense in which the term is opposed to scientific—that is, they are mere summaries of results obtained under more or less accidental circumstances.

Our next chapter will be devoted to explicit consideration of the historic philosophies of empiricism and rationalism about the nature of knowledge. Before passing to this theme, we conclude with a summary statement of the more important results reached in the present phase of discussion. First, the active and productive character of ideas, of thought, is manifest. The motivating desire of idealistic systems of philosophy is justified. But the constructive office of thought is empirical—that is, experimental. "Thought" is not a property of something termed intellect or reason apart from nature. It is a mode of directed overt action. Ideas are anticipatory plans and designs which take effect in concrete *re*constructions of antecedent conditions of existence. They are not innate properties of mind corresponding to ultimate prior traits of Being, nor are they *a priori* categories imposed on sense in a wholesale, once-for-all way, prior to experience so as to make it possible. The active power of ideas is a reality, but ideas and idealisms have an operative force in concrete experienced situations; their worth has to be tested by the specified consequences of their operation. Idealism is something experimental not abstractly rational; it is related to experienced needs and concerned with projection of operations which remake the actual content of experienced objects.

Secondly, ideas and idealisms are in themselves hypotheses not finalities. Being connected with operations to be performed, they are tested by the consequences of these operations, not by what exists prior to them. Prior experience supplies the conditions which evoke ideas and of which thought has to take account, with which it must reckon. It furnishes both obstacles to attainment of what is desired and the resources that must be used to attain it. Conception and systems of conceptions, ends in view and plans, are constantly making and remaking as fast as those already in use reveal their weaknesses, defects and positive values. There is no predestined course they must follow. Human experience consciously guided by ideas evolves its own standards and measures and each new experience constructed by their means is an opportunity for new ideas and ideals.

In the third place, action is at the heart of ideas. The experimental practice of knowing, when taken to supply the pattern of philosophic doctrine of mind and its organs, eliminates the age-old separation of theory and practice. It discloses that knowing is itself a kind of action, the only one which progressively and securely clothes natural existence with realized meanings. For the outcome of experienced objects which are begot by operations which define thinking, take into themselves, as part of their own funded and incorporated meaning, the relation to other things disclosed by thinking. There are no sensory or perceived objects fixed in themselves. In the course of experience, as far as that is an outcome influenced by thinking, objects perceived, used and enjoyed take up into their own meaning the results of thought; they become ever richer and fuller of meanings. This issue constitutes the last significance of the philosophy of experimental idealism. Ideas direct operations; the operations have a result in which ideas are no longer abstract, mere ideas, but where they qualify sensible objects. The road from a perceptible experience which is blind, obscure, fragmentary, meagre in meaning, to objects of sense which are also objects which satisfy, reward and feed intelligence is through ideas that are experimental and operative.

Our conclusion depends upon an analysis of what takes place in the experimental inquiry of natural science. It goes without saying that the wider scope of human experience, that which is concerned with distinctively human conditions and ends, does not comport, as it currently exists, with the result that the examination of natural science yields. The genuinely philosophic force, as distinct from a technical one, of the conclusion reached lies in precisely this incongruity. The fact that the most exacting type of experience has attained a marvelous treasury of working ideas that are used in control of objects is an indication of possibilities as yet unattained in less restricted forms of experience. Negatively, the result indicates the need of thoroughgoing revision of ideas of mind and thought and their connection with natural things that were formed before the rise of experimental inquiry; such is the critical task imposed on contemporary thought. Positively, the result achieved in science is a challenge to philosophy to consider the possibility of the extension of the method of operative intelligence to direction of life in other fields.

7. The Seat of Intellectual Authority

The dispute as to whether reason and conception or perception and sense are the source and test of ultimate knowledge is one of the most enduring in the history of thought. It has affected philosophy from the side of both the nature of the object of knowledge and the mental faculty operating to obtain it. From the side of the object those who put forward the claims of reason have placed the universal higher than the individual; those who have held to perception have reversed the order. From the side of mind, one school has emphasized the synthetic action of conceptions. The other school has dwelt upon the fact that in sensation the mind does not interfere with the action of objects in writing their own report. The opposition has extended to problems of conduct and society. On one hand, there is emphasis upon the necessity of control by rational standards; on the other hand, the dynamic quality of wants has been insisted upon together with the intimately personal character of their satisfaction as against the pale remoteness of pure thought. On the political side, there is a like division between the adherents of order and organization, those who feel that reason alone gives security, and those interested in freedom, innovation and progress, those who have used the claims of the individual and his desires as a philosophical basis.

The controversy is acute and longstanding. In consequence of it, philosophers have expended energy in controversy with one another, and the guidance they have given to practical affairs has been largely by way of support to partisans of contending forces. The situation raises a further point in our inquiry: What is the bearing of the experimental theory of knowing upon the rival contentions? The first point which presents itself is that the object of knowledge is eventual; that is, it is an outcome of directed experimental operations, instead of something in sufficient existence before the act of knowing. The further point to be presented is that, along with this change, sensible and rational factors cease to be competitors for primary rank. They are allies, cooperating to make knowledge possible. Isolation from each other is an expression of the isolation of each from organic connection with action. When theory is placed in opposition to practice, there is ground for dispute as to whether primacy in theory shall go to sense or intellect. Directed activity demands ideas which go beyond the results of past perceptions, for it goes out to meet future and as yet unexperienced situations. But it deals, both in origin and outcome, with things which can be had only directly, through immediate perception and enjoyment.

The three chief contending doctrines in this field are sensational empiricism, rationalism and Kantianism, with its compromise of the factors isolated in the two other schools. The doctrine of Kant has a superficial resemblance to the one just stated; it insists upon the necessity of both perception and ideas if there is to be knowledge. It is convenient, accordingly, to begin discussion with it. The element of similarity is suggested by Kant's well known saying that perception without conception is blind, conception without perception empty. His doctrine none the less is fundamentally different from that which results from an analysis of experimental knowing. The fundamental difference lies in the fact that, according to the latter, the distinction of sense and thought occurs *within* the process of reflective inquiry, and the two are connected together by means of operations overtly performed. In the Kantian scheme, the two originally exist in independence of each other, and their connection is established by operations that are covert and are performed in the hidden recesses of mind, once for all. As to their original difference, sense-material is impressed from without, while connective conceptions are supplied from within the understanding. As to connection, synthesis takes place not intentionally and by means of the controlled art of investigation, but automatically and all at once.

From the experimental point of view, the art of knowing demands skill in selecting appropriate sense-data on one side and connecting principles, or conceptual theories, on the other. It requires a developed and constantly progressive technique to settle upon both the observational data and the idea that assist inquiry in reaching a conclusion in any particular case. But in Kant's view, the distinction and the connection between the two, while necessary to anything which may be termed cognition, have nothing to do with the validity of any particular enterprise of knowing. Illusion and error exemplify the synthesis of sense and understanding quite as much as does the soundest instance of scientific discovery. In one case, the heart of the whole matter is the exercise of a *differential* control which makes the difference between good and bad knowing. In Kant's scheme the blessings of the categories descend upon the material of sense without reference to making a distinction between the true and the false.

We summarize the differences as follows. 1. In experimental knowing, the antecedent is always the subject-matter of some experience which has its origin in natural causes, but which, not having been controlled in its occurrence, is uncertain and problematic. Original objects of experience are produced by the natural interactions of organism and environment, and in themselves are neither sensible, conceptual nor a mixture of the two. They are precisely the qualitative material of all our ordinary untested experiences. 2. The distinction between sense-data and interpretive ideas is deliberately instituted by the process of inquiry, for sake of carrying it forward to an adequately tested conclusion, one with a title to acceptance. 3. Hence each term of the distinction is not absolute and fixed, but is contingent and tentative. Each is subject to revision as we find observational data which supply better evidence, and as the growth of science provides better directive hypotheses to draw upon. 4. Hence the material selected to serve as data and as regulative principles constantly check one another; any advance in one brings about a corresponding improvement in the other. The two are constantly working together to effect a rearrangement of the original experienced material in the construction of a new object having the properties that make it understood or *known*.

These statements are formal, but their meaning is not recondite. Any scientific investigation illustrates their significance. The astronomer, chemist, botanist, start from the material of gross unanalyzed experience, that of the "common-sense" world in which we live, suffer, act and enjoy; from familiar stars, suns, moons, from acids, salts and metals, trees, mosses and growing plants. Then the process of investigation divides into two kinds of operations. One is that of careful and analytic observation to determine exactly what there is which is indubitably seen, touched and heard. An operation takes place to discover what the sure data of the problem are, the evidence which theoretical explanation must reckon with. The other operation consists in searching through previous knowledge to obtain ideas which may be used to interpret this observed material and to suggest the initiation of new experiments. By these latter, more data are had, and the additional evidence they supply suggests new ideas and more experiments until the problem is resolved. The investigator never makes the division between perceptual and conceptual material at large or wholesale. He is careful at each stage of inquiry to discriminate between what he has observed and what is a matter of theory and ideas, using the latter as means of directing further observations, the results of which test the application of the ideas and theories employed. Finally, the original material is reorganized into a coherent and settled form capable of entering integrally into the general system of science.

A physician, for example, is called by a patient. His original material of experience is thereby provided; it requires a stretch of useless imagination to fancy that the ill man is a mass of sense data organized by categories. This experienced object sets the problem of inquiry. Certain clinical operations are performed, sounding, tapping, getting registrations of pulse, temperature, respiration, etc. These constitute the symptoms; they supply the evidence to be interpreted. The philosopher or logician, looking on, sees they are that part of the original object which is capable of being presented in observation as that is sensibly present. The results are not all that is or can be observed, but are those phases and portions of the experienced whole that are judged to be relevant to making an inference as to the nature of the ailment. The observations mean something not in and of themselves, but are given meaning in the light of the systematized knowledge of medicine as far as that is at the command of the practitioner. He calls upon his store of knowledge to suggest ideas that may aid him in reaching a judgment as to the nature of the trouble and its proper treatment. The analytic philosopher, looking on, notes that the interpreting material, by means of which the scattered data of sense are bound together into a coherent whole, is not itself directly sensibly present. So he calls it ideational or conceptual.

Sense data are signs which direct this selection of ideas; the ideas when suggested arouse new observations; the two together determine his final judgment or diagnosis and his procedure. Something is then added to the store of the clinical material of medical art so that subsequent observations of symptoms are refined and extended, and the store of material from which to draw ideas is further enlarged. To this process of cooperation of observation and conceptual or general ideas there is no limit. In no case are the data the whole of the original object; they are material selected for the purpose of serving as evidence and signs. In no case do general ideas, principles, laws, conceptions, determine the conclusion—although just as some men collect fragmentary observations without trying to find out what they mean, so in other cases an unskilled worker permits some preconceived idea to control his decision instead of using it as a hypothesis.

The case seems simple enough, so simple indeed that it may be supposed that we have overlooked the conditions which have created perplexity and controversy. But the source of these complications is that theories about the mind, about sensation and perception, about reason, the intellect, conceptions and perception, were framed and established in philosophy before the rise of experimental knowing. It is difficult to break loose from habits thus engendered so as to turn attention in a whole-hearted way to actual inquiry. While it may seem presumptuous to set up the case of the physician or some other concrete inquirer over against the elaborate machinery of the *Critique of Pure Reason* and the countless tomes of commentary it has called forth, our picture has behind it the whole weight of the experimental practices by which science has been actually advanced.

More specifically, it may be asserted that the Kantian theory went wrong because it took distinctions that are genuine and indispensable out of their setting and function in actual inquiry. It generalized them into fixed and wholesale distinctions, losing sight of their special roles in attainment of those tested beliefs which give security. Consequently artificial complications were engendered, and insoluble puzzles created.

Take for example the fragmentary and isolated character of sense-data. Taken in isolation from a context in a particular inquiry they undoubtedly have this character. Hence when they are generalized into a character at large, the result is the doctrine of the disconnected "atomicity" of sense-data. This doctrine is common to sensationalism and to some forms of the new realism, along with Kantianism. As a matter of fact, smells, tastes, sounds, pressures, colors, etc., are not isolated; they are bound together by all kinds of interactions or connections, among which are included the habitual responses of the one having the experience. Some connections are organic, flowing from the constitution of the subject. Others have become engrained in habit because of education and the customary state of culture. But these habitual connections are obstacles rather than aids. Some of them are irrelevant and misleading. In any case, they fail to provide the clews, the evidence, which is wanted in the particular inquiry in hand. Consequently, sense qualities are artificially isolated from their ordinary connections so that the inquirer is free to see them in a new light or as constituents of a new object.

Since the very need for inquiry shows that there is a *problem* set by the existing situation, there can be no understanding of it achieved until there are new connections established. The fragmentary and isolated character of sense-data does not therefore describe anything belonging to them intrinsically, but marks a transitory, although necessary, stage in the progress of inquiry. The isolation of sense-data from their status and office in furthering the objective of knowing is responsible for treating them as a kind of isolated atomic existence. If we keep an eye on the actual enterprise of knowing, it is clear that only sense-data can supply evidential subject-matter; ideas of what is not presented in sense *interpret* evidence, but they cannot constitute it. The whole history of science shows, however, that material *directly* and originally observed does not furnish *good* evidential material; as we saw, it was the essential mistake of ancient science to suppose that we can base inference upon observed objects without an artificial prior analytic resolution. Hence there is need of a distinctive type of experimental operations which detach *some* qualities of the object; these form sense-data in the technical meaning of the word.

Traditional empiricism was accordingly right in insisting that no amount of conceptions, of thought material, could by itself deliver any knowledge of existence, no matter how elaborate be the conceptual system and how internally coherent. We cannot derive existence from thought—*pace* idealism. Observed material is necessary to suggest ideas and it is equally necessary to test them. The senses are, existentially speaking, the organs by which we obtain the material of observation. But, as we have previously noted, this material is significant and effective for purposes of knowing only as it is connected with operations of which it is the product. *Merely* physical interactions, whether of external things or of the organism, yield observations that form the material of inquiry; a problematic material. Only operations intentionally performed and attentively noted *in connection* with their products give observed material a positive intellectual value, and this condition is satisfied only by thought: ideas *are* the perception of this connection. Even non-scientific experience, as far as it has meaning, is neither mere doing nor mere undergoing, but is an acknowledgment of the *connection* between something done and something undergone in consequence of the doing.

In its later history, empiricism tended to identify sensory consequences with "mental" or psychical states and processes; this identification was the logical conclusion of taking the object of science, in which these qualities are not found, as *the* real object. But the insistence, as by contemporary realists, that sense-data are external and not mental does not remedy the logical error. It repeats the isolation of sense-data from the intentional operations by which they are supplied and from the purpose and function of these operations. Hence it makes it necessary to call in the supplement of logical objects, now termed essences. What is even more important, no light is thrown upon the control of the course of actual inquiry. For there is still failure to see that the distinction between sense-data and objects of rational apprehension is one which occurs *within* reflective investigation, for the sake of regulating its procedure.

The history of the theory of knowledge or epistemology would have been very different if instead of the word "data" or "givens," it had happened to start with calling the qualities in question "takens." Not that the data are not existential and qualities of the ultimately "given"—that is, the total subject-matter which is had in non-cognitive experiences. But *as* data they are *selected* from this total original subject-matter which gives the impetus to knowing; they are discriminated for a purpose:—that, namely, of affording signs or evidence to define and locate a problem, and thus give a clew to its resolution.

If we recur to the instance of the patient and the inquiries of the physician, it is evident that the presence of a man who is ill is the "given," and that this given is complex, marked by all kinds of diverse qualities. Only the assumption—such as is made by Kant in common with traditional theories—that all experience is inherently cognitive leads to the doctrine that perception of the patient is a case of knowledge. In reality the original perception furnishes the *problem* for knowing; it is something *to be* known, not an object of knowing. And in knowing, the first thing to be done is to select from the mass of presented qualities those which, in distinction from other qualities, throw light upon the nature of the trouble. As they are deliberately selected, being discriminated by special technical operations, they become data; these are called sensible simply because of the role of sense organs in their *generation*. They may *then* be formulated as the subject-matter of primitive existential propositions. But even so, there is no class of such propositions *in general*. Each inquiry yields its own primitive existential propositions, even though they all agree in having for their objects qualities which investigation reveals to be connected with the use of organs of sense. Moreover, these primitive propositions are such only in a logical sense as distinct from being empirically primitive, and they are only hypothetical or conditional. This statement does not imply that their *existence* is hypothetical; perception, as far as it is properly conducted, warrants their existence. But their status in inquiry is tentative. Many, perhaps most, errors in physical inference arise from taking as data things that are not data for the problem in hand; they undoubtedly exist, but they are not the evidence that is demanded. In some respects, the more undoubted the existence of sensory qualities, the less certain is their meaning for inference; the very fact that a quality is glaringly obvious in perception exercises an undue influence, leading thought to take its evident presence as an equivalent of evidential value. The reader of detective stories is aware that it is a common device to have the inquirer misled by the too patent character of given "clews"; genuine clews are usually obscure and have to be searched out. The conditional character of sense-data in inferential inquiry means, then, that they have to be tested by their consequences. They are good clews or evidence when they instigate operations whose effect is to solve the problem in hand.

It is hardly necessary to repeat the criticisms of the rationalistic doctrine of conceptions that have been brought out in previous chapters. The doctrine stood for a positive truth:—the necessity of relations, of connectivity in existence and knowledge, and it noted the fact of the connection of relations with thought. For while *some* connections are always found in the material of experienced things, the fact that as experienced these things are problematic and not definitively known, means that important relations are *not* presented in them as they stand. These relations have to be projected in anticipation if the reactions of the inquiries are not blind fumblings—if they are genuinely experimental. *Such* relations must be *thought*; they are present conceptually, not sensibly. They represent possible consequences of operations, and the possible and the conceivable are one. Just as sensationalism ignores the functional role and hypothetical status of sensible qualities in an inquiry, so rationalism makes a fixed and independent matter out of the utility of conceptions in directing inquiry to solve particular problems.

The object of this criticism of historical theories of knowledge is not just to cast discredit upon them. It is to direct attention to the source of their errors. As soon as and whenever it is assumed that the office of knowledge is to lay hold of existence which is prior to and apart from the operations of inquiry and their consequences, one or other of these errors or some combination of both of them is inevitable. Either logical characters belonging to the operations of effective inquiry are read into antecedent existence; or the world as known is reduced to a pulverized multiplicity of atomically isolated elements, a Kantian "manifold"; or some machinery is devised, whether of an "idealistic" or a "realistic" sort, to bring the two together.

When, on the other hand, it is seen that the object of *knowledge* is prospective and eventual, being the result of inferential or reflective operations which redispose what was antecedently existent, the subject-matters called respectively sensible and conceptual are seen to be complementary in effective direction of inquiry to an intelligible conclusion.

There is another way of discussing the fundamental issue which does not involve so much going over topics worn threadbare by previous discussion. In effect, traditional theories treat all reflective or inferential knowing as cases of "explanation," and by explanation is meant making some seemingly new object or problem plain and clear by identifying its elements with something previously known, ultimately something said to be known immediately and intuitively, or without inference. In traditional theory, "discursive" knowledge, that involving reflection, must always be referred for its validation back to what is immediately known. It cannot bring its credentials with it and test its results in the very process of reaching them. There is postulated identity implicit or explicit of the results of inference with things known without inference. Making the identity explicit constitutes proof.

There are many different and opposed theories regarding the way in which this identification takes place. There is a doctrine that the operation is one of subsumption of given particulars under given universals; that it is classificatory definition; that it is a kind of Platonic reminiscence in which perceptual material is cognized by being identified with *a priori* forms; that it is a case of schematization *à la* Kant; that it is an assimilation of present sensations to images that revive previous sensations. These theories differ widely among themselves; they are irreconcilable with one another. But they all have one premise in common. They all assume that the conclusions of reflective inference must be capable of reduction to things already known if they are to be proved. The quarrel between them is strictly domestic, all in the family. The differences between them concern the character of the original immediately known objects with which the conclusions of reflection must be identified in order to be really known. They all involve the supposed necessity that whatever is a product of inference must, in order to be valid knowledge, be reducible to something already known immediately. Thus they all take the element of *knowledge* found in inferential conclusions to be simply a matter of restatement.[1]

The especial significance of the experimental procedure is that

1. The logic of Stuart Mill is the classic logic of sensational empiricism. Yet he demanded "canons" of proof for induction as rigorous as those of Aristotle were for syllogistic reasoning. The essence of these canons is that proof consists in identification of the results of inference with particulars given in sense, just as with Aristotle demonstration consisted in subsuming them under independently given universals. That the latter was influenced by Euclidean geometry with its assumption of axioms as self-evident truths we have already noticed. Mathematicians now recognize that indemonstrables and indefinables are starting points of operations and that in themselves they have neither meaning nor "truth."

it scraps once for all the notion that the results of inference must be validated by operations of *identification* of whatever sort. When we compare the premise which underlies all the different theories that assume a primitive mode of direct knowledge (knowledge which does not include reflection) with the practice of experimental science, according to which *only the conclusion of reflective inquiry is known*, we find three marked points of contrast. The first difference is that the traditional theories make all reflective knowledge to be a case of recognition going back to an earlier more certain form of knowledge. The second is that they have no place for genuine discovery, or creative novelty. The third point concerns the dogmatic character of the assumption regarding what is said to be immediately known, in contrast with the experimentally tested character of the object known in consequence of reflection.

We begin with the last point. When it is stated that the conclusions of knowledge involving inference must be subordinated to knowledge which is had directly and immediately, and must be carried to the latter for proof and verification, we are at once struck by the multitude of theories regarding what is immediately and infallibly known. The diversity and contradictions give ground for a suspicion that in no case is the "knowledge" in question as self-evident as it is asserted to be. And there is good theoretical ground for the suspicion. Suppose a man "explains" the eclipse of the moon by saying it is due to the attempt of a dragon to devour it. To him the devouring dragon is a more evident fact than is the darkening of the moon. To us the existence of an animal capable of such a feat is the doubtful matter. It will be objected that it is unfair to take such an absurd case as an instance: dragons are not the sort of thing which any philosopher has asserted to be the object of direct and certain noninferential knowledge. But the illustration still serves a purpose.

The thing to be known is "explained" by identification with something else. What guarantees this something else? If it too has to be guaranteed by identification with something else, there is an infinite regress. To avoid this regress, we stop short and assert that this or that object or truth is directly known, by sense intuition, by rational intuition, as a direct deliverance of consciousness, or in some other way. But what is such a procedure except the essence of what Bentham called *ipse dixitism*? What is it but arbitrary dogmatism? Who guards the guardians? The theory which places knowledge in rounded out conclusions is in no such dilemma. It admits the hypothetical status of all data and premises and appeals for justification to operations capable, when they are repeated, of yielding like results. The antecedents do not have to be substantiated by being carried back to earlier antecedents and so on; they are good and sound if they do what is wanted of them: if they lead to an observable result which satisfies the conditions set by the nature of the problem in hand.

The significance of this point comes out more clearly in dealing with the genuineness of discovery or new knowledge. By terms of the traditional theories, this is impossible in the case of inference and reflective inquiry. We know, according to them, only when we have assimilated the seemingly new to something previously known immediately. In consequence, all distinctive individual, or non-repeated, traits of things are incapable of being known. What cannot be treated as a case of something else stays outside knowledge. Individualized characteristics are unknowable surds.

According to this doctrine, reflective inquiry may hit upon new instances of laws, new specimens of old truths, new members of old classes, but not upon intrinsically new objects of knowledge. As far as empiricism is concerned the case of Locke is instructive. His *Essay on Human Understanding* is one continued effort to test all reflective beliefs and ideas whatever by reduction to original "simple ideas" that are infallibly known in isolation from any inferential undertaking—a point in which many of the new realisms are still Lockeian.

If one looks at the course of science, we find a very different story told. Important conclusions of science are those which distinctly refuse to be identified with anything previously known. Instead of having to be proved by being assimilated to the latter, they rather occasion revision of what men thought they previously knew. The recent crisis in physical science is a case in point. The experimental discovery that the velocity of light remains the same when measured either with or against the direction of the earth's movement was totally unaccountable on the basis of previous knowing. But scientific men accepted the *consequences* of their experimental operations as constituting the known object, rather than feeling under obligation to "prove" them by identification with what was said to be antecedently known. Inferential inquiry in scientific procedure is an adventure in which conclusions confound expectation and upset what has been accepted as facts. It takes time for these new facts to be assimilated: to become familiar. Assimilation of the new to the familiar is doubtless a precondition for our finding ourselves at home in the new and being able to handle it freely. But the older theories virtually made this personal and psychological phase of assimilation of new and old into a test of knowledge itself.

The third point, that cognition is recognition, only presents the same difficulty in another way. It presents it in a light which brings out a distinctive point. The theory that knowledge due to reflection consists in identifying something with what is already known or possessed confuses the psychological trait of familiarity, the quality of finding ourselves at ease in a situation, with knowledge. The conception originated when experimental knowing occurred only occasionally and as if by accident; when discoveries were regarded as gifts of the gods or as special inspirations: when men were governed by custom and were uneasy in the presence of change and afraid of the unknown. It was rationalized into a theory when the Greeks succeeded in identifying natural phenomena with rational ideas and were delighted with the identification because their esthetic interest made them at home in a world of such harmony and order as that identification involved. They called the result science, although in fact it fastened wrong beliefs about nature upon Europe for well nigh two thousand years.

Newtonian science, as we have seen in another connection, in effect only substituted one set of identifying objects, the mathematical, for those previously employed. It set up permanent substances, the particles or atoms having inherent mathematical properties, as ultimate realities, and alleged that reflective thought yields knowledge when it translates phenomena into these properties. Thus it retained unimpaired the theory that knowing signifies a process of identification. It required over two centuries for the experimental method to reach a point where men were forced to realize that progress in science depends upon choice of operations performed and not upon the properties of objects which were alleged to be so antecedently certain and fixed that all detailed phenomena might be reduced to them.

This conception of knowledge still dominates thinking in social and moral matters. When it is realized that in these fields as in the physical, we know what we intentionally construct, that everything depends upon determination of methods of operation and upon observation of the consequences which test them, the progress of knowledge in these affairs may also become secure and constant.

What has been said does not imply that previous knowledge is not of immense importance in obtaining new knowledge. What is denied is that this previous knowledge need be immediate or intuitive, and that it provides the measure and standard of conclusions obtained by inferential operations. Inferential inquiry is continuous; one phase passes into the next which uses, tests and expands conclusions already obtained. More particularly, the conclusions of prior knowledge are the *instruments* of new inquiries, not the norm which determines their validity. Objects of previous knowledge supply working hypotheses for new situations; they are the source of suggestion of new operations; they direct inquiry. But they do not enter into reflective knowing by way of providing its premises in a logical sense. The tradition of classic logic persists in leading philosophers to call premises what in effect are regulative and instrumental points of view for conducting new observations.

We are constantly referring to what is already known to get our bearings in any new situation. Unless there is some reason to doubt whether presumptive knowledge is really knowledge, we take it as a net product. It would be a waste of time and energy to repeat the operations in virtue of which the object is a known object unless there were ground for suspecting its validity. Every adult, irrespective of whether he is a man of science or not, carries in his head a large store of things known in virtue of earlier operations. When a new problem comes up, one habitually refers to what is already known to get a start in dealing with it. Such objects, until we have occasion to doubt them, are settled, assured; the given situation is dubious, but they are secure. Hence we take them for granted, we take them as a matter of course. Then if we question them, we tend to fall back upon something else already known. What is too easily overlooked (especially in quest for certainty by attachment to the fixed) is that the objects we thus fall back upon are themselves known in virtue of previous operations of inferential inquiry and test, and that their "immediacy" as objects of reference marks an assured product of reflection. It is also overlooked that they are referred to as instruments, rather than as fixed in and of themselves. The case is similar to the use of tools previously manufactured when we are dealing with the conditions of a new situation; only when they prove defective does invention of new tools demand recurrence to the operations by which they were originally constructed.

This act of taking and using objects already known is *practically* justified; it is like eating a fruit without asking how it was grown. But many theories of knowledge take this retrospective use of things known in virtue of earlier operations as typical of the nature of knowledge itself. Being reminded of something we already know is taken as *the* pattern of all knowing. When the thing of which we are now retrospectively aware was in process of being known, it was prospective and eventual to inquiry, not something already "given." And it has *cognitive* force in a new inquiry whose objective and ultimate object is *now* prospective. Taking what is already known or pointing to it is no more a case of knowledge than taking a chisel out of a tool-box is the making of the tool. Because some theories of knowledge have taken the operations that yield the known object to be merely mental or psychical instead of overt redispositions of antecedent subject-matter (and thus have terminated in some form of "idealism") is no reason for denying the mediated character of all known objects.

Thus we are led by another road to the conclusion that the basic error of traditional theories of knowledge resides in the isolation and fixation of some phase of the whole process of inquiry in resolving problematic situations. Sometimes sense-data are so taken; sometimes, conceptions; sometimes, objects previously known. An episode in a series of operational acts is fastened upon, and then in its isolation and consequent fragmentary character is made the foundation of the theory of knowing in its entirety.

Reflective knowing certainly involves identification. But identity itself has to be defined operationally. There are as many meanings of identity and identification as there are types of operation by which they are determined. There is identification of an object as a member of a class, of a plant as belonging to a certain species: taxonomic identity. The classic theory of definition took this to be the sole valid type of logical definition. There are identifications that are historic, that are concerned with individuals as such. They define the identity of an individual throughout a series of successive temporal changes, while the other type is purely static. This kind of identity is secured by operations that introduce temporal continuity into what is otherwise discrete: it yields genetic and generative definitions. For the identity of an individual is constituted by continued absorption and incorporation of materials previously external—as in the growth of a person, a nation or a social movement. It demands operations that redispose and organize what antecedently exists. Identifications effected by inferential operations are of this type. They are not reductions of the new object or situation to terms of something already known. Traditional theories treat them as if they were of the static and subsumptive type.

Hence these theories have no way of accounting for the discrimination and differentiation, the novel elements, involved in the conclusions of inferential knowing. They must be viewed as mere surds, cognitively speaking. Identifications through processes of temporal growth are, on the contrary, differentiations; new and previously external material is incorporated; otherwise there is no growth, no development. All reflective inquiry starts from a problematic situation, and no such situation can be settled in its own terms. It evolves into a resolved situation only by means of introduction of material not found in the situation itself. Imaginative survey, comparison with things already known, is the first step. This does not eventuate in complete *knowledge*, however, until some overt experimental act takes place by means of which an existential incorporation and organization is brought about. Merely "mental" revisions remain in the status of thought as distinct from knowledge. Identification through operations that rearrange what is antecedently given is a process of additive discrimination; it alone is synthetic in the true sense of that word, involving likeness-and-difference.

Objective idealisms have insisted upon the conjoint presence of identity and difference in objects of knowledge, as in the doctrine of the "concrete universal." But they have ignored the phase of *temporal* reconstruction with its necessity for overt existential interaction.

A further implication of the experimental determination of the known object concerns its office in the verification of hypotheses. It is often supposed that the value of experiment lies merely in the fact that it confirms, refutes or modifies a hypothesis. From the standpoint of the personal interest of the inquirer such an interpretation often holds good. He is interested in a theory, and views the eventually disclosed state of facts solely in its bearing upon the theory he is entertaining. To him, at the time, the cognitive value of the results of experimental operation lies in the test they afford of the claims of his hypothesis. Even so, however, verification, or the opposite, is attained only because experimentation effects a transition of a problematical situation into a resolved one. In this development new individual objects with new features are brought to light. As far as the objective course of knowledge is concerned, as distinct from the personal interest of the investigator, *this* result is the important one; in comparison with it the verification of a hypothesis is secondary and incidental. The institution of a new object of experience is the essential fact. It would not occur to any one surveying the body of scientific knowledge as a whole to think that its value lay in the corroboration it provides for a number of hypotheses. Taken in the large, the significance of the body of subject-matter as a whole clearly resides in the fact that it marks an added depth, range and fullness of meaning conferred upon objects of ordinary experience.

This consequence is the only intelligible end that can be assigned to processes of reflective inquiry. It marks a gain that during their course hypotheses have gained increased solidity. But the eventual object of activity with tools is not to perfect tools, but is found in what tools accomplish, the products they turn out. When a person working on the basis of a certain idea succeeds in making an invention, his idea is verified. But verification was not the purpose of making the invention, nor does it constitute its value when made. The same may be said of physicians working upon a certain hypothesis in cure of a disease. Only an ultra-specialist would regard a successful outcome simply as verification of a theory. Since a hypothesis is itself instrumental to inquiry, its verification cannot constitute the whole significance of inquiry.

Hypotheses which have later been rejected have often proved

serviceable in discovery of new facts, and thus advanced knowledge. A poor tool is often better than none at all. It has even been doubted whether any hypothesis ever entertained has not turned out later to have been erroneous in important respects. It is still questioned whether many of the objects of the most valuable and indispensable hypotheses in present use have actual existence; the existential status of the electron is still, for example, a matter of controversy. In many cases, as in the older theory of the nature of atoms, it is now clear that their worth was independent of the existential status imputed to their subject-matter; that indeed this imputation was irrelevant and as far as it went injurious. As we have seen, progress beyond the Newtonian scheme was made possible when the ascription of antecedently existing inherent properties was dropped out, and concepts were regarded as designations of operations to be performed.

These considerations have a practical importance with respect to the attitude of disdain often affected—usually in behalf of preservation of some dogma—toward the course of science. It is pointed out that scientific men are constantly engaged in furbishing and refurbishing their theories, rejecting those to which they have been devoted, and putting new ones in their place only in time to reject these also. Then it is demanded why we should put our trust in science self-confessed to be unstable rather than in some old dogma which men have continued to believe without change. It is overlooked that the instability affects the intellectual apparatus which is employed, conceptions which are frankly hypothetical. What remains and is not discarded but is added to is the body of concrete knowledge and of definite controls constructed by conceptions no longer tenable. No one would dream of reflecting adversely upon the evolution of mechanical inventions because the sickle had been discarded for the mowing machine, and the mechanized tractor substituted for the horse-drawn mower. We are obviously confronted with betterment of the instrumentalities that are employed to secure consequences.

The adverse criticism of science just mentioned attaches only to some of the philosophic interpretations which have been advanced. If scientific conceptions were valid in the degree in which they are revelations of antecedent properties of real Being and existence (as the Newtonian scheme took them to be), there would be something disturbing in their continual revamping.

The claim of any one of them to be valid would suffer discredit. Not so, if they are instrumentalities which direct operations of experimental observations, and if the knowledge-property resides in conclusions. Fruits remain and these fruits are the abiding advance of knowledge. Thus the breaking down of the traditional barrier between theory, supposed to be concerned with prior reality and practice concerned with production of consequences, protects the actual results of theory from cavil.

At the same time, it does away once for all with the grounds upon which wholesale skeptical and agnostic philosophies have rested. As long as theories of knowledge are framed in terms of organs assigned to mind or consciousness, whether sense or reason or any combination of the two, organs occupied, it is alleged, in reproducing or grasping antecedent reality, there will continue to exist such generalized skeptical philosophies. Phenomenalism, which holds that impressions and ideas come between the knower and things to be known, will have plenty of support as long as sensations and ideas are supposed to be valid only when they report to mind something prior to them. Phenomenalism may be objected to on the ground that data, ideas, essences, are means of knowing, not its objects. But as long as they are regarded as merely mental means rather than as means which through overt acts effect actual redisposition of antecedent things, the retort will have the character of an arbitrary *tour de force*; it will be a pious doctrine rather than a conclusion empirically verified.

It is always in place to be doubtful or skeptical about particular items of supposed knowledge when evidence to the contrary presents itself. There is no knowledge self-guaranteed to be infallible, since all knowledge is the product of special acts of inquiry. Agnosticism as confession of ignorance about special matters, in the absence of adequate evidence, is not only in place under such circumstances but is an act of intellectual honesty. But such skepticism and agnosticism are particular and depend upon special conditions; they are not wholesale; they do not issue from a generalized impeachment of the adequacy of the organs of knowing to perform their office. Theories which assume that the knowing subject, that mind or consciousness, have an inherent capacity to disclose reality, a capacity operating apart from any overt interactions of the organism with surrounding conditions, are invitations to general philosophical doubt.

The case stands radically otherwise when it is seen that "mental" states and acts are organs of knowing things not directly but through the overt actions which they evoke and direct. For the *consequences* of these acts constitute the object said to be known; and these consequences are public and open. Doubt and skepticism attach only to the adequacy of the operations used in achieving the issue which transforms a problematic situation into a settled or resolved one. Instead of being impotent and paralyzing, they are opportunities for bettering concrete *methods* of inquiry.

Once more, we recur to the problem raised concerning the possibility of carrying over the essential elements of the pattern of experimental knowing into the experience of man in its everyday traits. A statement that judgments about regulative ends and values, the creeds that are to govern conduct in its important interests, are upon the whole matters of tradition, dogma and imposition from alleged authorities, hardly requires argument in its support. It is equally patent that skepticism is rife as to the value of purposes and policies of life thus supplied; the skepticism often extends to complete agnosticism as to the possibility of any regulative ends and standards whatever. The course of human experience in such matters is supposed to be inherently chaotic. Even more precious than the special conclusions of scientific inquiry is its proof that intelligent experimental inquiry is possible which, when it is used, will develop expansion of ideas and regulation of securely tested consequences. It is, once more, a hypothesis rather than a settled fact that extension and transfer of experimental method is generally possible. But like other hypotheses it is to be tried in action, and the future history of mankind is at stake in the trial.

8.   The Naturalization of Intelligence

Every student of philosophy is aware of the number of seeming impasses into which the theory of knowledge has been led. There are four general types of subject-matter whose rival claims to be the objects of true knowledge have to be either disposed of or in some way accommodated to one another. At one pole, are immediate sense-data which are said to be the immediate and accordingly most certain objects in knowledge of existence: the original material from which knowledge of nature must set out. At the other pole, are mathematical and logical objects. Somewhere between them lie the objects of physical science, the products of an elaborate technique of reflective inquiry. Then there are the objects of everyday experience, the concrete things of the world in which we live and which, from the standpoint of our practical affairs, our enjoyments and sufferings, form the world we live in. To common sense these are the most important if not the most real of all objects of knowing. Recent philosophy has been increasingly occupied with the problems which grow out of the titles of these various kinds of objects to jurisdiction over the field of knowledge. From some point of view, the pretensions of each seem to be supreme.

The problem, however, is far from being a purely technical one. There has been repeated occasion to note that the claim of physical objects, the objects in which the physical sciences terminate, to constitute the real nature of the world, places the objects of value with which our affections and choices are concerned at an invidious disadvantage. The mathematician often doubts the claims of physics to be a science in the full sense of the word; the psychologist may quarrel with both; and the devotees of physical inquiry are suspicious of the claims of those who deal with human affairs, historians and students of social life. The biological subjects which stand between and form a connecting link are often refused the title of science if they adopt principles and categories different from those of strict physics. The net practical effect is the creation of the belief that science exists only in the things which are most remote from any significant human concern, so that as we approach social and moral questions and interests we must either surrender hope of the guidance of genuine knowledge or else purchase a scientific title and authority at the expense of all that is distinctly human.

Those who have followed the previous discussions will not be surprised to hear that, from the standpoint of experimental knowing, all of the rivalries and connected problems grow from a single root. They spring from the assumption that the true and valid object of knowledge is that which has being prior to and independent of the operations of knowing. They spring from the doctrine that knowledge is a grasp or beholding of reality without anything being done to modify its antecedent state—the doctrine which is the source of the separation of knowledge from practical activity. If we see that knowing is not the act of an outside spectator but of a participator inside the natural and social scene, then the true object of knowledge resides in the consequences of directed action. When we take this point of view, if only by way of a hypothesis, the perplexities and difficulties of which we have been speaking vanish. For on this basis there will be as many kinds of known objects as there are kinds of effectively conducted operations of inquiry which result in the consequences intended.

The result of one operation will be as good and true an object of knowledge as is any other, provided it is good at all: provided, that is, it satisfies the conditions which induced the inquiry. For if consequences are the object of knowing, then an archetypal antecedent reality is not a model to which the conclusions of inquiry must conform. One might even go as far as to say that there are as many kinds of valid knowledge as there are conclusions wherein distinctive operations have been employed to solve the problems set by antecedently experienced situations. For operations dealing with different problems never exactly repeat one another and do not determine exactly the same consequences. However, as far as logical theory is concerned, operations fall into certain kinds or types. It is the bearing of our principle upon the validity of these kinds that we are directly concerned with.

It is only repeating what has been said to assert that no problem can be solved without a determination of the data which define and locate it and which furnish clews or evidence. In so far, when we secure dependable sense-data, we know truly. Again, the systematic progress of inquiry in dealing with physical problems requires that we determine those metric properties by means of which correlations of changes are instituted so as to make predictions possible. These form the objects of physical science, and if our operations are adequate they are truly known. We develop operations, through symbols, which connect possible operations with one another; their outcome gives the *formal* objects of mathematics and logic. As consequences of suitable operations these too are truly known. Finally, when these operations, or some combination of them, are used to solve the problems which arise in connection with the things of ordinary perceived and enjoyed objects, the latter, as far as they are consequences of these operations, are themselves truly known. We know whenever we do know; that is, whenever our inquiry leads to conclusions which settle the problem out of which it grew. This truism is the end of the whole matter—upon the condition that we frame our theory of knowledge in accord with the pattern set by experimental methods.

The conclusions, however, are not truistic; they certainly are not trivial. The more complex the conditions with which operations are concerned, the fuller and richer are their consequences. Consequently, the more significant, although not the truer, is the resulting knowledge. The advantage of physical knowledge depends upon the fact that it deals with fewer conditions, those of a narrower and more isolated range, by means of operations that are more precise and more technical. There is no difference in principle between knowledge of them and knowledge of the most complex human affairs, but there is a decided practical difference. To be an object of specifically physical knowledge is the same thing as being an object of operations that discriminate definitely fundamental relations of the experienced world from others, and that deal with them in their discriminated character. The gain is great. But the objects thus known lay no claim to be final. When used as factors for inquiring into phenomena of life and society they become instrumental; they cease to be inclusive, and become part of a method for understanding more complex phenomena.

From this point of view, the objects of our common sense world (by which is signified that in which we live, with our loves and hates, our defeats and achievements, our choices, strivings and enjoyments) have a double status. When they *precede* operations of competent directed inquiry, they are not matters of knowledge; they are experienced just as they happen to occur. They thus set problems for inquiry, problems of varied scope. But they are of such a nature that things of the most limited range, the purely physical, are the first to be successfully dealt with. But in the degree in which fuller and more complex social and moral affairs—which of course include physical and biological conditions and relations within themselves—are transformed by becoming consequences of operations made possible by the limited forms of knowing, they also are objects of knowledge. While they are not more real, they are richer and more significant objects than are those of any other type of knowledge.

The special results of science are always finding their way back into the natural and social environment of daily life and modifying it. This fact does not of itself cause the latter to be known objects. A typical example is the effect of physical science upon a worker in a factory; he may merely become an attachment to a machine for a number of hours a day. Physical science has had its effect in changing social conditions. But there has been no correspondingly significant increase of intelligent understanding. The application of physical knowledge has taken place in a technical way for the sake of limited consequences. But when the operations in which physical science is used are such as to transform distinctively human values in behalf of a human interest, those who participate in these consequences have a knowledge of the things of ordinary perception, use and enjoyment as genuine and fuller and deeper than that of the scientist in his laboratory. Were we to define science not in the usual technical way, but as a knowledge that accrues when methods are employed which deal competently with problems that present themselves, the physician, engineer, artist, craftsman, lay claim to scientific knowing.

These statements go contrary to the philosophic tradition. They do so for just one reason. They rest upon the idea that known objects exist as the consequences of directed operations, not because of conformity of thought or observation with something antecedent. We may, for reasons which I hope will appear later, give the name intelligence to these directed operations. Using this term, we may say that the worth of any object that lays claim to being an object of knowledge is dependent upon the intelligence employed in reaching it. In saying this, we must bear in mind that intelligence means operations actually performed in the modification of conditions, including all the guidance that is given by means of ideas, both direct and symbolic.

The statement may sound strange. But it is only a way of saying that the value of any cognitive conclusion depends upon the *method* by which it is reached, so that the perfecting of method, the perfecting of intelligence, is the thing of supreme value. If we judge the work of a scientific inquirer by what he does and not by his speech when he talks about his work (when he is likely to talk in terms of traditional notions that have become habitual) we shall have little difficulty, I think, in accepting the idea that he determines the cognitive claims of anything presented to him on the basis of the method by which it is reached. The import of this doctrine is simple. It becomes complicated, however, the moment we contrast it with the doctrines which have dominated thought. For these all rest on the notion that a reality in Being independently of the operations of inquiry is the standard and measure of anything said to be known. Viewed in this connection, the conception just advanced involves hardly less than a revolutionary transformation of many of our most cherished convictions. The essential difference is that between a mind which beholds or grasps objects from outside the world of things, physical and social, and one which is a participant, interacting with other things and knowing them provided the interaction is regulated in a definable way.

In discussion up to this point we have depended upon the general pattern of experimental knowing. It is asserted that when we frame our theory of knowledge and the known object after this pattern, the conclusion is inevitable. But the point is of such importance that we may gratefully acknowledge the support given the conclusion by one of the definite conclusions reached in recent physical science. For this one result is of a crucially decisive nature. It is known technically as Heisenberg's principle of indeterminacy. The basic philosophy of the Newtonian system of the universe is closely connected with what is termed the principle of canonic conjugates. The fundamental principle of the mechanical philosophy of nature is that it is possible to determine exactly (in principle if not in actual practice) both the position and the velocity of any body. Knowing this for each particle which enters into any change, as a motion, it is possible to calculate mathematically, that is exactly, just what will happen. The laws or physical equations that express the relations of the particles and bodies under different conditions are then assumed to be a "governing" framework of nature to which all particular phenomena conform. Knowing volumes and momenta in a particular case we can by the aid of fixed laws predict the subsequent course of events.

The philosophy in question assumed that these positions and velocities are there in nature independent of our knowing, of our experiments and observations, and that we have scientific knowledge in the degree in which we ascertain them exactly. The future and the past belong to the same completely determinate and fixed scheme. Observations, when correctly conducted, merely register this fixed state of changes according to laws of objects whose essential properties are fixed. The implications of the positions are expressed in Laplace's well-known saying that were there a knowledge (in mechanical terms) of the state of the universe at any one time its whole future could be predicted—or deduced. It is this philosophy which Heisenberg's principle has upset, a fact implied in calling it a principle of indeterminacy.

It is true that critics had attacked the Newtonian scheme on the basis of a logical flaw in it. It first postulates that the position and velocity of any particle can be determined in isolation from all others. Then it postulates that there is a complete and continuous interaction of all these particles with one another. Logically, the two postulates nullify each other. But as long as the principles involved gave satisfactory results this objection was brushed aside or ignored. Heisenberg's principle compels a recognition of the fact that interaction prevents an accurate measurement of velocity and position for *any* body, the demonstration centering about the role of the interaction of the observer in determining what actually happens.

The scientific data and the mathematical reasonings which led him to his conclusion are technical. But fortunately they do not concern us. The logic of the matter is not complicated. He showed that if we fix, metrically, velocity, then there is a range of indeterminateness in the assignment of position, and vice-versa. When one is fixed, the other is defined only within a specified limit of probability. The element of indeterminateness is not connected with defect in the method of observation but is intrinsic. The particle observed does not *have* fixed position or velocity, for it is changing all the time because of interaction: specifically, in this case, interaction with the act of observing, or more strictly, with the conditions under which an observation is possible; for it is not the "mental" phase of observation which makes the difference. Since either position or velocity may be fixed at choice, leaving the element of indeterminacy on the other side, both of them are shown to be conceptual in nature. That is, they belong to our intellectual apparatus for *dealing with* antecedent existence, not to fixed properties of that existence. An isolation of a particle for measurement is essentially a device for regulation of subsequent perceptual experience.

Technically, the principle of Heisenberg is connected with recent determinations regarding observation of phenomena of light. The principle as far as the role of the conditions of observation is concerned is simple. We should all, I suppose, recognize that when we perceive an object by means of touch, the contact introduces a slight modification in the thing touched. Although in dealing with large bodies this change would be insignificant, it would be considerable if we touched a minute body and one moving at high speed. It might be thought that we could calculate the displacement thus effected, and by making allowances for it determine exactly the position and momentum of the thing touched. But this result would be theoretical, and would have to be confirmed by another observation. The effect of the last observation cannot be eliminated. Failure to generalize this conclusion was due presumably to two facts. Until recently physics dealt mainly with bodies of relatively large volume and relatively low velocity. Experiences with these bodies were carried over to minute particles of any velocity; these were treated as mathematical points located at fixed, unchanging, instants of time. The second cause is that vision does not involve interaction with the thing seen as obviously as does touch.

But the situation changed when it came to dealing with minute bodies moving at high speed. Also, it became clear that a continuous field or even flow of light cannot be observed and measured. Light can be observed only as an individual object, a drop, pellet or bullet. The presence of at least one such bullet is required to make, say, an electron visible, and its action displaces to some extent the object observed; the displacement or jog, being involved in the observation, cannot be measured by it. As Bridgman says: "A cat may look at a king but at least one bullet of light must pass if any light at all passes, and the king cannot be observed without the exertion of that minimum amount of mechanical repulsion which corresponds to the single bullet."[1]

To a layman the full import of the discovery may not seem at first sight very great. In the subject-matter of scientific thought it calls for only slight changes of formulation, insignificant for all macroscopic bodies. The change for the underlying philosophy and logic of science is, however, very great. In relation to the metaphysics of the Newtonian system it is hardly less than revolutionary. What is known is seen to be a product in which the act of observation plays a necessary role. Knowing is seen to be a participant in what is finally known. Moreover, the metaphysics of existence as something fixed and therefore capable of literally exact mathematical description and prediction is undermined. Knowing is, for philosophical theory, a case of specially directed activity instead of something isolated from practice. The quest for certainty by means of exact possession in mind of immutable reality is exchanged for search for security by means of active control of the changing course of events. Intelligence in operation, another name for method, becomes the thing most worth winning.

The principle of indeterminacy thus presents itself as the final step in the dislodgment of the old spectator theory of knowledge. It marks the acknowledgment, within scientific procedure itself, of the fact that knowing is one kind of interaction which goes on within the world. Knowing marks the conversion of undirected changes into changes directed toward an intended conclusion. There are left for philosophy but two alternatives. Either

1. In the March, 1929, number of *Harper's Magazine*, in an article entitled "The New Vision of Science."

knowledge defeats its own purpose; or the objective of knowing *is* the consequences of operations purposely undertaken, provided they fulfill the conditions for the sake of which they are carried on. If we persist in the traditional conception, according to which the thing to be known is something which exists prior to and wholly apart from the act of knowing, then discovery of the fact that the act of observation, necessary in existential knowing, modifies that preexistent something, is proof that the act of knowing gets in its own way, frustrating its own intent. If knowing is a form of doing and is to be judged like other modes by its eventual issue, this tragic conclusion is not forced upon us. Fundamentally, the issue is raised whether philosophy is willing to surrender a theory of mind and its organs of knowing which originated when the practice of knowing was in its infancy.

One important result of acknowledgment of the philosophic modification involved in the principle of indeterminacy is a definite change in our conception of natural laws. The individually observed case becomes the measure of knowledge. Laws are intellectual instrumentalities by which that individual object is instituted and its meaning determined. This change involves a reversal of the theory which has dominated thought since the Newtonian system obtained full sway. According to the latter, the aim of science is to ascertain laws; individual cases are known only as they are reduced to instances of laws. For, as we saw earlier, the Newtonian philosophy allowed itself to become entangled in the Greek metaphysics according to which the immutable is the truly real and our thought is adequate in the degree in which it approximates a grasp of what is antecedently fixed in existence.

In content, or subject-matter, Newton's philosophy effected a revolutionary change. The unchanging reality had been thought to consist of forms and species. According to Newtonian science, it consists of fixed relations, temporal and spatial, designated by exact enumeration of changes between fixed ultimate substances, the masses of atoms. The discovery that mass varies with velocity was the beginning of the end. It deprived physical knowledge of its supposedly ultimate permanent coefficient, one having nothing to do with configuration or motion, and one in terms of which all interactions were to be exactly described. All "laws" were statements of these ultimate and rigid uniformities of being.

While perhaps there was felt to be something metaphorical in speaking of laws as if they "governed" changes and of the latter as if they "obeyed" laws, there was nothing figurative in the notion that laws stated the ultimate unchanging properties of natural existence, and that all individual cases, those observed, were only specimen instances of the antecedent properties of the real world formulated in laws. The principle of indeterminacy brings to fruition the scientific transformation initiated in the discovery that the supposition of a permanent coefficient of mass is illusory—a survival, when judged in historical terms, of the old notion that something immutable is the true object of knowledge.

In technical statement, laws on the new basis are *formulae for the prediction of the probability of an observable occurrence.* They are designations of relations sufficiently stable to allow of the occurrence of forecasts of individualized situations—for every observed phenomenon is individual—within limits of specified probability, not a probability of error, but of probability of actual occurrence. Laws are inherently conceptual in character, as is shown in the fact that either position or velocity may be fixed at will. To call them conceptual is not to say that they are merely "mental" and arbitrary. It is to say that they are *relations* which are thought not observed. The subject-matter of the conceptions which constitute laws is not arbitrary, for it is determined by the interactions of what exists. But determination of them is very different from that denoted by conformity to fixed properties of unchanging substances. Any instrument which is to operate effectively in existence must take account of what exists, from a fountain pen to a self-binding reaper, a locomotive or an airplane. But "taking account of," paying heed to, is something quite different from literal conformity to what is already in being. It is an adaptation of what previously existed to accomplishment of a purpose.

The eventual purpose in knowledge is observation of a new phenomenon, an object actually experienced by way of perception. Thus the supposed immutable law supposed to govern phenomena becomes a way of transacting business effectively with concrete existences, a mode of regulation of our relations with them. There is no difference in principle between their use in "pure" science and in an art. We may recur to the case of a physician to which reference was made. The physician in diagnosing a case of disease deals with something individualized. He draws upon a store of general principles of physiology, etc., already at command. Without this store of conceptual material he is helpless. But he does not attempt to reduce the case to an exact specimen of certain laws of physiology and pathology, or do away with its unique individuality. Rather he uses general statements as aids to direct his observation of the particular case, so as to discover what it is *like*. They function as intellectual tools or instrumentalities.

The recognition that laws are means of calculating the probability of observation of an event signifies that in basic logic there is no difference in the two kinds of cases. The full and eventual reality of knowledge is carried in the individual case, not in general laws isolated from use in giving an individual case its meaning. Thus the empirical or observational theory of knowledge comes to its own, although in quite a different way from that imagined by traditional empiricism.

It is an old remark that human progress is a zigzag affair. The idea of a universal reign of law, based on properties immutably inhering in things and of such a nature as to be capable of exact mathematical statement was a sublime idea. It displaced once for all the notion of a world in which the unaccountable and the mysterious have the first and last word, a world in which they constantly insert themselves. It established the ideal of regularity and uniformity in place of the casual and sporadic. It gave men inspiration and guidance in seeking for uniformities and constancies where only irregular diversity was experienced. The ideal extended itself from the inanimate world to the animate and then to social affairs. It became, it may fairly be said, the great article of faith in the creed of scientific men. From this point of view, the principle of indeterminacy seems like an intellectual catastrophe. In compelling surrender of the doctrine of exact and immutable laws describing the fixed antecedent properties of things, it seems to involve abandonment of the idea that the world is fundamentally intelligible. A universe in which fixed laws do not make possible exact predictions seems from the older standpoint to be a world in which disorder reigns.

The feeling is psychologically natural. But it arises from the hold which intellectual habits have over us. The traditional conception displaced in fact lingers in imagination as a picture of what the world ought to be; we are uneasy because the fact turns out not to be in accord with the picture in our minds. As a matter of fact, the change, viewed in a perspective of distance, is nothing like so upsetting. All the facts that were ever known are still known, and known with greater accuracy than before. The older doctrine was in effect an offshoot not of science but of a metaphysical doctrine which taught that the immutable is the truly real, and of a theory of knowledge which held that rational conceptions rather than observations are the vehicle of knowledge. Newton foisted a fundamental "rationalism" upon the scientific world all the more effectually because he did it in the name of empirical observation.

Moreover, like all generalizations which go beyond the range of possible as well as of actual experience, a price was paid for the sublime and inspiring ideal of a reign of universal and exact law: the sacrifice of the individual to the general, of the concrete to the relational. Spinoza's magnificently sweeping dictum that "the order and connection of ideas is the order and connection of things" was in effect, although not avowedly as it was with Spinoza, the current measure of the intelligibility of nature. And a universe whose essential characteristic is fixed order and connection has no place for unique and individual existences, no place for novelty and genuine change and growth. It is, in the words of William James, a block universe. The fact that in detailed content it is a thoroughly mechanistic world is, one may say, a mere incident attending the fact that it is a fixed and closed world.

Probably everyone has heard of the child who expressed surprise at the fact that rivers or bodies of water are always located conveniently near great cities. Suppose every one had had engrained in his mind the notion that cities, like rivers, are works of nature. Suppose it was then suddenly ascertained that cities were man made and were located near bodies of water in order that the activities of men in industry and commerce might be better carried on and human purposes and needs be better served. We can imagine that the discovery would bring with it a shock. It would be upsetting because it would seem unnatural; for the ordinary measure of the natural is psychological; it is what we have become accustomed to. But in time the new idea in becoming familiar would also become "natural." If men had always previously conceived of the connection between cities and rivers as one which was intrinsic and fixed by nature, instead of being a product of human art, it is moreover probable that in time a liberation would be experienced by discovery that the contrary was the case. Men would be led to take fuller advantage of the facilities afforded by natural conditions. These would be used in new and more diversified ways when it was realized that cities were near them because of and for the sake of the uses they provide.

The analogy suggested seems to me close. From the standpoint of traditional notions, it appears that nature, intrinsically, is *irrational*. But the quality of irrationality is imputed only because of conflict with a prior definition of rationality. Abandon completely the notion that nature *ought* to conform to a certain definition, and nature intrinsically is neither rational nor irrational. Apart from the use made of it in knowing, it exists in a dimension irrelevant to either attribution, just as rivers inherently are neither located near cities nor are opposed to such location. Nature is intellig*ible* and understand*able*. There are operations by means of which it *becomes* an object of knowledge, and is turned to human purposes, just as rivers provide conditions which *may* be utilized to promote human activities and to satisfy human need.

Moreover, just as commerce, carried on by natural bodies of water, signifies interactions within nature, by which changes are effected in natural conditions—the building of docks and harbors, erection of warehouses and factories, construction of steamships and also in invention of new modes of interaction—so with knowing and knowledge. The organs, instrumentalities and operations of knowing are inside nature, not outside. Hence they are changes of what previously existed: the object of knowledge is a constructed, existentially produced, object. The shock to the traditional notion that knowledge is perfect in the degree in which it grasps or beholds without change some thing previously complete in itself is tremendous. But in effect it only makes us aware of what we have always done, as far as ever we have actually succeeded in knowing: it clears away superfluous and irrelevant accompaniments and it concentrates attention upon the agencies which are actually effective in obtaining knowledge, eliminating waste and making actual knowing more controllable. It installs man, thinking man, within nature.

The doctrine that nature is inherently rational was a costly one. It entailed the idea that reason in man is an outside spectator of a rationality already complete in itself. It deprived reason in man of an active and creative office; its business was simply to copy, to re-present symbolically, to view a given rational structure. Ability to make a transcript of this structure in mathematical formulae gives great delight to those who have the required ability. But it *does* nothing; it makes no difference in nature. In effect, it limits thought in man to retraversing in cognition a pattern fixed and complete in itself. The doctrine was both an effect of the traditional separation between knowledge and action and a factor in perpetuating it. It relegated practical making and doing to a secondary and relatively irrational realm.

Its paralyzing effect on human action is seen in the part it played in the eighteenth and nineteenth century in the theory of "natural laws" in human affairs, in social matters. These natural laws were supposed to be inherently fixed; a science of social phenomena and relations was equivalent to discovery of them. Once discovered, nothing remained for man but to conform to them; they were to rule his conduct as physical laws govern physical phenomena. They were the sole standard of conduct in economic affairs; the laws of economics are the "natural" laws of all political action; other so-called laws are artificial, man-made contrivances in contrast with the normative regulations of nature itself.

Laissez-faire was the logical conclusion. For organized society to attempt to regulate the course of economic affairs, to bring them into service of humanly conceived ends, was a harmful interference.

This doctrine is demonstratively the offspring of that conception of universal laws that phenomena must observe which was a heritage of the Newtonian philosophy. But if man in knowing is a participator in the natural scene, a factor in generating things known, the fact that man participates as a factor in social affairs is no barrier to knowledge of them. On the contrary, a certain method of directed participation is a precondition of his having any genuine understanding. Human intervention for the sake of effecting ends is no interference, and it is a means of knowledge.

There is thus involved more than a verbal shift if we say that the new scientific development effects an exchange of reason for intelligence. In saying this, "reason" has the technical meaning given to it in classic philosophic tradition, the *nous* of the Greeks, the *intellectus* of the scholastics. In this meaning, it designates both an inherent immutable order of nature, superempirical in character, and the organ of mind by which this universal order is grasped. In both respects, reason is with respect to changing things the ultimate fixed standard—the law physical phenomena obey, the norm human action should obey. For the marks of "reason" in its traditional sense are necessity, universality, superiority to change, domination of the occurrence and the understanding of change.

Intelligence on the other hand is associated with *judgment*; that is, with selection and arrangement of means to effect consequences and with choice of what we take as our ends. A man is intelligent not in virtue of having reason which grasps first and indemonstrable truths about fixed principles, in order to reason deductively from them to the particulars which they govern, but in virtue of his capacity to estimate the possibilities of a situation and to act in accordance with his estimate. In the large sense of the term, intelligence is as practical as reason is theoretical. Wherever intelligence operates, things are judged in their capacity of signs of other things. If scientific knowledge enables us to estimate more accurately the worth of things as signs, we can afford to exchange a loss of theoretical certitude for a gain in practical judgment. For if we can judge events as indications of other events, we can prepare in all cases for the coming of what is anticipated. In some cases, we can forestall a happening; desiring one event to happen rather than another, we can intentionally set about institution of those changes which our best knowledge tells us to be connected with that which we are after.

What has been lost in the theoretical possibility of exact knowledge and exact prediction is more than compensated for by the fact that the knowing which occurs within nature involves possibility of direction of change. This conclusion gives intelligence a foothold and a function within nature which "reason" never possessed. That which acts outside of nature and is a mere spectator of it is, by definition, not a participator in its changes. Therefore it is debarred from taking part in directing them. Action may follow but it is only an external attachment to knowing, not an inherent factor in it. As a mechanical addendum, it is inferior to knowledge. Moreover, it must either issue automatically from knowledge or else there must be some intervening act of "will" to produce it. In any case, because of its externality it adds nothing to intelligence or knowledge. It can only increase personal shrewdness in prudential manipulation of conditions.

We may, indeed, engage during knowing in experimentation. But according to the classic logic the effect was not to reorganize prior conditions, but merely to bring about a change in our own subjective or mental attitude. The act no more entered into the constitution of the known object than traveling to Athens to see the Parthenon had any effect on architecture. It makes a change in our own personal attitude and posture so that we can see better what was there all the time. It is a practical concession to the weakness of our powers of apprehension. The whole scheme hangs together with the traditional depreciation of practical activity on the part of the intellectual class. In reality, it also condemns intelligence to a position of impotency. Its exercise is an enjoyable use of leisure. The doctrine of its supreme value is largely a compensation for the impotency that attached to it in contrast with the force of executive acts.

The realization that the observation necessary to knowledge enters into the natural object known cancels this separation of knowing and doing. It makes possible and it demands a theory in which knowing and doing are intimately connected with each other. Hence, as we have said, it domesticates the exercise of intelligence within nature. This is part and parcel of nature's own continuing interactions. Interactions go on anyway and produce changes. Apart from intelligence, these changes are not directed. They are effects but not consequences, for consequences imply means deliberately employed. When an interaction intervenes which directs the course of change, the scene of natural interaction has a new quality and dimension. This added type of interaction *is* intelligence. The intelligent activity of man is not something brought to bear upon nature from without; it is nature realizing its own potentialities in behalf of a fuller and richer issue of events. Intelligence within nature means liberation and expansion, as reason outside of nature means fixation and restriction.

The change does not mean that nature has lost intelligibility. It rather signifies that we are in position to realize that the term intellig*ible* is to be understood literally. It expresses a potentiality rather than an actuality. Nature is capable of being understood. But the possibility is realized not by a mind thinking about it from without but by operations conducted from within, operations which give it new relations summed up in production of a new individual object. Nature *has* intelligible order as its possession in the degree in which we by our own overt operations realize potentialities contained in it. The change from intrinsic rationality in the traditional sense to an intelligibility to be realized by human action places responsibility upon human beings. The devotion we show to the ideal of intelligence determines the extent in which the actual order of nature is congenial to mind.

These conclusions connect directly with the question raised at the outset of this chapter. When knowledge is defined from the standpoint of a reality to which the conclusions of thought must accommodate themselves, as a photograph must be faithful to its original, there will always be disputes as to whether this or that subject can possibly be treated scientifically. But if the measure of knowledge is the quality of intelligence manifested in dealing with problems presented by any experienced subject-matter, the issue takes on a different aspect. The question always at issue is the possibility of developing a method adequate to cope with problems. The conclusions of physical knowledge do indeed set a standard for knowing. But it is because of their elaboration of competent method that this statement is true, not because of any superior claim to reality on the part of physical subject-matter. All materials of experience are equally real; that is, all are existential; each has a right to be dealt with in terms of its own especial characteristics and its own problems. To use philosophical terminology, each type of subject-matter is entitled to its own characteristic categories, according to the questions it raises and the operations necessary to answer them.

The difference between various types of knowledge thus turns out to be a difference in fullness and range of conditions involved in subject-matter dealt with. When one considers the success of astronomy in attaining understanding of phenomena occurring at enormous distances one may well be lost in admiration. But we should also reflect upon how much is omitted from inquiry and conclusion. Our knowledge of human affairs on this earth is inexact and unorganized as compared with *some* things which we know about bodies distant many, many, light years. But there are vast multitudes of things about these bodies that astronomy makes no pretense of inquiring into. The relative perfection of its conclusions is connected with the strict limitation of the problems it deals with. The case of astronomy is typical of physical science in general as compared with knowledge of human affairs. The essence of the latter is that we cannot indulge in the selective abstractions that are the secret of the success of physical knowing. When we introduce a like simplification into social and moral subjects we eliminate the distinctively human factors:— reduction to the physical ensues.

The principle is exemplified in the difference which is found between results obtained in the laboratory and in manufacturing processes carried on for commercial purposes. The same materials and relations may be involved. But under laboratory conditions elements are isolated and treated under a control not possible in the factory, where the same rigid isolation would defeat the aim of cheap production on a large scale. Nevertheless, in the end, the researches of scientific inquiries transform industrial production. Possibilities of new operations are suggested, and the laboratory results indicate ways of eliminating wasteful operations and make manifest conditions which have to be attended to. *Artificial simplification or abstraction is a necessary precondition of securing ability to deal with affairs which are complex, in which there are many more variables and where strict isolation destroys the special characteristics of the subject-matter.* This statement conveys the important distinction which exists between physical and social and moral objects. The distinction is one of methods of operation not of kinds of reality.

In other words, what is meant by "physical" in distinction from other adjectives that are prefixed to subject-matter is precisely an abstraction of a limited range of conditions and relations out of a total complex. The same principle applies to mathematical objects. The use of symbols designating possible operations makes possible a greater degree of exactness and intellectual organization. There is no disparagement of abstraction involved. Abstraction is simply an instance of the economy and efficiency involved in all intelligent practice:—Deal first with matters that can be effectively handled, and then use the results to go on to cope with more complex affairs. Objection comes in, and comes in with warranted force, when the results of an abstractive operation are given a standing which belongs only to the total situation from which they have been selected. All specialization breeds a familiarity which tends to create an illusion. Material dealt with by specialized abstractive processes comes to have a psychological independence and completion which is converted—hypostatized—into objective independence and self-sufficiency.

In addition there is a definite social reason for abstractive simplification. Intercourse of human individuals with one another makes it necessary to find common ground. Just because individuals are individuals, there is much in the experience of each which is unique; being incommunicable in and of itself, it is in so far a bar to entering into relations with others. For the purposes of communication, dissection is necessary. Otherwise the personal element is a bar to agreement and understanding. If one follows out this line of thought, it will be evident that the more widely extended is the notion of mutual comprehensibility, the more completely all individual traits tend to get excluded from the object of thought. In arriving at statements which hold for all possible experiencers and observers under all possible varying individual circumstances we arrive at that which is most remote from any one concrete experience. In this sense, the abstractions of mathematics and physics represent the common denominators in all things experienceable. Taken by themselves they seem to present a *caput mortuum*. Erected into complete statements of reality as such, they become hallucinatory obsessions. But in practice, there is always an accompanying reverse movement. These generalized findings are employed to enrich the meanings of individualized experiences, and to afford, within limits of probability, an increased control of them.

It is in this sense that all reflective knowledge as such is instrumental. The beginning and the end are things of gross everyday experience. But apart from knowledge the things of our ordinary experience are fragmentary, casual, unregulated by purpose, full of frustrations and barriers. In the language previously used, they are problematic, obstructive, and challenges to thought. By ignoring for a time their concrete and qualitative fullness, by making abstractions and generalizations, we ascertain certain basic relations upon which occurrence of the things experienced depend. We treat them as mere events, that is, as changes brought about in a system of relationships, ignoring their individualizing qualities. But the qualities are still there, are still experienced, although as such they are not the objects of knowledge. But we return from abstractive thought to experience of them with added meaning and with increased power to regulate our relations to them.

Reflective knowledge is the *only* means of regulation. Its value as instrumental is unique. Consequently philosophers, themselves occupied in a fascinating branch of reflective knowledge, have isolated knowledge and its results. They have ignored its context of origin and function and made it coextensive with all valid experience. The doctrine was thus formed that all experience of worth is inherently cognitive; that other modes of experienced objects are to be tested, not here and there as occasion demands but universally by reduction to the terms of known objects. This assumption of the proper ubiquity of knowledge is the great intellectualistic fallacy. It is the source of all disparagement of everyday qualitative experience, practical, esthetic, moral. It is the ultimate source of the doctrine that calls subjective and phenomenal all objects of experience that cannot be reduced to properties of objects of knowledge.

From this derogation of the things we experience by way of love, desire, hope, fear, purpose and the traits characteristic of human individuality, we are saved by the realization of the purposefully instrumental and abstract character of objects of reflective knowledge. One mode of experience is as real as any other. But apart from the exercise of intelligence which yields knowledge, the realities of our emotional and practical life have fragmentary and inconsistent meanings and are at the mercy of forces beyond our control. We have no choice save to accept them or to flee from them. Experience of that phase of objects which is constituted by their relations, their interactions, with one another, makes possible a new way of dealing with them, and thus eventually creates a new kind of experienced objects, not more real than those which preceded but more significant, and less overwhelming and oppressive.

Thus the recognition that intelligence is a method operating within the world places physical knowledge in respect to other kinds of knowing. It deals with those relations which are of the broadest scope. It affords a sure foundation for other more specialized forms of knowing:—not in the sense that these must be reduced to the objects in which physical knowledge terminates, but in the sense that the latter supply intellectual points of departure, and suggest operations to be employed. There is no kind of inquiry which has a monopoly of the honorable title of knowledge. The engineer, the artist, the historian, the man of affairs attain knowledge in the degree they employ methods that enable them to solve the problems which develop in the subject-matter they are concerned with. As philosophy framed upon the pattern of experimental inquiry does away with all wholesale skepticism, so it eliminates all invidious monopolies of the idea of science. By their fruits we shall know them.

The marking off of certain conclusions as alone truly science, whether mathematical or physical, is an historical incident. It sprang originally from man's desire for a certainty and peace which he could not attain practically in the absence of the arts of management and direction of natural conditions. When modern physical inquiry began, it had a hard time to get a hearing, or even to be permitted to carry on. The temptation was practically irresistible to treat it as an exclusive and esoteric undertaking. Moreover, as it progressed, it required more and more specialized technical preparation. The motive of defense from social attack and the motive of glorification of a specialized calling conspired together. All the eulogistic connotations that gather about "truth" were called into play.

Thus "science," meaning physical knowledge, became a kind of sanctuary. A religious atmosphere, not to say an idolatrous one, was created. "Science" was set apart; its findings were supposed to have a privileged relation to the real. In fact, the painter may know colors as well as the physicist; the poet may know stars, rain and clouds as well as the meteorologist; the statesman, educator and dramatist may know human nature as truly as the professional psychologist; the farmer may know soils and plants as truly as the botanist and mineralogist. For the criterion of knowledge lies in the method used to secure consequences and not in metaphysical conceptions of the nature of the real. Nevertheless in the end thinkers in all lines are dependent upon the mathematician and the physical inquirer for perfecting of the tools employed in their respective callings.

That "knowledge" has many meanings follows from the operational definition of conceptions. There are as many conceptions of knowledge as there are distinctive operations by which problematic situations are resolved. When it is asserted that *reflective* knowledge as such is instrumental, it is not meant that there is an *a priori* form of non-reflective knowledge, one which is immediately given. What is signified is that there is a direct possession and enjoyment of meanings to be had in that experience of objects which issues *from* reflective knowledge. It is futile to argue whether the conclusions of reflective method as such or the eventual objects enriched in meaning which are capable of direct perception and use more truly deserve the title of knowledge. It is congenial to our idiom to call the reflective conclusions of competent methods by the name of science. But science thus conceived is not a final thing. The final thing is appreciation and use of things of direct experience. These are *known* in as far as their constituents and their form are the result of science. But they are also more than science. They are natural objects experienced in relations and continuities that are summed up in rich and definite individual forms.

9.   The Supremacy of Method

Uncertainty is primarily a practical matter. It signifies uncertainty of the *issue* of present experiences; these are fraught with future peril as well as inherently objectionable. Action to get rid of the objectionable has no warrant of success and is itself perilous. The intrinsic troublesome and uncertain quality of situations lies in the fact that they hold outcomes in suspense; they move to evil or to good fortune. The natural tendency of man is to do something at once; there is impatience with suspense, and lust for immediate action. When action lacks means for control of external conditions, it takes the form of acts which are the prototypes of rite and cult. Intelligence signifies that direct action has become indirect. It continues to be overt, but it is directed into channels of examination of conditions, and doings that are tentative and preparatory. Instead of rushing to "do something about it," action centres upon finding out something about obstacles and resources and upon projecting inchoate later modes of definite response. Thinking has been well called deferred action. But not all action is deferred; only that which is final and in so far productive of irretrievable consequences. Deferred action is present exploratory action.

The first and most obvious effect of this change in the quality of action is that the dubious or problematic situation becomes *a* problem. The risky character that pervades a situation as a whole is translated into an object of inquiry that locates what the trouble is, and hence facilitates projection of methods and means of dealing with it. Only after expertness has been gained in special fields of inquiry does the mind set out at once from problems: even then in novel cases, there is a preliminary period of groping through a situation which is characterized throughout by confusion, instead of presenting a clear-cut problem for investigation.

Many definitions of mind and thinking have been given. I know of but one that goes to the heart of the matter:—response to the doubtful as such. No inanimate thing reacts to things *as* problematic. Its behavior to other things is capable of description in terms of what is determinately there. Under given conditions, it just reacts or does not react. Its reactions merely enstate a new set of conditions, in which reactions continue without regard to the nature of their outcome. It makes no difference, so to say, to a stone what are the results of its interactions with other things. It enjoys the advantage that it makes no difference how it reacts, even if the effect is its own pulverization. It requires no argument to show that the case is different with a living organism. To live signifies that a connected continuity of acts is effected in which preceding ones prepare the conditions under which later ones occur. There is a chain of cause and effects, of course, in what happens with inanimate things. But for living creatures, the chain has a particular cumulative continuity, or else death ensues.

As organisms become more complex in structure and thus related to a more complex environment, the importance of a particular act in establishing conditions favorable to subsequent acts that sustain the continuity of the life process, becomes at once more difficult and more imperative. A juncture may be so critical that the right or wrong present move signifies life or death. Conditions of the environment become more ambivalent: it is more uncertain what sort of action they call for in the interests of living. Behavior is thus compelled to become more hesitant and wary, more expectant and preparatory. In the degree that responses take place to the doubtful *as* the doubtful, they acquire *mental* quality. If they are such as to have a directed tendency to change the precarious and problematic into the secure and resolved, they are *intellectual* as well as mental. Acts are then relatively more instrumental and less consummatory or final; even the latter are haunted by a sense of what may issue from them.

This conception of the mental brings to unity various modes of response; emotional, volitional and intellectual. It is usual to say that there is no fundamental difference among these activities—that they are all different phases or aspects of a common action of mind. But I know of but one way of making this assertion good: that in which they are seen to be distinctive modes of response to the uncertain. The emotional aspect of responsive behavior is its *immediate* quality. When we are confronted with the precarious, an ebb and flow of emotion marks a disturbance of the even tenor of existence. Emotions are conditioned by the indeterminateness of present situations with respect to their issue. Fear and hope, joy and sorrow, aversion and desire, as perturbations, are qualities of a divided response. They involve concern, solicitude, for what the present situation may *become*. "Care" signifies two quite different things: fret, worry and anxiety, and cherishing attention to that in whose potentialities we are interested. These two meanings represent different poles of reactive behavior to a present having a future which is ambiguous. Elation and depression, moreover, manifest themselves only under conditions wherein not everything from start to finish is completely determined and certain. They may occur at a final moment of triumph or defeat, but this moment is one of victory or frustration in connection with a previous course of affairs whose issue was in suspense. Love for a Being so perfect and complete that our regard for it can make no difference to it is not so much affection as (a fact which the scholastics saw) it is concern for the destiny of our own souls. Hate that is sheer antagonism without any element of uncertainty is not an emotion, but is an energy devoted to ruthless destruction. Aversion is a state of affectivity only in connection with an obstruction offered by the disliked object or person to an end made uncertain by it.

The volitional phase of mental life is notoriously connected with the emotional. The only difference is that the latter is the immediate, the cross-sectional, aspect of response to the uncertain and precarious, while the volitional phase is the tendency of the reaction to modify indeterminate, ambiguous conditions in the direction of a preferred and favored outcome; to actualize one of its possibilities rather than another. Emotion is a hindrance or an aid to resolute will according as it is overwhelming in its immediacy or as it marks a gathering together of energy to deal with the situation whose issue is in doubt. Desire, purpose, planning, choice, have no meaning save in conditions where something is at stake, and where action in one direction rather than another may eventuate in bringing into existence a new situation which fulfills a need.

The intellectual phase of mental action is identical with an *in-*

direct mode of response, one whose purpose is to locate the nature of the trouble and form an idea of how it may be dealt with—so that operations may be directed in view of an intended solution. Take any incident of experience you choose, seeing a color, reading a book, listening to conversation, manipulating apparatus, studying a lesson, and it has or has not intellectual, cognitive, quality according as there is deliberate endeavor to deal with the indeterminate so as to dispose of it, to settle it. Anything that may be called knowledge, or a known object, marks a question answered, a difficulty disposed of, a confusion cleared up, an inconsistency reduced to coherence, a perplexity mastered. Without reference to this mediating element, what is called knowledge is but direct and unswerving action or else a possessive enjoyment. Similarly, thinking is the actual transition from the problematic to the secure, as far as that is intentionally guided. There is no separate "mind" gifted in and of itself with a faculty of thought; such a conception of thought ends in postulating the mystery of a power outside of nature and yet able to intervene within it. Thinking is objectively discoverable as that mode of serial responsive behavior to a problematic situation in which transition to the relatively settled and clear is effected.

The concrete pathologies of belief, its failures and perversions, whether of defect or excess, spring from failure to observe and adhere to the principle that knowledge is the completed resolution of the inherently indeterminate or doubtful. The commonest fallacy is to suppose that since the state of doubt is accompanied by a feeling of uncertainty, knowledge arises when this feeling gives way to one of assurance. Thinking then ceases to be an effort to effect change in the objective situation and is replaced by various devices which generate a change in feeling or "consciousness." Tendency to premature judgment, jumping at conclusions, excessive love of simplicity, making over of evidence to suit desire, taking the familiar for the clear, etc., all spring from confusing the feeling of certitude with a certified situation. Thought hastens toward the settled and is only too likely to force the pace. The natural man dislikes the dis-ease which accompanies the doubtful and is ready to take almost any means to end it. Uncertainty is got rid of by fair means or foul. Long exposure to danger breeds an overpowering love of security. Love for security, translated into a desire not to be disturbed and unsettled, leads to dogmatism, to acceptance of beliefs upon authority, to intolerance and fanaticism on one side and to irresponsible dependence and sloth on the other.

Here is where ordinary thinking and thinking that is scrupulous diverge from each other. The natural man is impatient with doubt and suspense: he impatiently hurries to be shut of it. A disciplined mind takes delight in the problematic, and cherishes it until a way out is found that approves itself upon examination. The questionable becomes an active questioning, a search; desire for the emotion of certitude gives place to quest for the objects by which the obscure and unsettled may be developed into the stable and clear. The scientific attitude may almost be defined as that which is capable of enjoying the doubtful; scientific method is, in one aspect, a technique for making a productive use of doubt by converting it into operations of definite inquiry. No one gets far intellectually who does not "love to think," and no one loves to think who does not have an interest in problems as such. Being on the alert for problems signifies that mere organic curiosity, the restless disposition to meddle and reach out, has become a truly intellectual curiosity, one that protects a person from hurrying to a conclusion and that induces him to undertake active search for new facts and ideas. Skepticism that is not such a search is as much a personal emotional indulgence as is dogmatism. Attainment of the relatively secure and settled takes place, however, only with respect to *specified* problematic situations; quest for certainty that is universal, applying to everything, is a compensatory perversion. One question is disposed of; another offers itself and thought is kept alive.

When we compare the theory of mind and its organs which develops from analysis of what takes place when precarious situations are translated into statement and resolution of problems, with other theories, the outstanding difference is that the first type of theory introduces no elements save such as are public, observable, and verifiable. In general, when there is discourse about the mental organs and processes of knowing we are told about sensations, mental images, consciousness and its various states, as if these were capable of identification in and of themselves. These mental organs having had meaning assigned to them in isolation from the operations of resolving a problematic situation, are then used to give an account of the actual operations of knowing. The more evident and observable is thus "explained" in terms of the obscure, the obscurity being hidden from view because of habits that have the weight of tradition behind them.

We do not need to repeat the results of the previous discussion. They are all connected with the theory that inquiry is a set of operations in which problematic situations are disposed of or settled. Theories which have been criticized all rest upon a different supposition; namely, that the properties of the states and acts of mind involved in knowing are capable of isolated determination—of description apart from overt acts that resolve indeterminate and ambiguous situations. The fundamental advantage of framing our account of the organs and processes of knowing on the pattern of what occurs in experimental inquiry is that nothing is introduced save what is objective and is accessible to examination and report. If it is objected that such an examination itself involves mind and its organs, the rejoinder is that the theory we have advanced is self-applying. Its only "assumption" is that something is done, done in the ordinary external sense of that word, and that this doing has consequences. We define mind and its organs in terms of this doing and its results, just as we define or frame ideas of stars, acids, and digestive tissues in terms of *their* behavior. If it be urged that we do not know whether the results of the directed operations are really knowledge or not, the answer is the objection assumes that we have some kind of advance intimation of what sort of a thing knowledge must be, and hence can use this conception as a standard for judging particular conclusions. The theory in question makes no such assumption. It asserts that by some operations conclusions emerge in which objects once uncertain and confused are rendered clear and stable. Alter names as much as you please; refuse to call one set of consequences knowledge and another error, or reverse the appellations, and these consequences remain just what they are. They present the difference between resolved and clarified situations and disordered and obscure ones. A rose by another name would smell as sweet; the gist of the theory advanced is to point to operations performed and to the consequences which issue from them.

Another point of difference is that traditional theories of mind and its organs of knowledge isolate them from continuity with the natural world. They are, in the literal sense of the word, super-natural or extra-natural. The problem of mind and body, of how it happens that bodily structures are involved in observing and thinking, is then unavoidable. When little was known about organic structures, one reason for looking down upon perception was that its connection with bodily organs, the eye and ear and hand, could not escape notice, while thought could be regarded as a purely spiritual act. But now we are aware that the exercise of thought bears the same relation to the brain that perception bears to sense organs, and that there is no separation, structural or functional, between the eye and ear and the central organs. Consequently it is impossible to think of sense as quasi-physical and thought as purely mental, as if the mental meant just the non-material. Yet we retain theories about the mental formed before we had this knowledge. Consequently, since those theories isolate knowing from doing, the dependence of knowing upon bodily organs becomes a mystery—a "problem."

But if knowing is one mode of doing, then it, as well as other modes of doing, properly involves bodily instruments. The metaphysical problem of the relation of mind and body is converted into a question, to be solved by observation of facts, of a differentiation of actions into those on a strictly physiological level, and those which, because of directed quality and distinctive consequences, are mental.

While traditional theories regard mind as an intruder from without into the natural development, or evolution, of organic structures, or else in the interest of natural continuity feel compelled to deny that mental behavior has any differential features, the theory that organic responses have mental quality in the degree in which they deal with the uncertain recognizes both continuity and difference. It can, in principle if not as yet in detail, give a genetic account of the development of mental and intellectual processes. There is neither a sudden jump from the merely organic to the intellectual, nor is there complete assimilation of the latter to primitive modes of the former.

On the objective side, the great difference between the conception proposed and that of traditional theory consists in recognition of the objective character of indeterminateness: it is a real property of some natural existences. Greek thought at least acknowledged the presence of contingency in natural existence, although it used this property of uncertainty to assign to natural existence a lower status than that which belongs to necessary Being. Modern thought, largely under the influence of a Newtonian philosophy of nature, tended to treat all existence as wholly determinate. The inherently incomplete was eliminated from nature along with qualities and ends. In consequence, the mental was sharply marked off from the physically natural; for the mental was obviously characterized by doubt and uncertainty. Mind was placed outside of nature; its relation to nature in knowing the latter became a dark mystery; the uncertain and indeterminate were said to be merely subjective. The contrast between the doubtful and the determinate became one of the chief marks by which objective and subjective were demarcated from each other and placed in opposition.

According to this doctrine, *we* are doubtful, puzzled, confused, undecided; *objects* are complete, assured, fixed. It is not easy to reconcile this notion with the fact that in order to relieve our doubt, to "make up" our minds, we have to modify in some way, in imaginative or overt experimentation, the situation in which uncertainty is experienced. Moreover, the procedure of science is conclusive. If doubt and indeterminateness were wholly within the mind—whatever that may signify—purely mental processes ought to get rid of them. But experimental procedure signifies that actual alteration of an external situation is necessary to effect the conversion. A *situation* undergoes, through operations directed by thought, transition from problematic to settled, from internal discontinuity to coherency and organization.

If we define "mental" through exclusion of overt acts that terminate in a changed environment, nothing merely mental can actually resolve doubt or clarify confusion. At most it can produce only a *feeling of certainty*—something best obtained by withdrawing from the real world and cultivating fantasies. The idea that doubt and assurance are merely subjective is contradicted by the coincidence of the progress of physical inquiry with invention and use of physical instruments. In principle, the correspondence of what we do when a situation is *practically* unsatisfactory with what happens in the case of intellectual doubt is complete. If a man finds himself in a situation which is practically annoying and troublesome, he has just two courses open to him. He can make a change in himself either by running away from trouble or by steeling himself to Stoic endurance; or he can set to work to do something so as to change the conditions of which unsatisfactoriness is a quality. When the latter course is impossible, nothing remains but the former.

Some change of personal attitude is the part of wisdom in any case, for there are few if any cases of trouble into which a personal factor of desire or aversion does not enter as a productive cause. But the idea that this causal factor can be changed by purely direct means, by an exercise of "will" or "thought" is illusory. A change of desire and purpose can itself be effected only indirectly, by a change in one's actual relation to environment. This change implies definite acts. The technological appliances and agencies that man has constructed to make these acts effective correspond to the development of instruments of scientific inquiry by which outer conditions are intentionally varied.

The relegation of the problematic to the "subjective" is a product of the habit of isolating man and experience from nature. Curiously enough, modern science has joined with traditional theology in perpetuating this isolation. If the physical terms by which natural science deals with the world are supposed to constitute that world, it follows as a matter of course that qualities we experience and which are the distinctive things in human life, fall outside of nature. Since some of these qualities are the traits that give life purpose and value, it is not surprising that many thinkers are dissatisfied with thinking of them as *merely* subjective; nor that they have found in traditional religious beliefs and in some elements of the classic philosophic tradition means by which these traits can be used to substantiate the being of a reality higher than nature, one qualified by the purpose and value that are extruded from natural existence. Modern idealism cannot be understood apart from the conditions that have generated it. Fundamentally, these conditions are the fusion of the positive results of the older metaphysics with the negative conclusions of modern science:—negative, that is to say, when, because of the persistence of earlier notions about mind and the office of knowledge, science is taken to disclose an antecedent natural world.

The organism is a part of the natural world; its interactions with it are genuine additive phenomena. When, with the development of symbols, also a natural occurrence, these interactions are directed towards anticipated consequences, they gain the quality of intelligence, and knowledge accrues. Problematic situations when they are resolved then gain the meaning of all the relations which the operations of thought have defined. Things that were causally effective in producing experienced results became means to consequences; these consequences incorporate in themselves all the meanings found in the causes which *intentionally* produce them. The supposed grounds for opposing human experience to the reality of nature disappear. Situations have problematic and resolved characters in and through the actual interactions of the organism and the environment. To refuse to treat these qualities as characteristic of nature itself is due to an arbitrary refusal to ascribe to some modes of interaction the existential character which is assigned as a matter of course to others.

We have seen that situations are precarious and perilous because the persistence of life-activity depends upon the influence which present acts have upon future acts. The continuity of a life-process is secured only as acts performed render the environment favorable to subsequent organic acts. The formal generalized statement of this fact is as follows: The occurrence of problematic and unsettled situations is due to the *characteristic union of the discrete or individual and the continuous or relational.* All perceived objects are individualized. They are, as such, wholes complete in themselves. Everything directly experienced is qualitatively unique; it has its own focus about which subject-matter is arranged, and this focus never exactly recurs. While every such situation shades off indefinitely, or is not sharply marked off from others, yet the pattern of arrangement of content is never exactly twice alike.

If the interactions involved in having such an individualized situation in experience were wholly final or consummatory, there would be no such thing as a situation which is problematic. In being individual and complete in itself, just what it is and nothing else, it would be discrete in the sense in which discreteness signifies complete isolation. Obscurity, for example, would be a final quality, like any other quality and as good as any other— just as the dusk of twilight is enjoyed instead of being troublesome until we need to see something the dusk interferes with seeing. Every situation has vagueness attending it, as it shades off from a sharper focus into what is indefinite; for vagueness is added quality and not something objectionable except as it obstructs gaining an eventual object.

There are situations in which self-enclosed, discrete, individualized characters dominate. They constitute the subject-matter of esthetic experience; and every experience is esthetic in as far as it is final or arouses no search for some other experience. When this complete quality is conspicuous the experience is denominated esthetic. The fine arts have as their purpose the construction of objects of just such experiences; and under some conditions the completeness of the object enjoyed gives the experience a quality so intense that it is justly termed religious. Peace and harmony suffuse the entire universe gathered up into the situation having a particular focus and pattern. These qualities mark any experience in as far as its final character dominates; in so far a mystic experience is simply an accentuated intensification of a quality of experience repeatedly had in the rhythm of experiences.

Interactions, however, are not isolated. No experienced situation can retain indefinitely its character of finality, for the interrelations that constitute it are, because they are interactions, themselves changing. They produce a change in what is experienced. The effort to maintain directly a consummatory experience or to repeat it exactly is the source of unreal sentimentality and of insincerity. In the continuous ongoing of life, objects part with something of their final character and become conditions of subsequent experiences. There is regulation of the change in the degree in which a causal character is rendered preparatory and instrumental.

In other words, all experienced objects have a double status. They are individualized, consummatory, whether in the way of enjoyment or of suffering. They are also involved in a continuity of interactions and changes, and hence are causes and potential means of later experiences. Because of this dual capacity, they become problematic. Immediately and directly they are just what they are; but as transitions to and possibilities of later experiences they are uncertain. There is a divided response; part of the organic activity is directed to them for what they immediately are, and part to them as transitive means of other experienced objects. We react to them both as finalities and in preparatory ways, and the two reactions do not harmonize.

This two-fold character of experienced objects is the source of their problematic character. Each of us can recall many occasions when he has been perplexed by disagreement between things directly present and their potential value as signs and means; when he has been torn between absorption in what is now enjoyed and the need of altering it so as to prepare for something likely to come. If we state the point in a formal way, it is signified that there is an incompatibility between the traits of an object in its direct individual and unique nature and those traits that belong to it in its relations or continuities. This incompatibility can be removed only by actions which temporally reconstruct what is given and constitute a new object having both individuality and the internal coherence of continuity in a series.

Previous discussion has been a statement of the chief factors that operate in bringing about this reconstruction—of resolving a problematic situation: Acts of analytic reduction of the gross total situation to determine data—qualities that locate the nature of the problem; formation of ideas or hypotheses to direct further operations that reveal new material; deductions and calculations that organize the new and old subject-matter together; operations that finally determine the existence of a new integrated situation with added meaning, and in so doing test or prove the ideas that have been employed.

Without retraversing that discussion, I wish to add a few words on one point involved in it. Nothing is more familiar than the standardized objects of reference designated by common nouns. Their distinction from proper names shows that they are not singular or individual, not existing things. Yet "*the* table" is both more familiar and seemingly more substantial than *this* table, the individual. "This" undergoes change all the time. It is interacting with other things and with me, who am not exactly the same person as when I last wrote upon it. "This" is an indefinitely multiple and varied series of "thises."

But save in extreme cases, these changes are indifferent, negligible, from the standpoint of means for consequences. *The* table is precisely the constancy among the serial "thises" of whatever serves as an instrument for a single end. *Knowledge* is concerned wholly with this constant, this standardized and averaged set of properties and relations:—just as esthetic perception is occupied with "this" in its individuality, irrespective of value in use. In the degree in which reactions are inchoate and unformed, "this" tends to be the buzzing, blooming confusion of which James wrote. As habits form, action is stereotyped into a fairly constant series of acts having a common end in view; *the* table serves a single use, in spite of individual variations. A group of properties is set aside, corresponding to the abiding end and single mode of use which form *the* object, in distinction from "this" of unique experiences. *The* object is an abstraction, but unless it is hypostatized it is not a vicious abstraction. It designates selected relations of things which, with respect to their mode of operation, are constant within the limits practically important. Moreover, the abstracted object has a consequence *in* the individualized experiences, one that is immediate and not merely instrumental to them. It marks an ordering and organizing of responses in a single focused way in virtue of which the original blur is definitized and rendered significant. Without habits dealing with recurrent and constant uses of things for abiding purposes, immediate esthetic perception would have neither rich nor clear meanings immanent within it.

The scientific or physical object marks an extension of the same sort of operation. *The* table, as *not* a table but as a swarm of molecules in motions of specified velocities and accelerations, corresponds to a liberated generalization of the purposes which *the* object may serve. "Table" signifies a definite but restricted set of uses; stated in the physical terms of science it is thought of in a wider environment and free from any specified set of uses; out of relation to any particular individualized experience. The abstraction is as legitimate as is that which gives rise to the idea of *the* table, for it consists of standardized relations or interactions. It is even more useful or more widely instrumental. For it has connection with an indefinite variety of unspecified but possible consummatory individual observations and enjoyments. It waits like a servant, idle for a time, but ready to be called upon as special occasion arises. When this standardized constant, the result of series of operations and expressing an indefinite multitude of possible relations among concrete things, is treated as the reality of nature, an instrument made for a purpose is hypostatized into a substance complete and self-sufficient in isolation. Then the fullness of qualities present in individual situations have to be

treated as subjective impressions mysteriously produced in mind
by the real object or else as products of a mysterious creative faculty of consciousness.

The bearing of the conclusion upon the qualitative values of
experienced objects is evident. Interactions of things with the organism eventuate in objects perceived to be colored and sonorous.
They also result in qualities that make the object hateful or delightful. All these qualities, taken as directly perceived or enjoyed, are terminal effects of natural interactions. They are individualized culminations that give static quality to a network of
changes. Thus "tertiary" qualities (as they have been happily
termed by Mr. Santayana), those which, in psychological analysis, we call affectional and emotional, are as much products of
the doings of nature as are color, sound, pressure, perceived size
and distance. But their very consummatory quality stands in the
way of using the things they qualify as signs of other things. Intellectually they are even more in the way than are "secondary"
qualities. With respect to preparatory acts they are useless; when
they are treated as signs and means they work injury to thought
and discovery. When not experienced, they are projected in
thought as ends to be reached and in that dependence upon
thought they are felt to be peculiarly mental. But only if *the* object, the physical object, instrumental in character, is supposed
to define "the real" in an exhaustive way, do they cease to be
for the philosopher what they are for the common man:—real
qualities of natural objects. This view forms the only complete
and unadulterated realism.

The problem which is supposed to exist between two tables,
one that of direct perception and use and the other that of physics (to take the favorite illustration of recent discussion) is thus
illusory. The perceived and used table is the only table, for it
alone has both individuality of form—without which nothing
can exist or be perceived—and also includes within itself a con-
tinuum of relations or interactions brought to a focus. We may
perhaps employ more instructively an illustration derived from
the supposed contrast between an object experienced in perception as it is rendered by a poet and the same object described by
a physicist. There is the instance of a body of water where the
movement of the wind over its surface is reflected in sunlight. As
an object of science, it is reported as follows: "Aethereal vibra-

tions of various wave-lengths, reflected at different angles from the disturbed interface between air and water, reached our eyes and by photoelectric action caused appropriate stimuli to travel along optic nerves to a brain-centre." Such a statement, however, includes ordinary objects of individual perceptions; water, air, brain and nerves. Consequently, it must be reduced still further; when so reduced it consists of mathematical functions between certain physical constants having no counterpart in ordinary perception.[1]

It is worth while at this point to recur to the metric character of the physical object. Defining metric traits are reached by a series of operations of which they express the statistically constant outcome; they are not the result of a single act. Hence the physical object cannot be taken to be a single or individual thing in existence. Metric definitions are also, in large measure, reached by indirect measurements, by calculation. In other words, the conception of the physical object is, in considerable degree, the outcome of complex operations of comparison and translation. In consequence, while the physical object is *not* any one of the things compared, it enables things qualitatively unlike and individual to be treated as if they were members of a comprehensive, homogeneous, or non-qualitative system. The possibility of control of the *occurrence* of individualized objects is thereby increased. At the same time, the latter gain added meaning, for the import of the scheme of continuity of relationships with other things is incorporated within them. The procedure of physics itself, not any metaphysical or epistemological theory, discloses that physical objects cannot be individual existential objects. In consequence, it is absurd to put them in opposition to the qualitatively individual objects of concrete experience.

The vogue of the philosophy that identifies the object of knowledge as such with the reality of the subject-matter of experience makes it advisable to carry the discussion further. Physical science submits the things of ordinary experience to specifiable op-

---

1. The illustration is borrowed from Eddington, *The Nature of the Physical World*; see pp. 316–319. It is indicative of the hold which the older tradition of knowledge as the exclusive revelation of reality has obtained, that Eddington finds no way to combine this account with the poetic account, save to suppose that while the scientific statement describes reality as it is "in itself," the creative activity of mind adds to this skeleton the qualities characterizing an object in direct experience.

erations. The result is objects of thought stated in numbers, where the numbers in question permit inclusion within complex systems of equations and other mathematical functions. In the physical object everything is ignored but the relations expressed by these numbers. It is safe to assert that no physicist *while at work* ever thought of denying the full reality of the things of ordinary, coarse experience. He pays no attention to their qualities except as they are signs of operations to be performed and of inference to relations to be drawn. But in these capacities he has to admit their full reality on pain of having, logically, to deny reality to the conclusions of his operative inferences. He takes the instruments he employs, including his own sensory-motor organs and measuring instruments, to be real in the ordinary sense of the word. If he denied the reality of these things as they are had in ordinary non-cognitive perceptual experience, the conclusions reached by them would be equally discredited. Moreover, the numbers which define his metric object are themselves results of noting interactions or connections among perceived things. It would be the height of absurdity to assert the reality of these relations while denying the reality of the things between which they hold. If the latter are "subjective" what becomes of the former? Finally, observation is resorted to for verification. It is a strange world in which the conception of the real has to be corroborated by reference to that the reality of which is made dubious by the conception. To common sense these comments may seem wholly superfluous. But since common sense may also hold the doctrine from which flow the conclusions to which the critical comments are apposite, common sense should first ask whether it holds that knowledge is a disclosure of the antecedently real? If it entertains this belief, then the dismissal by science of the experienced object to a limbo of unreality, or subjectivity or the phenomenal—whatever terms be used—results logically from his own position.

Our discussion involves a summary as well as some repetition of points previously made. Its significance lies in the liberation which comes when knowing, in all its phases, conditions and organs, is understood after the pattern provided by experimental inquiry, instead of upon the groundwork of ideas framed before such knowing had a systematic career opened to it. For according to the pattern set by the practice of knowing, knowledge is the fruit of the undertakings that transform a problematic situation into a resolved one. Its procedure is public, a part and partner of the Nature in which all interactions exist. But experienced situations come about in two ways and are of two distinct types. Some take place with only a minimum of regulation, with little foresight, preparation and intent. Others occur because, in part, of the prior occurrence of intelligent action. Both kinds are *had*; they are undergone, enjoyed or suffered. The first are not known; they are not understood; they are dispensations of fortune or providence. The second have, as they are experienced, meanings that present the funded outcome of operations that substitute definite continuity for experienced discontinuity and for the fragmentary quality due to isolation. Dream, insanity and fantasy are natural products, as "real" as anything else in the world. The acts of intentional regulation which constitute thinking are also natural developments, and so are the experienced things in which they eventuate. But the latter are resolutions of the problems set by objects experienced without intent and purpose; hence they have a security and fullness of meaning the first lack. Nothing happens, as Aristotle and the scholastics said, without an end—without a terminal effectuation. *Every* experienced object is, in some sense, such a closing and consummatory closing episode: alike the doubtful and secure, the trivial and significant, the true and mistaken, the confused and ordered. Only when the ends are closing termini of *intelligent operations* of thinking are they ends in the honorific sense. We always experience individual objects, but only the individual things which are fruits of intelligent action have in them intrinsic order and fullness of qualities.

The conditions and processes of nature generate uncertainty and its risks as truly as nature affords security and means of insurance against perils. Nature is characterized by a constant mixture of the precarious and the stable. This mixture gives poignancy to existence. If existence were either completely necessary or completely contingent, there would be neither comedy nor tragedy in life, nor need of the will to live. The significance of morals and politics, of the arts both technical and fine, of religion and of science itself as inquiry and discovery, all have their source and meaning in the union in Nature of the settled and the unsettled, the stable and the hazardous. Apart from this union, there are no such things as "ends," either as consummations or as those ends-in-view we call purposes. There is only a block universe, either something ended and admitting of no change, or else a predestined march of events. There is no such thing as fulfillment where there is no risk of failure, and no defeat where there is no promise of possible achievement.

Any philosophy that in its quest for certainty ignores the reality of the uncertain in the ongoing processes of nature denies the conditions out of which it arises. The attempt to include all that is doubtful within the fixed grasp of that which is theoretically certain is committed to insincerity and evasion, and in consequence will have the stigmata of internal contradiction. Every such philosophy is marked at some point by a division of its subject-matter into the truly real and the merely apparent, a subject and an object, a physical and a mental, an ideal and an actual, that have nothing to do with one another, save in some mode which is so mysterious as to create an insoluble problem.

Action is the means by which a problematic situation is resolved. Such is the net outcome of the method of science. There is nothing extraordinary about this conclusion. Interaction is a universal trait of natural existence. "Action" is the name given to one mode of this interaction, namely, that named from the standpoint of an organism. When interaction has for its consequence the settling of future conditions under which a life-process goes on, it is an "act." If it be admitted that knowing is something which occurs within nature, then it follows as a truism that knowing is an existential overt act. Only if the one who engages in knowing be outside of nature and behold it from some external locus can it be denied that knowing is an act which modifies what previously existed, and that its worth consists in the consequences of the modification. The spectator theory of knowing may, humanly speaking, have been inevitable when thought was viewed as an exercise of a "reason" independent of the body, which by means of purely logical operations attained truth. It is an anachronism now that we have the model of experimental procedure before us and are aware of the role of organic acts in all mental processes.

Our discussion has for the most part turned upon an analysis of knowledge. The theme, however, is the relation of knowledge and action; the final import of the conclusions as to knowledge resides in the changed idea it enforces as to action. The dis-

tinction once made between theory and practice has meaning as
a distinction between two kinds of action: blind and intelligent.
Intelligence is a quality of some acts, those which are directed;
and directed action is an achievement not an original endow-
ment. The history of human progress is the story of the transformation of acts which, like the interactions of inanimate things,
take place unknowingly to actions qualified by understanding of
what they are about; from actions controlled by external conditions to actions having guidance through their intent:—their
insight into their own consequences. Instruction, information,
knowledge, is the only way in which this property of intelligence
comes to qualify acts originally blind.

This conclusion is decisive for the significance of purpose and
mechanism in nature. The doctrine that knowledge is ideally or
in its office a disclosure of antecedent reality resulted, under the
impact of the results of natural science, in relegating purpose to
the purely subjective, to states of consciousness. An unsolved
problem then developed out of the question as to how purpose
could be efficacious in the world. Now intelligent action is purposive action; if it is a natural occurrence, coming into being under complex but specifiable conditions of organic and social interaction, then purpose like intelligence is within nature; it is a
"category" having objective standing and validity. It has this status in a direct way through the place and operation of human art
within the natural scene; for distinctively human conduct can be
interpreted and understood only in terms of purpose. Purpose is
the dominant category of anything truly denominated history,
whether in its enacting or in the writing of it, since action which
is *distinctively* human is marked by intent.

Indirectly, purpose is a legitimate and necessary idea in describing Nature itself in the large. For man is continuous with
nature. As far as natural events culminate in the intelligent arts of
mankind, nature itself has a history, a movement toward consequences. When for convenience of study, nature is broken up
into disconnected bits the parts of which are taken to have a relation to one another in isolation from other parts, the concept
of purpose has no application. It is excluded by the very method
of intellectual approach. Science is full of abstractions of this
sort. For example, water is a combination of hydrogen and oxy-

gen in definite proportions. This is a statement about "water" in general, not about the occurrence of any particular portion which takes place under conditions in which more than hydrogen and oxygen exist. Any individualized water is a phase of an indefinitely varied and extensive course of things. Generically, however, "water" is treated in relation to its defining constituents as if it were a complete universe in itself. As a statement of a relation that is stable amid a multitude of varying changes, each having its own individualized history, it is an instrument of control. When it is treated as if it provided a model for framing a general theory of nature, the result converts an instrument of control into a view of the world in which there is neither history nor purpose.

Generalized facts, when they are taken to be individual events complete in themselves, lead to a picture of the universe in which occurrences are exactly like one another. There is repetition but no development; mechanical production but no cumulative movement toward an integrated consequence. We take out of our logical package what we have put into it, and then convert what we draw out to be a literal description of the actual world. Things lose their individuality and are "instances" of a general law. When, however, events are viewed in their connections, as it is surely the province of philosophy to view them, nature is seen to be marked by histories, some of which terminate in the existence of human beings and finally in their intelligent activities. This issue, as the consequence of a cumulative integration of complex interactions, is such as to give anterior processes a purposive meaning. Everything depends whether we take short-sections of the course of nature in isolation, or whether we take the course of events over a span of time sufficiently long to disclose the integration of a multitude of processes toward a single outcome.[2]

A machine is a striking instance of mechanism. It is an equally striking instance of something to be understood in terms of purpose, use or function. Nature *has* mechanism. This mechanism forms the content of the objects of physical science for it fulfills

2. *Purposive Evolution*, New York, 1926, by Edmund Noble, contains by far the best statement known to me of considerations of which a brief summary is given in this paragraph.

the instrumental office to be performed by knowledge. If the interactions and connections involved in natural occurrences were not sufficiently like one another, sufficiently constant and uniform, so that inference and prediction from one to another were possible, control and purpose would be non-existent. Since constant relations among changes are the subject-matter of scientific thought, that subject-matter is the mechanism of events. The net effect of modern inquiry makes it clear that these constancies, whether the larger ones termed laws or the lesser ones termed facts, are statistical in nature. They are the products of averaging large numbers of observed frequencies by means of a series of operations. They are not descriptions of the exact structure and behavior of any *individual* thing, any more than the actuarial "law" of the frequency of deaths of persons having a certain age is an account of the life of one of the persons included in the calculation. Nature *has* a mechanism sufficiently constant to permit of calculation, inference and foresight. But only a philosophy which hypostatizes isolated results and results obtained for a purpose, only a substantiation of the function of being a tool, concludes that nature *is* a mechanism and only a mechanism.

It has long been recognized that some physical laws are statistical, instead of being reports of behavior of individuals as such. Heisenberg's principle, together with the discovery that mass varies with velocity, mark the generalized conclusion that all physical laws are of this character. They are, as we have noted, predictions of the *probability* of an observable event. They mark the culmination of a qualified prediction of Maxwell's so remarkable as to be worth quoting in full.

The theory of atoms and void leads us to attach more importance to the doctrines of integral numbers and definite proportions; but, in applying dynamic principles to the motion of immense numbers of atoms, the limitation of our faculties forces us to abandon the attempt to express the exact history of each atom and to be content with estimating the average condition of a group of atoms large enough to be visible. This method of dealing with groups of atoms, which I might call the statistical method, and which in the present state of our knowledge, is the only available method of studying the properties of real bodies, involves an abandonment of strict dynamical principles, and an adoption of the mathematical methods belonging to the theory of probability. It is probable that important results will be obtained by the application of this method, which is, as yet, little known and is not familiar to our minds. If the actual history of Science had been different, and if the scientific doctrines most familiar to us had been those which must be expressed in this way, it is probable that we might have considered the existence of a certain kind of contingency as a self-evident truth and treated the doctrine of philosophical necessity as a mere sophism.[3]

That which Maxwell felt that he must look upon as a trait due to the "limitation of our faculties" turns out to be a trait of natural events themselves. No mechanically exact science of an individual is possible. An individual is a history unique in character. But constituents of an individual are known when they are regarded not as qualitative, but as statistical constants derived from a series of operations.

This fact has an obvious bearing on freedom in action. Contingency is a necessary although not, in mathematical phrase, a sufficient condition of freedom. In a world which was completely tight and exact in all its constituents, there would be no room for freedom. Contingency while it gives room for freedom does not fill that room. Freedom is an actuality when the recognition of relations, the stable element, is combined with the uncertain element, in the knowledge which makes foresight possible and secures intentional preparation for probable consequences. We are free in the degree in which we act knowing what we are about. The identification of freedom with "freedom of will" locates contingency in the wrong place. Contingency of will would mean that uncertainty was uncertainly dealt with; it would be a resort to chance for a decision. The business of "will" is to be resolute; that is, to resolve, under the guidance of thought, the indeterminateness of uncertain *situations*. Choice wavers and is brought to a head arbitrarily only when circumstances compel action and yet we have no intelligent clew as to how to act.

The doctrine of "free-will" is a desperate attempt to escape

---

3. J. C. Maxwell, *Scientific Papers*, Vol. II, p. 253. I am indebted to Dr. Charles Hartshorne for this reference.

from the consequences of the doctrine of fixed and immutable objective Being. With dissipation of that dogma, the need for such a measure of desperation vanishes. Preferential activities characterize every individual as individual or unique. In themselves these are differential in a *de facto* sense. They become true choices under the direction of insight. Knowledge, instead of revealing a world in which preference is an illusion and does not count or make a difference, puts in our possession the instrumentality by means of which preference may be an intelligent or intentional factor in constructing a future by wary and prepared action. Knowledge of special conditions and relations is instrumental to the action which is in turn an instrument of production of situations having qualities of added significance and order. To be capable of such action is to be free.

Physical inquiry has been taken as typical of the nature of knowing. The selection is justified because the operations of physical knowledge are so perfected and its scheme of symbols so well devised. But it would be misinterpreted if it were taken to mean that science is the only valid kind of knowledge; it is just an intensified form of knowing in which are written large the essential characters of any knowing. It is in addition the most powerful tool we possess for developing other modes of knowledge. But we know with respect to any subject-matter whatsoever in the degree in which we are able deliberately to transform doubtful situations into resolved ones. Physical knowledge has the advantage of its specialized character, its whole-hearted devotion to a single purpose. The attitude involved in it, its method, has not as yet gone far beyond its own precincts. Beliefs current in morals, politics and religion, are marked by dread of change and by the feeling that order and regulative authority can be had only through reference to fixed standards accepted as finalities, because referring to fixed antecedent realities. Outside of physical inquiry, we shy from problems; we dislike uncovering serious difficulties in their full depth and reach; we prefer to accept what is and muddle along. Hence our social and moral "sciences" consist largely in putting facts as they are into conceptual systems framed at large. Our logic in social and humane subjects is still largely that of definition and classification as until the seventeenth century it was in natural science. For the most part the lesson of experimental inquiry has still to be learned in the things of chief concern.

We are, socially, in a condition of division and confusion because our best authenticated knowledge is obtained by directed practice, while this method is still limited to things aloof from man or concerning him only in the technologies of industries. The rest of our practice in matters that come home to us most closely and deeply is regulated not by intelligent operations, but by tradition, self-interest and accidental circumstance. The most significant phase of physical science, that which concerns its method, is unapplied in social practice, while its technical results are utilized by those in positions of privileged advantage to serve their own private or class ends. Of the many consequences that result, the state of education is perhaps the most significant. As the means of the general institution of intelligent action, it holds the key to orderly social reconstruction. But inculcation of fixed conclusions rather than development of intelligence as a method of action still dominates its processes. Devotion to training in technical and mechanical skills on one hand and to laying in a store of abstract information on the other is to one who has the power to read the scene an almost perfect illustration of the significance of the historic separation of knowledge and action, theory and practice. As long as the isolation of knowledge and practice holds sway, this division of aims and dissipation of energy, of which the state of education is typical, will persist. The effective condition of the integration of all divided purposes and conflicts of belief is the realization that intelligent action is the sole ultimate resource of mankind in every field whatsoever.

It is not claimed, therefore, that there is *no* philosophical problem of the relation of physical science to the things of ordinary experience. It is asserted that the problem *in the form* in which it has chiefly occupied modern philosophy is an artificial one, due to the continued assumption of premises formed in an earlier period of history and now having no relevancy to the state of physical inquiry. Clearing the ground of this unreal problem, however, only imposes upon philosophy the consideration of a problem which is urgently practical, growing out of the conditions of contemporary life. What revisions and surrenders of current beliefs about authoritative ends and values are demanded by the method and conclusions of natural science? What possibilities of controlled transformation of the content of present belief and practice in human institutions and associations are indicated by the control of natural energies which natural science has effected? These questions are as genuine and imperative as the traditional problem is artificial and futile.

10. The Construction of Good

We saw at the outset of our discussion that insecurity generates the quest for certainty. Consequences issue from every experience, and they are the source of our interest in what is present. Absence of arts of regulation diverted the search for security into irrelevant modes of practice, into rite and cult; thought was devoted to discovery of omens rather than of signs of what is to occur. Gradually there was differentiation of two realms, one higher, consisting of the powers which determine human destiny in all important affairs. With this religion was concerned. The other consisted of the prosaic matters in which man relied upon his own skill and his matter-of-fact insight. Philosophy inherited the idea of this division. Meanwhile in Greece many of the arts had attained a state of development which raised them above a merely routine state; there were intimations of measure, order and regularity in materials dealt with which give intimations of underlying rationality. Because of the growth of mathematics, there arose also the ideal of a purely rational knowledge, intrinsically solid and worthy and the means by which the intimations of rationality within changing phenomena could be comprehended within science. For the intellectual class the stay and consolation, the warrant of certainty, provided by religion was henceforth found in intellectual demonstration of the reality of the objects of an ideal realm.

With the expansion of Christianity, ethico-religious traits came to dominate the purely rational ones. The ultimate authoritative standards for regulation of the dispositions and purposes of the human will were fused with those which satisfied the demands for necessary and universal truth. The authority of ultimate Being was, moreover, represented on earth by the Church; that which in its nature transcended intellect was made known by a revelation of which the Church was the interpreter and guardian. The system endured for centuries. While it endured, it provided an integration of belief and conduct for the western world. Unity of thought and practice extended down to every detail of the management of life; efficacy of its operation did not depend upon thought. It was guaranteed by the most powerful and authoritative of all social institutions.

Its seemingly solid foundation was, however, undermined by the conclusions of modern science. They effected, both in themselves and even more in the new interests and activities they generated, a breach between what man is concerned with here and now and the faith concerning ultimate reality which, in determining his ultimate and eternal destiny, had previously given regulation to his present life. The problem of restoring integration and cooperation between man's beliefs about the world in which he lives and his beliefs about the values and purposes that should direct his conduct is the deepest problem of modern life. It is the problem of any philosophy that is not isolated from that life.

The attention which has been given to the fact that in its experimental procedure science has surrendered the separation between knowing and doing has its source in the fact that there is now provided within a limited, specialized and technical field the possibility and earnest, as far as theory is concerned, of effecting the needed integration in the wider field of collective human experience. Philosophy is called upon to be the theory of the practice, through ideas sufficiently definite to be operative in experimental endeavor, by which the integration may be made secure in actual experience. Its central problem is the relation that exists between the beliefs about the nature of things due to natural science and beliefs about values—using that word to designate whatever is taken to have rightful authority in the direction of conduct. A philosophy which should take up this problem is struck first of all by the fact that beliefs about values are pretty much in the position in which beliefs about nature were before the scientific revolution. There is either a basic distrust of the capacity of experience to develop its own regulative standards, and an appeal to what philosophers call eternal values, in order to ensure regulation of belief and action; or there is acceptance of enjoyments actually experienced irrespective of the method or operation by which they are brought into existence. Complete bifurcation between rationalistic method and an empirical method has its final and most deeply human significance in the ways in which good and bad are thought of and acted for and upon.

As far as technical philosophy reflects this situation, there is division of theories of values into two kinds. On the one hand, goods and evils, in every region of life, as they are concretely experienced, are regarded as characteristic of an inferior order of Being—intrinsically inferior. Just because they are things of human experience, their worth must be estimated by reference to standards and ideals derived from ultimate reality. Their defects and perversion are attributed to the same fact; they are to be corrected and controlled through adoption of methods of conduct derived from loyalty to the requirements of Supreme Being. This philosophic formulation gets actuality and force from the fact that it is a rendering of the beliefs of men in general as far as they have come under the influence of institutional religion. Just as rational conceptions were once superimposed upon observed and temporal phenomena, so eternal values are superimposed upon experienced goods. In one case as in the other, the alternative is supposed to be confusion and lawlessness. Philosophers suppose these eternal values are known by reason; the mass of persons that they are divinely revealed.

Nevertheless, with the expansion of secular interests, temporal values have enormously multiplied; they absorb more and more attention and energy. The sense of transcendent values has become enfeebled; instead of permeating all things in life, it is more and more restricted to special times and acts. The authority of the church to declare and impose divine will and purpose has narrowed. Whatever men say and profess, their tendency in the presence of actual evils is to resort to natural and empirical means to remedy them. But in formal belief, the old doctrine of the inherently disturbed and unworthy character of the goods and standards of ordinary experience persists. This divergence between what men do and what they nominally profess is closely connected with the confusions and conflicts of modern thought.

It is not meant to assert that no attempts have been made to replace the older theory regarding the authority of immutable and transcendent values by conceptions more congruous with the practices of daily life. The contrary is the case. The utilitarian theory, to take one instance, has had great power. The idealistic school is the only one in contemporary philosophies, with the exception of one form of neo-realism, that makes much of the notion of a reality which is all one with ultimate moral and religious values. But this school is also the one most concerned with the conservation of "spiritual" life. Equally significant is the fact that empirical theories retain the notion that thought and judgment are concerned with values that are experienced independently of them. For these theories, emotional satisfactions occupy the same place that sensations hold in traditional empiricism. Values are constituted by liking and enjoyment; to be enjoyed and to be a value are two names for one and the same fact. Since science has extruded values from its objects, these empirical theories do everything possible to emphasize their purely subjective character of value. A psychological theory of desire and liking is supposed to cover the whole ground of the theory of values; in it, immediate feeling is the counterpart of immediate sensation.

I shall not object to this empirical theory as far as it connects the theory of values with concrete experiences of desire and satisfaction. The idea that there is such a connection is the only way known to me by which the pallid remoteness of the rationalistic theory, and the only too glaring presence of the institutional theory of transcendental values can be escaped. The objection is that the theory in question holds down value to objects *antecedently* enjoyed, apart from reference to the method by which they come into existence; it takes enjoyments which are casual because unregulated by intelligent operations to be values in and of themselves. Operational thinking needs to be applied to the judgment of values just as it has now finally been applied in conceptions of physical objects. Experimental empiricism in the field of ideas of good and bad is demanded to meet the conditions of the present situation.

The scientific revolution came about when material of direct and uncontrolled experience was taken as problematic; as supplying material to be transformed by reflective operations into known objects. The contrast between experienced and known objects was found to be a temporal one; namely, one between empirical subject-matters which were had or "given" prior to the acts of experimental variation and redisposition and those which succeeded these acts and issued from them. The notion of an act whether of sense or thought which supplied a valid measure of thought in immediate knowledge was discredited. Consequences of operations became the important thing. The suggestion almost imperatively follows that escape from the defects of transcendental absolutism is not to be had by setting up as values enjoyments that happen anyhow, but in defining value by enjoyments which are the consequences of intelligent action. Without the intervention of thought, enjoyments are not values but problematic goods, becoming values when they re-issue in a changed form from intelligent behavior. The fundamental trouble with the current empirical theory of values is that it merely formulates and justifies the socially prevailing habit of regarding enjoyments as they are actually experienced as values in and of themselves. It completely side-steps the question of regulation of these enjoyments. This issue involves nothing less than the problem of the directed reconstruction of economic, political and religious institutions.

There was seemingly a paradox involved in the notion that if we turned our backs upon the immediately perceived qualities of things, we should be enabled to form valid conceptions of objects, and that these conceptions could be used to bring about a more secure and more significant experience of them. But the method terminated in disclosing the connections or interactions upon which perceived objects, viewed as events, depend. Formal analogy suggests that we regard our direct and original experience of things liked and enjoyed as only *possibilities* of values to be achieved; that enjoyment becomes a value when we discover the relations upon which its presence depends. Such a causal and operational definition gives only a conception of a value, not a value itself. But the utilization of the conception in action results in an object having secure and significant value.

The formal statement may be given concrete content by pointing to the difference between the enjoyed and the enjoyable, the desired and the desirable, the satis*fying* and the satis*factory*. To say that something is enjoyed is to make a statement about a fact, something already in existence; it is not to judge the value of that fact. There is no difference between such a proposition and one which says that something is sweet or sour, red or black. It is just correct or incorrect and that is the end of the matter. But to call an object a value is to assert that it satisfies or fulfills certain conditions. Function and status in meeting conditions is a different matter from bare existence. The fact that something is desired only raises the *question* of its desirability; it does not settle it. Only a child in the degree of his immaturity thinks to settle the question of desirability by reiterated proclamation: "I want it, I want it, I want it." What is objected to in the current empirical theory of values is not connection of them with desire and enjoyment but failure to distinguish between enjoyments of radically different sorts. There are many common expressions in which the difference of the two kinds is clearly recognized. Take for example the difference between the ideas of "satisfying" and "satisfactory." To say that something satisfies is to report something as an isolated finality. To assert that it is satis*factory* is to define it in its connections and interactions. The fact that it pleases or is immediately congenial poses a problem to judgment. How shall the satisfaction be rated? Is it a value or is it not? Is it something to be prized and cherished, *to be* enjoyed? Not stern moralists alone but everyday experience informs us that finding satisfaction in a thing may be a warning, a summons to be on the lookout for consequences. To declare something satis*factory* is to assert that it meets specifiable conditions. It is, in effect, a judgment that the thing "will do." It involves a prediction; it contemplates a future in which the thing will continue to serve; it *will* do. It asserts a consequence the thing will actively institute; it will *do*. That it is satisfying is the content of a proposition of fact; that it is satisfactory is a judgment, an estimate, an appraisal. It denotes an attitude *to be* taken, that of striving to perpetuate and to make secure.

It is worth notice that besides the instances given, there are many other recognitions in ordinary speech of the distinction. The endings "able," "worthy" and "ful" are cases in point. Noted and notable, noteworthy; remarked and remarkable; advised and advisable; wondered at and wonderful; pleasing and beautiful; loved and lovable; blamed and blameable, blameworthy; objected to and objectionable; esteemed and estimable; admired and admirable; shamed and shameful; honored and honorable; approved and approvable, worthy of approbation, etc. The multiplication of words adds nothing to the force of the distinction. But it aids in conveying a sense of the fundamental character of the distinction; of the difference between mere report of an already existent fact and judgment as to the importance and need of bringing a fact into existence; or, if it is already there, of sustaining it in existence. The latter is a genuine practical judgment, and marks the only type of judgment that has to do with the direction of action. Whether or no we reserve the term "value" for the latter, (as seems to me proper) is a minor matter; that the distinction be acknowledged as the key to understanding the relation of values to the direction of conduct is the important thing.

This element of direction by an idea of value applies to science as well as anywhere else. For in every scientific undertaking, there is passed a constant succession of estimates; such as "it is worth treating these facts as data or evidence; it is advisable to try this experiment; to make that observation; to entertain such and such a hypothesis; to perform this calculation," etc.

The word "taste" has perhaps got too completely associated with arbitrary liking to express the nature of judgments of value. But if the word be used in the sense of an appreciation at once cultivated and active, one may say that the formation of taste is the chief matter wherever values enter in, whether intellectual, esthetic or moral. Relatively immediate judgments, which we call tact or to which we give the name of intuition, do not precede reflective inquiry, but are the funded products of much thoughtful experience. Expertness of taste is at once the result and the reward of constant exercise of thinking. Instead of there being no disputing about tastes, they are the one thing worth disputing about, if by "dispute" is signified discussion involving reflective inquiry. Taste, if we use the word in its best sense, is the outcome of experience brought cumulatively to bear on the intelligent appreciation of the real worth of likings and enjoyments. There is nothing in which a person so completely reveals himself as in the things which he judges enjoyable and desirable. Such judgments are the sole alternative to the domination of belief by impulse, chance, blind habit and self-interest. The formation of a cultivated and effectively operative good judgment or taste with respect to what is esthetically admirable, intellectually acceptable and morally approvable is the supreme task set to human beings by the incidents of experience.

Propositions about what is or has been liked are of instrumental value in reaching judgments of value, in as far as the conditions and consequences of the thing liked are thought about. In themselves they make no claims; they put forth no demand upon subsequent attitudes and acts; they profess no authority to direct. If one likes a thing he likes it; that *is* a point about which there can be no dispute:—although it is not so easy to state just *what* is liked as is frequently assumed. A judgment about what is *to be* desired and enjoyed is, on the other hand, a claim on future action; it possesses *de jure* and not merely *de facto* quality. It is a matter of frequent experience that likings and enjoyments are of all kinds, and that many are such as reflective judgments condemn. By way of self-justification and "rationalization," an enjoyment creates a tendency to assert that the thing enjoyed is a value. This assertion of validity adds authority to the fact. It is a decision that the object has a right to exist and hence a claim upon action to further its existence.

The analogy between the status of the theory of values and the theory of ideas about natural objects before the rise of experimental inquiry may be carried further. The sensationalistic theory of the origin and test of thought evoked, by way of reaction, the transcendental theory of *a priori* ideas. For it failed utterly to account for objective connection, order and regularity in objects observed. Similarly, any doctrine that identifies the mere fact of being liked with the value of the object liked so fails to give direction to conduct when direction is needed that it automatically calls forth the assertion that there are values eternally in Being that are the standards of all judgments and the obligatory ends of all action. Without the introduction of operational thinking, we oscillate between a theory that, in order to save the objectivity of judgments of values, isolates them from experience and nature, and a theory that, in order to save their concrete and human significance, reduces them to mere statements about our own feelings.

Not even the most devoted adherents of the notion that enjoyment and value are equivalent facts would venture to assert that because we have once liked a thing we should go on liking it; they are compelled to introduce the idea that *some* tastes are to be cultivated. Logically, there is no ground for introducing the idea of cultivation; liking is liking, and one is as good as another. If enjoyments *are* values, the judgment of value cannot regulate the form which liking takes; it cannot regulate its own conditions. Desire and purpose, and hence action, are left without guidance, although the question of regulation of their formation is the supreme problem of practical life. Values (to sum up) may be connected inherently with liking, and yet not with *every* liking but only with those that judgment has approved, after examination of the relation upon which the object liked depends. A casual liking is one that happens without knowledge of how it occurs nor to what effect. The difference between it and one which is sought because of a judgment that it is worth having and is to be striven for, makes just the difference between enjoyments which are accidental and enjoyments that have value and hence a claim upon our attitude and conduct.

In any case, the alternative rationalistic theory does not afford the guidance for the sake of which eternal and immutable norms are appealed to. The scientist finds no help in determining the probable truth of some proposed theory by comparing it with a standard of absolute truth and immutable being. He has to rely upon definite operations undertaken under definite conditions— upon method. We can hardly imagine an architect getting aid in the construction of a building from an ideal at large, though we can understand his framing an ideal on the basis of knowledge of actual conditions and needs. Nor does the ideal of perfect beauty in antecedent Being give direction to a painter in producing a particular work of art. In morals, absolute perfection does not seem to be more than a generalized hypostatization of the recognition that there is a good to be sought, an obligation to be met—both being concre matters. Nor is the defect in this respect merely negative. An examination of history would reveal, I am confident, that these general and remote schemes of value actually obtain a content definite enough and near enough to concrete situations as to afford guidance in action only by consecrating some institution or dogma already having social currency. Concreteness is gained, but it is by protecting from inquiry some accepted standard which perhaps is outworn and in need of criticism.

When theories of values do not afford intellectual assistance in framing ideas and beliefs about values that are adequate to direct action, the gap must be filled by other means. If intelligent method is lacking, prejudice, the pressure of immediate circumstance, self-interest and class-interest, traditional customs, institutions of accidental historic origin, are *not* lacking, and they tend to take the place of intelligence. Thus we are led to our main proposition: *Judgments about values are judgments about the conditions and the results of experienced objects; judgments about that which should regulate the formation of our desires, affections and enjoyments.* For whatever decides their formation will determine the main course of our conduct, personal and social.

If it sounds strange to hear that we should frame our judgments as to what has value by considering the connections in existence of what we like and enjoy, the reply is not far to seek. As long as we do not engage in this inquiry enjoyments (values if we choose to apply that term) are casual; they are given by "nature," not constructed by art. Like natural objects in their qualitative existence, they at most only supply material for elaboration in rational discourse. A *feeling* of good or excellence is as far removed from goodness in fact as a feeling that objects are intellectually thus and so is removed from their being actually so. To recognize that the truth of natural objects can be reached only by the greatest care in selecting and arranging directed operations, and then to suppose that values can be truly determined by the mere fact of liking seems to leave us in an incredible position. All the serious perplexities of life come back to the genuine difficulty of forming a judgment as to the values of the situation; they come back to a conflict of goods. Only dogmatism can suppose that serious moral conflict is between something clearly bad and something known to be good, and that uncertainty lies wholly in the will of the one choosing. Most conflicts of importance are conflicts between things which are or have been satisfying, not between good and evil. And to suppose that we can make a hierarchical table of values at large once for all, a kind of catalogue in which they are arranged in an order of ascending or descending worth, is to indulge in a gloss on our inability to frame intelligent judgments in the concrete. Or else it is to dignify customary choice and prejudice by a title of honor.

The alternative to definition, classification and systematization of satisfactions just as they happen to occur is judgment of them by means of the relations under which they occur. If we know the conditions under which the act of liking, of desire and enjoyment, takes place, we are in a position to know what are the consequences of that act. The difference between the desired and the desirable, admired and the admirable, becomes effective at just this point. Consider the difference between the proposition "That thing has been eaten," and the judgment "That thing is edible." The former statement involves no knowledge of any relation except the one stated; while we are able to judge of the edibility of anything only when we have a knowledge of its interactions with other things sufficient to enable us to foresee its probable effects when it is taken into the organism and produces effects there.

To assume that anything can be known in isolation from its connections with other things is to identify knowing with merely having some object before perception or in feeling, and is thus to lose the key to the traits that distinguish an object as known. It is futile, even silly, to suppose that some quality that is directly present constitutes the whole of the thing presenting the quality. It does not do so when the quality is that of being hot or fluid or heavy, and it does not when the quality is that of giving pleasure, or being enjoyed. Such qualities are, once more, effects, ends in the sense of closing termini of processes involving causal connections. They are something to be investigated, challenges to inquiry and judgment. The more connections and interactions we ascertain, the more we *know* the object in question. Thinking is search for these connections. Heat experienced as a consequence of directed operations has a meaning quite different from the heat that is casually experienced without knowledge of how it came about. The same is true of enjoyments. Enjoyments that issue from conduct directed by insight into relations have a meaning and a validity due to the way in which they are experienced. Such enjoyments are not repented of; they generate no after-taste of bitterness. Even in the midst of direct enjoyment, there is a sense of validity, of authorization, which intensifies the enjoyment. There is solicitude for perpetuation of the *object* having value which is radically different from mere anxiety to perpetuate the *feeling* of enjoyment.

Such statements as we have been making are, therefore, far from implying that there are values apart from things actually enjoyed as good. To find a thing enjoy*able* is, so to say, a *plus* enjoyment. We saw that it was foolish to treat the scientific object as a rival to or substitute for the perceived object, since the former is intermediate between uncertain and settled situations and those experienced under conditions of greater control. In the same way, judgment of the value of an object to be experienced is instrumental to appreciation of it when it is realized. But the notion that every object that happens to satisfy has an equal claim with every other to be a value is like supposing that every object of perception has the same cognitive force as every other. There is no knowledge without perception; but objects perceived are *known* only when they are determined as consequences of connective operations. There is no value except where there is satisfaction, but there have to be certain conditions fulfilled to transform a satisfaction into a value.

The time will come when it will be found passing strange that we of this age should take such pains to control by every means at command the formation of ideas of physical things, even those most remote from human concern, and yet are content with haphazard beliefs about the qualities of objects that regulate our deepest interests; that we are scrupulous as to methods of forming ideas of natural objects, and either dogmatic or else driven by immediate conditions in framing those about values. There is, by implication, if not explicitly, a prevalent notion that values are already well known and that all which is lacking is the will to cultivate them in the order of their worth. In fact the most profound lack is not the will to act upon goods already known but the will to know what they are.

It is not a dream that it is possible to exercise some degree of regulation of the occurrence of enjoyments which are of value. Realization of the possibility is exemplified, for example, in the technologies and arts of industrial life—that is, up to a definite limit. Men desired heat, light, and speed of transit and of communication beyond what nature provides of itself. These things have been attained not by lauding the enjoyment of these things and preaching their desirability, but by study of the conditions of their manifestation. Knowledge of relations having been obtained, ability to produce followed, and enjoyment ensued as a matter of course. It is, however, an old story that enjoyment of these things as goods is no warrant of their bringing only good in their train. As Plato was given to pointing out, the physician knows how to heal and the orator to persuade, but the ulterior knowledge of whether it is better for a man to be healed or to be persuaded to the orator's opinion remains unsettled. Here there appears the split between what are traditionally and conventionally called the values of the baser arts and the higher values of the truly personal and humane arts.

With respect to the former, there is no assumption that they can be had and enjoyed without definite operative knowledge. With respect to them it is also clear that the degree in which we value them is measurable by the pains taken to control the conditions of their occurrence. With respect to the latter, it is assumed that no one who is honest can be in doubt what they are; that by revelation, or conscience, or the instruction of others, or immediate feeling, they are clear beyond question. And instead of action in their behalf being taken to be a measure of the extent to which things *are* values to us, it is assumed that the difficulty is to persuade men to act upon what they already know to be good. Knowledge of conditions and consequences is regarded as wholly indifferent to judging what is of serious value, though it is useful in a prudential way in trying to actualize it. In consequence, the existence of values that are by common consent of a secondary and technical sort are under a fair degree of control, while those denominated supreme and imperative are subject to all the winds of impulse, custom and arbitrary authority.

This distinction between higher and lower types of value is itself something to be looked into. Why should there be a sharp division made between some goods as physical and material and others as ideal and "spiritual"? The question touches the whole dualism of the material and the ideal at its root. To denominate anything "matter" or "material" is not in truth to disparage it. It is, if the designation is correctly applied, a way of indicating that the thing in question is a condition or means of the existence of something else. And disparagement of effective means is practically synonymous with disregard of the things that are termed, in eulogistic fashion, ideal and spiritual. For the latter terms if they have any concrete application at all signify something which is a desirable consummation of conditions, a cherished fulfillment of means. The sharp separation between material and ideal good thus deprives the latter of the underpinning of effective support while it opens the way for treating things which should be employed as means as ends in themselves. For since men cannot after all live without some measure of possession of such matters as health and wealth, the latter things will be viewed as values and ends in isolation unless they are treated as integral constituents of the goods that are deemed supreme and final.

The relations that determine the occurrence of what human beings experience, especially when social connections are taken into account, are indefinitely wider and more complex than those that determine the events termed physical; the latter are the outcome of definite selective operations. This is the reason why we know something about remote objects like the stars better than we know significantly characteristic things about our own bodies and minds. We forget the infinite number of things we do not know about the stars, or rather that what we call a star is itself the product of the elimination, enforced and deliberate, of most of the traits that belong to an actual existence. The amount of knowledge we possess about stars would not seem very great or very important if it were carried over to human beings and exhausted our knowledge of them. It is inevitable that genuine knowledge of man and society should lag far behind physical knowledge.

But this difference is not a ground for making a sharp division between the two, nor does it account for the fact that we make so little use of the experimental method of forming our ideas and beliefs about the concerns of man in his characteristic social relations. For this separation religions and philosophies must admit some responsibility. They have erected a distinction between a narrower scope of relations and a wider and fuller one into a difference of kind, naming one kind material, and the other mental and moral. They have charged themselves gratuitously with the office of diffusing belief in the necessity of the division, and with instilling contempt for the material as something inferior in kind in its intrinsic nature and worth. Formal philosophies undergo evaporation of their technical solid contents; in a thinner and more viable form they find their way into the minds of those who know nothing of their original forms. When these diffuse and, so to say, airy emanations re-crystallize in the popular mind they form a hard deposit of opinion that alters slowly and with great difficulty.

What difference would it actually make in the arts of conduct, personal and social, if the experimental theory were adopted not as a mere theory, but as a part of the working equipment of habitual attitudes on the part of everyone? It would be impossible, even were time given, to answer the question in adequate detail, just as men could not foretell in advance the consequences for knowledge of adopting the experimental method. It is the nature of the method that it has to be tried. But there are generic lines of difference which, within the limits of time at disposal, may be sketched.

Change from forming ideas and judgments of value on the basis of conformity to antecedent objects, to constructing enjoyable objects directed by knowledge of consequences, is a change from looking to the past to looking to the future. I do not for a moment suppose that the experiences of the past, personal and social, are of no importance. For without them we should not be able to frame any ideas whatever of the conditions under which objects are enjoyed nor any estimate of the consequences of esteeming and liking them. But past experiences are significant in giving us intellectual instrumentalities of judging just these points. They are tools, not finalities. Reflection upon what we have liked and have enjoyed is a necessity. But it tells us nothing about the *value* of these things until enjoyments are themselves reflectively controlled, or, until, as they are recalled, we form the best judgment possible about what led us to like this sort of thing and what has issued from the fact that we liked it.

We are not, then, to get away from enjoyments experienced in the past and from recall of them, but from the notion that they are the arbiters of things to be further enjoyed. At present, the arbiter is found in the past, although there are many ways of interpreting what in the past is authoritative. Nominally, the most influential conception doubtless is that of a revelation once had or a perfect life once lived. Reliance upon precedent, upon institutions created in the past, especially in law, upon rules of morals that have come to us through unexamined customs, upon uncriticized tradition, are other forms of dependence. It is not for a moment suggested that we can get away from customs and established institutions. A mere break would doubtless result simply in chaos. But there is no danger of such a break. Mankind is too inertly conservative both by constitution and by education to give the idea of this danger actuality. What there is genuine danger of is that the force of new conditions will produce disruption externally and mechanically: this is an ever present danger.

The prospect is increased, not mitigated, by that conservatism which insists upon the adequacy of old standards to meet new conditions. What is needed is intelligent examination of the consequences that are actually effected by inherited institutions and customs, in order that there may be intelligent consideration of the ways in which they are to be intentionally modified in behalf of generation of different consequences.

This is the significant meaning of transfer of experimental method from the technical field of physical experience to the wider field of human life. We trust the method in forming our beliefs about things not directly connected with human life. In effect, we distrust it in moral, political and economic affairs. In the fine arts, there are many signs of a change. In the past, such a change has often been an omen and precursor of changes in other human attitudes. But, generally speaking, the idea of actively adopting experimental method in social affairs, in the matters deemed of most enduring and ultimate worth, strikes most persons as a surrender of all standards and regulative authority. But in principle, experimental method does not signify random and aimless action; it implies direction by ideas and knowledge. The question at issue is a practical one. Are there in existence the ideas and the knowledge that permit experimental method to be effectively used in social interests and affairs?

Where will regulation come from if we surrender familiar and traditionally prized values as our directive standards? Very largely from the findings of the natural sciences. For one of the effects of the separation drawn between knowledge and action is to deprive scientific knowledge of its proper service as a guide of conduct—except once more in those technological fields which have been degraded to an inferior rank. Of course, the complexity of the conditions upon which objects of human and liberal value depend is a great obstacle, and it would be too optimistic to say that we have as yet enough knowledge of the scientific type to enable us to regulate our judgments of value very extensively. But we have more knowledge than we try to put to use, and until we try more systematically we shall not know what are the important gaps in our sciences judged from the point of view of their moral and humane use.

For moralists usually draw a sharp line between the field of the natural sciences and the conduct that is regarded as moral. But a moral that frames its judgments of value on the basis of consequences must depend in a most intimate manner upon the conclusions of science. For the knowledge of the relations between changes which enable us to connect things as antecedents and consequences *is* science. The narrow scope which moralists often give to morals, their isolation of some conduct as virtuous and vicious from other large ranges of conduct, those having to do with health and vigor, business, education, with all the affairs in which desires and affection are implicated, is perpetuated by this habit of exclusion of the subject-matter of natural science from a role in formation of moral standards and ideals. The same attitude operates in the other direction to keep natural science a technical specialty, and it works unconsciously to encourage its use exclusively in regions where it can be turned to personal and class advantage, as in war and trade.

Another great difference to be made by carrying the experimental habit into all matter of practice is that it cuts the roots of what is often called subjectivism, but which is better termed egoism. The subjective attitude is much more widespread than would be inferred from the philosophies which have that label attached. It is as rampant in realistic philosophies as in any others, sometimes even more so, although disguised from those who hold these philosophies under the cover of reverence for and enjoyment of ultimate values. For the implication of placing the standard of thought and knowledge in antecedent existence is that our thought makes no difference in what is significantly real. It then affects only our own attitude toward it.

This constant throwing of emphasis back upon a change made in ourselves instead of one made in the world in which we live seems to me the essence of what is objectionable in "subjectivism." Its taint hangs about even Platonic realism with its insistent evangelical dwelling upon the change made within the mind by contemplation of the realm of essence, and its depreciation of action as transient and all but sordid—a concession to the necessities of organic existence. All the theories which put conversion "of the eye of the soul" in the place of a conversion of natural and social objects that modifies goods actually experienced, are a retreat and escape from existence—and this retraction into self is, once more, the heart of subjective egoisms. The typical example is perhaps the other-worldliness found in religions whose chief concern is with the salvation of the personal soul. But other-worldliness is found as well in estheticism and in all seclusion within ivory towers.

It is not in the least implied that change in personal attitudes, in the disposition of the "subject," is not of great importance. Such change, on the contrary, is involved in any attempt to modify the conditions of the environment. But there is a radical difference between a change in the self that is cultivated and valued as an end, and one that is a means to alteration, through action, of objective conditions. The Aristotelian-medieval conviction that highest bliss is found in contemplative possession of ultimate Being presents an ideal attractive to some types of mind; it sets forth a refined sort of enjoyment. It is a doctrine congenial to minds that despair of the effort involved in creation of a better world of daily experience. It is, apart from theological attachments, a doctrine sure to recur when social conditions are so troubled as to make actual endeavor seem hopeless. But the subjectivism so externally marked in modern thought as compared with ancient is either a development of the old doctrine under new conditions or is of merely technical import. The medieval version of the doctrine at least had the active support of a great social institution by means of which man could be brought into the state of mind that prepared him for ultimate enjoyment of eternal Being. It had a certain solidity and depth which is lacking in modern theories that would attain the result by merely emotional or speculative procedures, or by any means not demanding a change in objective existence so as to render objects of value more empirically secure.

The nature in detail of the revolution that would be wrought by carrying into the region of values the principle now embodied in scientific practice cannot be told; to attempt it would violate the fundamental idea that we know only after we have acted and in consequences of the outcome of action. But it would surely effect a transfer of attention and energy from the subjective to the objective. Men would think of themselves as agents not as ends; ends would be found in experienced enjoyment of the fruits of a transforming activity. In as far as the subjectivity of modern thought represents a discovery of the part played by personal responses, organic and acquired, in the causal production of the qualities and values of objects, it marks the possibility of a decisive gain. It puts us in possession of some of the conditions that control the occurrence of experienced objects, and thereby it supplies us with an instrument of regulation. There is something querulous in the sweeping denial that things as experienced, as perceived and enjoyed, in any way depend upon interaction with human selves. The error of doctrines that have exploited the part played by personal and subjective reactions in determining what is perceived and enjoyed lies either in exaggerating this factor of constitution into the sole condition—as happens in subjective idealism—or else in treating it as a finality instead of, as with all knowledge, an instrument in direction of further action.

A third significant change that would issue from carrying over experimental method from physics to man concerns the import of standards, principles, rules. With the transfer, these, and all tenets and creeds about good and goods, would be recognized to be hypotheses. Instead of being rigidly fixed, they would be treated as intellectual instruments to be tested and confirmed—and altered—through consequences effected by acting upon them. They would lose all pretence of finality—the ulterior source of dogmatism. It is both astonishing and depressing that so much of the energy of mankind has gone into fighting for (with weapons of the flesh as well as of the spirit) the truth of creeds, religious, moral and political, as distinct from what has gone into effort to try creeds by putting them to the test of acting upon them. The change would do away with the intolerance and fanaticism that attend the notion that beliefs and judgments are capable of inherent truth and authority; inherent in the sense of being independent of what they lead to when used as directive principles. The transformation does not imply merely that men are responsible for acting upon what they profess to believe; that is an old doctrine. It goes much further. Any belief as such is tentative, hypothetical; it is not just to be acted upon, but is to be *framed* with reference to its office as a guide to action. Consequently, it should be the last thing in the world to be picked up casually and then clung to rigidly. When it is apprehended as a tool and only a tool, an instrumentality of direction, the same scrupulous attention will go to its formation as now goes into the making of instruments of precision in technical fields. Men, instead of being proud of accepting and asserting beliefs and "principles" on the ground of loyalty, will be as ashamed of that

222 THE QUEST FOR CERTAINTY

procedure as they would now be to confess their assent to a scientific theory out of reverence for Newton or Helmholtz or
whomever, without regard to evidence.

If one stops to consider the matter, is there not something
strange in the fact that men should consider loyalty to "laws,"
principles, standards, ideals to be an inherent virtue, accounted
unto them for righteousness? It is as if they were making up for
some secret sense of weakness by rigidity and intensity of insistent attachment. A moral law, like a law in physics, is not something to swear by and stick to at all hazards; it is a formula of the
way to respond when specified conditions present themselves. Its
soundness and pertinence are tested by what happens when it is
acted upon. Its claim or authority rests finally upon the impera-
tiveness of the situation that has to be dealt with, not upon its
own intrinsic nature—as any tool achieves dignity in the measure of needs served by it. The idea that adherence to standards
external to experienced objects is the only alternative to confusion and lawlessness was once held in science. But knowledge became steadily progressive when it was abandoned, and clews and
tests found within concrete acts and objects were employed. The
test of consequences is more exacting than that afforded by fixed
general rules. In addition, it secures constant development, for
when new acts are tried new results are experienced, while the
lauded immutability of eternal ideals and norms is in itself a denial of the possibility of development and improvement.

The various modifications that would result from adoption in
social and humane subjects of the experimental way of thinking
are perhaps summed up in saying that it would place *method
and means* upon the level of importance that has, in the past,
been imputed exclusively to ends. Means have been regarded as
menial, and the useful as the servile. Means have been treated
as poor relations to be endured, but not inherently welcome.
The very meaning of the word "ideals" is significant of the divorce which has obtained between means and ends. "Ideals" are
thought to be remote and inaccessible of attainment; they are
too high and fine to be sullied by realization. They serve vaguely
to arouse "aspiration," but they do not evoke and direct strivings
for embodiment in actual existence. They hover in an indefinite
way over the actual scene; they are expiring ghosts of a once sig-

nificant kingdom of divine reality whose rule penetrated to every detail of life.

It is impossible to form a just estimate of the paralysis of effort that has been produced by indifference to means. Logically, it is truistic that lack of consideration for means signifies that so-called ends are not taken seriously. It is as if one professed devotion to painting pictures conjoined with contempt for canvas, brush and paints; or love of music on condition that no instruments, whether the voice or something external, be used to make sounds. The good workman in the arts is known by his respect for his tools and by his interest in perfecting his technique. The glorification in the arts of ends at the expense of means would be taken to be a sign of complete insincerity or even insanity. Ends separated from means are either sentimental indulgences or if they happen to exist are merely accidental. The ineffectiveness in action of "ideals" is due precisely to the supposition that means and ends are not on exactly the same level with respect to the attention and care they demand.

It is, however, much easier to point out the formal contradiction implied in ideals that are professed without equal regard for the instruments and techniques of their realization, than it is to appreciate the concrete ways in which belief in their separation has found its way into life and borne corrupt and poisonous fruits. The separation marks the form in which the traditional divorce of theory and practice has expressed itself in actual life. It accounts for the relative impotency of arts concerned with enduring human welfare. Sentimental attachment and subjective eulogy take the place of action. For there is no art without tools and instrumental agencies. But it also explains the fact that in actual behavior, energies devoted to matters nominally thought to be inferior, material and sordid, engross attention and interest. After a polite and pious deference has been paid to "ideals," men feel free to devote themselves to matters which are more immediate and pressing.

It is usual to condemn the amount of attention paid by people in general to material ease, comfort, wealth, and success gained by competition, on the ground that they give to mere means the attention that ought to be given to ends, or that they have taken for ends things which in reality are only means. Criticisms of the

place which economic interest and action occupy in present life
are full of complaints that men allow lower aims to usurp the
place that belongs to higher and ideal values. The final source of
the trouble is, however, that moral and spiritual "leaders" have
propagated the notion that ideal ends may be cultivated in isolation from "material" means, as if means and material were not
synonymous. While they condemn men for giving to means the
thought and energy that ought to go to ends, the condemnation
should go to them. For they have not taught their followers to
think of material and economic activities as *really* means. They
have been unwilling to frame their conception of the values
that should be regulative of human conduct on the basis of the
actual conditions and operations by which alone values can be
actualized.

Practical needs are imminent; with the mass of mankind they
are imperative. Moreover, speaking generally, men are formed to
act rather than to theorize. Since the ideal ends are so remotely
and accidentally connected with immediate and urgent conditions that need attention, after lip service is given to them, men
naturally devote themselves to the latter. If a bird in the hand is
worth two in a neighboring bush, an actuality in hand is worth,
for the direction of conduct, many ideals that are so remote as to
be invisible and inaccessible. Men hoist the banner of the ideal,
and then march in the direction that concrete conditions suggest
and reward.

Deliberate insincerity and hypocrisy are rare. But the notion
that action and sentiment are inherently unified in the constitution of human nature has nothing to justify it. Integration is
something to be achieved. Division of attitudes and responses,
compartmentalizing of interests, is easily acquired. It goes deep
just because the acquisition is unconscious, a matter of habitual
adaptation to conditions. Theory separated from concrete doing
and making is empty and futile; practice then becomes an immediate seizure of opportunities and enjoyments which conditions
afford without the direction which theory—knowledge and
ideas—has power to supply. The problem of the relation of theory and practice is not a problem of theory alone; it is that, but it
is also the most practical problem of life. For it is the question of
how intelligence may inform action, and how action may bear
the fruit of increased insight into meaning: a clear view of the

values that are worth while and of the means by which they are to be made secure in experienced objects. Construction of ideals in general and their sentimental glorification are easy; the responsibilities both of studious thought and of action are shirked. Persons having the advantage of positions of leisure and who find pleasure in abstract theorizing—a most delightful indulgence to those to whom it appeals—have a large measure of liability for a cultivated diffusion of ideals and aims that are separated from the conditions which are the means of actualization. Then other persons who find themselves in positions of social power and authority readily claim to be the bearers and defenders of ideal ends in church and state. They then use the prestige and authority their representative capacity as guardians of the highest ends confers on them to cover actions taken in behalf of the harshest and narrowest of material ends.

The present state of industrial life seems to give a fair index of the existing separation of means and ends. Isolation of economics from ideal ends, whether of morals or of organized social life, was proclaimed by Aristotle. Certain things, he said, are conditions of a worthy life, personal and social, but are not constituents of it. The economic life of man, concerned with satisfaction of wants, is of this nature. Men have wants and they must be satisfied. But they are only prerequisites of a good life, not intrinsic elements in it. Most philosophers have not been so frank nor perhaps so logical. But upon the whole, economics has been treated as on a lower level than either morals or politics. Yet the life which men, women and children actually lead, the opportunities open to them, the values they are capable of enjoying, their education, their share in all the things of art and science, are mainly determined by economic conditions. Hence we can hardly expect a moral system which ignores economic conditions to be other than remote and empty.

Industrial life is correspondingly brutalized by failure to equate it as the means by which social and cultural values are realized. That the economic life, thus exiled from the pale of higher values, takes revenge by declaring that it is the only social reality, and by means of the doctrine of materialistic determination of institutions and conduct in all fields, denies to deliberate morals and politics any share of causal regulation, is not surprising.

When economists were told that their subject-matter was

merely material, they naturally thought they could be "scientific" only by excluding all reference to distinctively human values. Material wants, efforts to satisfy them, even the scientifically regulated technologies highly developed in industrial activity, are then taken to form a complete and closed field. If any reference to social ends and values is introduced it is by way of an external addition, mainly hortatory. That economic life largely determines the conditions under which mankind has access to concrete values may be recognized or it may not be. In either case, the notion that it is the means to be utilized in order to secure significant values as the common and shared possession of mankind is alien and inoperative. To many persons, the idea that the ends professed by morals are impotent save as they·are connected with the working machinery of economic life seems like deflowering the purity of moral values and obligations.

The social and moral effects of the separation of theory and practice have been merely hinted at. They are so manifold and so pervasive that an adequate consideration of them would involve nothing less than a survey of the whole field of morals, economics and politics. It cannot be justly stated that these effects are in fact direct consequences of the quest for certainty by thought and knowledge isolated from action. For, as we have seen, this quest was itself a reflex product of actual conditions. But it may be truly asserted that this quest, undertaken in religion and philosophy, has had results which have reinforced the conditions which originally brought it about. Moreover, search for safety and consolation amid the perils of life by means other than intelligent action, by feeling and thought alone, began when actual means of control were lacking, when arts were undeveloped. It had then a relative historic justification that is now lacking. The primary problem for thinking which lays claim to be philosophic in its breadth and depth is to assist in bringing about a reconstruction of all beliefs rooted in a basic separation of knowledge and action; to develop a system of operative ideas congruous with present knowledge and with present facilities of control over natural events and energies.

We have noted more than once how modern philosophy has been absorbed in the problem of effecting an adjustment between the conclusions of natural science and the beliefs and values that have authority in the direction of life. The genuine and poignant issue does not reside where philosophers for the most part have placed it. It does not consist in accommodation to each other of two realms, one physical and the other ideal and spiritual, nor in the reconciliation of the "categories" of theoretical and practical reason. It is found in that isolation of executive means and ideal interests which has grown up under the influence of the separation of theory and practice. For this, by nature, involves the separation of the material and the spiritual. Its solution, therefore, can be found only in action wherein the phenomena of material and economic life are equated with the purposes that command the loyalties of affection and purpose, and in which ends and ideals are framed in terms of the possibilities of actually experienced situations. But while the solution cannot be found in "thought" alone, it can be furthered by thinking which is operative—which frames and defines ideas in terms of what may be done, and which uses the conclusions of science as instrumentalities. William James was well within the bounds of moderation when he said that looking forward instead of backward, looking to what the world and life might become instead of to what they have been, is an alteration in the "seat of authority."

It was incidentally remarked earlier in our discussion that the serious defect in the current empirical philosophy of values, the one which identifies them with things actually enjoyed irrespective of the conditions upon which they depend, is that it formulates and in so far consecrates the conditions of our present social experience. Throughout these chapters, primary attention has perforce been given to the methods and statements of philosophic theories. But these statements are technical and specialized in formulation only. In origin, content and import they are reflections of some condition or some phase of concrete human experience. Just as the theory of the separation of theory and practice has a practical origin and a momentous practical consequence, so the empirical theory that values are identical with whatever men actually enjoy, no matter how or what, formulates an aspect, and an undesirable one, of the present social situation.

For while our discussion has given more attention to the other type of philosophical doctrine, that which holds that regulative and authoritative standards are found in transcendent eternal values, it has not passed in silence over the fact that actually the greater part of the activities of the greater number of human beings is spent in effort to seize upon and hold onto such enjoyments as the actual scene permits. Their energies and their enjoyments are controlled in fact, but they are controlled by external conditions rather than by intelligent judgment and endeavor. If philosophies have any influence over the thoughts and acts of men, it is a serious matter that the most widely held empirical theory should in effect justify this state of things by identifying values with the objects of any interest as such. As long as the only theories of value placed before us for intellectual assent alternate between sending us to a realm of eternal and fixed values and sending us to enjoyments such as actually obtain, the formulation, even as only a theory, of an experimental empiricism which finds values to be identical with goods that are the fruit of intelligently directed activity has its measure of practical significance.

The Copernican Revolution

Kant claimed that he had effected a Copernican revolution in philosophy by treating the world and our knowledge of it from the standpoint of the knowing subject. To most critics, the endeavor to make the known world turn on the constitution of the knowing mind, seems like a return to an ultra-Ptolemaic system. But Copernicus, as Kant understood him, effected a straightening out of astronomical phenomena by interpreting their perceived movements from their relation to the perceiving subject, instead of treating them as inherent in the things perceived. The revolution of the sun about the earth as it offers itself to sense-perception was regarded as due to the conditions of human observation and not to the movements of the sun itself. Disregarding the consequences of the changed point of view, Kant settled upon this one feature as characteristic of the method of Copernicus. He thought he could generalize this feature of Copernican method, and thus clear up a multitude of philosophical difficulties by attributing the facts in question to the constitution of the human subject in knowing.

That the consequence was Ptolemaic rather than Copernican is not to be wondered at. In fact, the alleged revolution of Kant consisted in making explicit what was implicit in the classic tradition. In words, the latter had asserted that knowledge is determined by the objective constitution of the universe. But it did so only after it had first assumed that the universe is itself constituted after the pattern of reason. Philosophers first constructed a rational system of nature and then borrowed from it the features by which to characterize their knowledge of it. Kant, in effect, called attention to the borrowing; he insisted that credit for the borrowed material be assigned to human reason instead of to divine. His "revolution" was a shift from a theological to a human authorship; beyond that point, it was an explicit acknowledgment of what philosophers in the classic line of descent had been doing unconsciously before him. For the basic assumption of this tradition was the inherent correspondence subsisting between *intellectus* and the structure of Nature—the principle so definitely stated by Spinoza. By the time of Kant difficulties in this rationalistic premise had become evident. He thought to maintain the underlying idea and remedy the perplexities it entailed by placing the locus of intellect in man as a knowing subject. The irritation which this performance arouses in some minds is due rather to this transfer than to any doubt about the valid function of reason in the constitution of nature.

Kant refers incidentally to the experimental method of Galileo as an illustration of the way in which thought actually takes the lead, so that an object is known because of conformity to a prior conception:—because of its conformity to the specifications of the latter. The reference makes clear by contrast the genuine reversal contained in the experimental way of knowing. It is true that experimentation proceeds on the basis of a directive idea. But the difference between the office of the idea in determining a known object and the office assigned to it in Kant's theory is as great as between the Copernican and the Ptolemaic systems. For an idea in experiment is tentative, conditional, not fixed and rigorously determinative. It controls an action to be performed, but the consequences of the operation determine the worth of the directive idea; the directive idea does not fix the nature of the object.

Moreover, in experiment everything takes place aboveboard, in the open. Every step is overt and capable of being observed. There is a specified antecedent state of things; a specified operation using means, both physical and symbolic, which are externally exhibited and reported. The entire process by which the conclusion is reached that such and such a judgment of an object is valid is overt. It can be repeated step by step by any one. Thus every one can judge for himself whether or not the conclusion reached as to the object justifies assertion of knowledge, or whether there are gaps and deflections. Moreover, the whole process goes on where other existential processes go on, in time. There is a temporal sequence as definitely as in any art, as in, say, the making of cotton cloth from ginning of raw material, through carding and spinning to the operation of the loom. A public and manifest series of definite operations, all capable of public notice and report, distinguishes scientific knowing from the knowing carried on by inner "mental" processes accessible only to introspection, or inferred by dialectic from assumed premises.

There is accordingly opposition rather than agreement between the Kantian determination of objects by thought and the determination by thought that takes place in experimentation. There is nothing hypothetical or conditional about Kant's forms of perception and conception. They work uniformly and triumphantly; they need no differential testing by consequences. The reason Kant postulates them is to secure universality and necessity instead of the hypothetical and the probable. Nor is there anything overt, observable and temporal or historical in the Kantian machinery. Its work is done behind the scenes. Only the result is observed, and only an elaborate process of dialectic inference enables Kant to assert the existence of his apparatus of forms and categories. These are as inaccessible to observation as were the occult forms and essences whose rejection was a prerequisite of development of modern science.

These remarks are not directed particularly against Kant. For, as has been already said, he edited a new version of old conceptions about mind and its activities in knowing, rather than evolved a brand new theory. But since he happens to be the author of the phrase "Copernican revolution," his philosophy forms a convenient point of departure for consideration of a genuine reversal of traditional ideas about the mind, reason, conceptions, and mental processes. Phases of this revolution have concerned us in the previous lectures. We have seen how the opposition between knowing and doing, theory and practice, has been abandoned in the actual enterprise of scientific inquiry, how knowing goes forward by means of doing. We have seen how the cognitive quest for absolute certainty by purely mental means has been surrendered in behalf of search for a security, having a high degree of probability, by means of preliminary active regulation of conditions. We have considered some of the definite steps by which security has come to attach to regulation of change rather than absolute certainty to the unchangeable. We have noted how in consequence of this transformation the standard of judgment has been transferred from antecedents to consequents, from inert dependence upon the past to intentional construction of a future.

If such changes do not constitute, in the depth and scope of their significance, a reversal comparable to a Copernican revolution, I am at a loss to know where such a change can be found or what it would be like. The old centre was mind knowing by means of an equipment of powers complete within itself, and merely exercised upon an antecedent external material equally complete in itself. The new centre is indefinite interactions taking place within a course of nature which is not fixed and complete, but which is capable of direction to new and different results through the mediation of intentional operations. Neither self nor world, neither soul nor nature (in the sense of something isolated and finished in its isolation) is the centre, any more than either earth or sun is the absolute centre of a single universal and necessary frame of reference. There is a moving whole of interacting parts; a centre emerges wherever there is effort to change them in a particular direction.

The reversal has many phases, and these are interconnected. It cannot be said that one is more important than another. But one change stands out with an extraordinary distinctness. Mind is no longer a spectator beholding the world from without and finding its highest satisfaction in the joy of self-sufficing contemplation. The mind is within the world as a part of the latter's own ongoing process. It is marked off as mind by the fact that wherever it is found, changes take place in a *directed* way, so that a movement in a definite one-way sense—from the doubtful and confused to the clear, resolved and settled—takes place. From knowing as an outside beholding to knowing as an active participant in the drama of an on-moving world is the historical transition whose record we have been following.

As far as philosophy is concerned, the first direct and immediate effect of this shift from knowing which makes a difference to the knower but none in the world, to knowing which is a directed change within the world, is the complete abandonment of what we may term the intellectualist fallacy. By this is meant something which may also be termed the ubiquity of knowledge as a measure of reality. Of the older philosophies, framed before experimental knowing had made any significant progress, it may be said that they made a definite separation between the world in which man thinks and knows and the world in which he lives and acts. In his needs and in the acts that spring from them, man *was* a part of the world, a sharer in its fortunes, sometimes willingly, sometimes perforce; he was exposed to its vicissitudes and at the mercy of its irregular and unforeseeable changes. By acting in and upon the world he made his earthly way, sometimes failing, sometimes achieving. He was acted upon by it, sometimes carried forward to unexpected glories and sometimes overwhelmed by its disfavor.

Being unable to cope with the world in which he lived, he sought some way to come to terms with the universe as a whole. Religion was, in its origin, an expression of this endeavor. After a time, a few persons with leisure and endowed by fortune with immunity from the rougher impacts of the world, discovered the delights of thought and inquiry. They reached the conclusion that through rational thought they could rise about the natural world in which, with their body and those mental processes that were connected with the body, they lived. In striving with the inclemencies of nature, suffering its buffetings, wresting sustenance from its resources, they were parts of Nature. But in knowledge, true knowledge which is rational, occupied with objects that are universal and immutable, they escaped from the world of vicissitude and uncertainty. They were elevated above the realm in which needs are felt and laborious effort imperative. In rising above this world of sense and time, they came into rational communion with the divine which was untroubled and perfect mind. They became true participants in the realm of ultimate reality. Through knowledge, they were without the world of chance and change, and within the world of perfect and unchanging Being.

How far this glorification by philosophers and scientific investigators of a life of knowing, apart from and above a life of doing, might have impressed the popular mind without adventitious aid there is no saying. But external aid came. Theologians of the Christian Church adopted this view in a form adapted to their religious purposes. The perfect and ultimate reality was God; to know Him was eternal bliss. The world in which man lived and acted was a world of trials and troubles to test and prepare him for a higher destiny. Through thousands of ways, including histories and rites, with symbols that engaged the emotions and imagination, the essentials of the doctrine of classic philosophy filtered its way into the popular mind.

It would be a one-sided view which held that this story gives the entire account of the elevation of knowing and its object above practical action and its objects. A contributing cause was found in the harshness, cruelties and tragic frustrations of the world of action. Were it not for its brutalities and failures, the motive for seeking refuge in a higher realm of knowledge would have been lacking. It was easy and, as we say, "natural" to associate these evils with the fact that the world in which we act is a realm of change. The generic fact of change was made absolute and the source of all the troubles and defects of the world in which we directly live. At the very best, good and excellence are insecure in a world of change; good can be securely at home only in a realm of fixed unchanging substance. When the source of evil was once asserted to reside in the inherent deficiencies of a realm of change, responsibility was removed from human ignorance, incapacity and insusceptibility. It remained only to change our own attitude and disposition, to turn the soul from perishable things toward perfect Being. In this idea religion stated in one language precisely what the great philosophic tradition stated in another.

Nor is this the whole of the story. There was, strangely enough, a definitely practical ground for the elevation of knowledge above doing and making. Whenever knowledge is actually obtained, a measure of security through ability to control ensues. There is a natural inclination to treat value as a measure of reality. Since knowledge is the mode of experience that puts in our hands the key to controlling our other dealings with experienced objects, it has a central position. There is no *practical* point gained in asserting that a thing *is* what it is *experienced* to be apart from knowledge. If a man has typhoid fever, he has it; he does not have to search for or pry into it. But to *know* it, he does have to search:—to *thought*, to intellect, the fever *is* what it is known to be. For when it is known, the various phenomena of *having* it, the direct experiences, fall into order; we have at least that kind of control called understanding, and with this comes the possibility of a more active control. The very fact that other experiences speak, so to say, for themselves makes it unnecessary to ask *what* they are. When the nature of an existence is in doubt and we have to seek for it, the idea of reality is consciously present. Hence the thought of existence becomes exclusively associated with knowing. Other ways of experiencing things exist so obviously that we do not *think* of existence in connection with them.

At all events, whatever the explanation, the idea that cognition is the measure of the reality found in other modes of experience is the most widely distributed premise of philosophies. The equation of the real and the known comes to explicit statement in idealistic theories. If we remind ourselves of the landscape with trees and grasses waving in the wind and waves dancing in sunlight, we recall how scientific thought of these things strips off the qualities significant in perception and direct enjoyment, leaving only certain physical constants stated in mathematical formulae. What is more natural, then, than to call upon mind to reclothe by some contributory act of thought or consciousness the grim skeleton offered by science? Then if only it can be shown that mathematical relations are themselves a logical construction of thought, the knowing mind is enstated as the constitutive author of the whole scheme. Realistic theories have protested against doctrines that make the knowing mind the source of the thing known. But they have held to a doctrine of a partial equation of the real and the known; only they have read the equation from the side of the object instead of the subject. Knowledge must be the grasp or vision of the real as it "is in itself," while emotions and affections deal with it as it is affected with an alien element supplied by the feeling and desiring subject. The postulate of the unique and exclusive relation among experienced things of knowledge and the real is shared by epistemological idealist and realist.

The meaning of a Copernican reversal is that we do not have to go to knowledge to obtain an exclusive hold on reality. The world as we experience it is a real world. But it is not in its primary phases a world that is known, a world that is understood, and is intellectually coherent and secure. Knowing consists of operations that give experienced objects a form in which the relations, upon which the onward course of events depends, are securely experienced. It marks a transitional redirection and rearrangement of the real. It is intermediate and instrumental; it comes between a relatively casual and accidental experience of existence and one relatively settled and defined. The knower is within the world of existence; his knowing, as experimental, marks an interaction of one existence with other existences. There is, however, a most important difference between it and other existential interactions. The difference is not between something going on within nature as a part of itself and something else taking place outside it, but is that between a regulated course of changes and an uncontrolled one. In knowledge, causes become means and effects become consequences, and thereby things have meanings. The known object is an antecedent object as that is intentionally rearranged and redisposed, an eventual object whose value is tested by the reconstruction it effects. It emerges, as it were, from the fire of experimental thought as a refined metal issues from operations performed on crude material. It is the same object but the same object with a difference, as a man who has been through conditions which try the temper of his being comes out the same man and a different man.

Knowledge then does not encompass the world as a whole. But the fact that it is not coextensive with experienced existence is no defect nor failure on its part. It is an expression of the fact that knowledge attends strictly to its own business:—transformation of disturbed and unsettled situations into those more controlled and more significant. Not all existence asks to be known, and it certainly does not ask leave from thought to exist. But some existences as they are experienced do ask thought to direct them in their course so that they may be ordered and fair and be such as to commend themselves to admiration, approval and appreciation. Knowledge affords the sole means by which this redirection can be effected. As the latter is brought about, parts of the experienced world have more luminous and organized meaning and their significance is rendered more secure against the gnawing tooth of time. The problem of knowledge is the problem of discovery of methods for carrying on this enterprise of redirection. It is a problem never ended, always in process; one problematic situation is resolved and another takes its place. The constant gain is not in approximation to universal solution but in betterment of methods and enrichment of objects experienced.

Man as a natural creature acts as masses and molecules act;

he lives as animals live, eating, fighting, fearing, reproducing. As he lives, some of his actions yield understanding and things take on meaning, for they become signs of one another; means of expectation and of recall, preparations for what is to come and celebrations of what has gone. Activities take on ideal quality. Attraction and repulsion become love of the admirable and hate of the harsh and ugly, and they seek to find and make a world in which they may be securely at home. Hopes and fears, desires and aversions, are as truly responses to things as are knowing and thinking. Our affections, when they are enlightened by understanding, are organs by which we enter into the meaning of the natural world as genuinely as by knowing, and with greater fullness and intimacy. This deeper and richer intercourse with things can be effected only by thought and its resultant knowledge; the arts in which the potential meanings of nature are realized demand an intermediate and transitional phase of detachment and abstraction. The colder and less intimate transactions of knowing involve temporary disregard of the qualities and values to which our affections and enjoyments are attached. But knowledge is an indispensable medium of our hopes and fears, of loves and hates, if desires and preferences are to be steady, ordered, charged with meaning, secure.

The glorification of knowledge as the exclusive avenue of access to what is real is not going to give way soon nor all at once. But it can hardly endure indefinitely. The more widespread become the habits of intelligent thought, the fewer enemies they meet from those vested interests and social institutions whose power depends upon immunity from inspection by intelligence,  in short, the more matter of course they become, the less need will there seem to be for giving knowledge an exclusive and monopolistic position. It will be prized for its fruits rather than for the properties assigned to it when it was a new and precarious enterprise. The common fact that we prize in proportion to rarity has a good deal to do with the exclusive esteem in which knowledge has been held. There is so much unintelligent appetite and impulse, so much routine action, so much that is dictated by the arbitrary power of other persons, so much, in short, that is not informed and enlightened by knowledge, that it is not surprising that action and knowledge should have been isolated in thought from one another, and knowledge treated as if it alone had dealings with real existence. I do not know when knowledge will become naturalized in the life of society. But when it is fully acclimatized, its instrumental, as distinct from its monopolistic, role in approach to things of nature and society will be taken for granted without need for such arguments as I have been engaging in. Meantime, the development of the experimental method stands as a prophecy of the possibility of the accomplishment of this Copernican Revolution.

Whenever anyone speaks about the relation of knowledge (especially if the word science be used) to our moral, artistic and religious interests, there are two dangers to which he is exposed. There exist on one hand efforts to use scientific knowledge to substantiate moral and religious beliefs, either with respect to some specific form in which they are current or in some vague way that is felt to be edifying and comforting. On the other hand, philosophers derogate the importance and necessity of knowledge in order to make room for an undisputed sway of some set of moral and religious tenets. It may be that preconceptions will lead some to interpret what has been said in one or other of these senses. If so, it is well to state that not a word has been said in depreciation of science; what has been criticized is a philosophy and habit of mind on the ground of which science is prized for false reasons. Nor does this negative statement cover the whole ground. Knowledge is instrumental. But the purport of our whole discussion has been in praise of tools, instrumentalities, means, putting them on a level equal in value to ends and consequences, since without them the latter are merely accidental, sporadic and unstable. To call known objects, in their capacity of being objects of knowledge, means is to appreciate them, not to depreciate them.

Affections, desires, purposes, choices are going to endure as long as man is man; therefore as long as man is man, there are going to be ideas, judgments, beliefs about values. Nothing could be sillier than to attempt to justify their existence at large; they are going to exist anyway. What is inevitable needs no proof for its existence. But these expressions of our nature need *direction*, and direction is possible only through knowledge. When they are informed by knowledge, they themselves constitute, in their directed activity, intelligence in operation. Thus as far as concerns particular value-beliefs, particular moral and religious ideas and creeds, the import of what has been said is that they need to be tested and revised by the best knowledge at command. The moral of the discussion is anything but a reservation for them of a position in which they are exempt from the impact, however disintegrative it may be, of new knowledge.

The relation between objects as known and objects with respect to value is that between the actual and the possible. "The actual" consists of given conditions; "the possible" denotes ends or consequences not now existing but which the actual may through its use bring into existence. The possible in respect to any given actual situation is thus an ideal for that situation; from the standpoint of operational definition—of thinking in terms of action—the ideal and the possible are equivalent ideas. Idea and ideal have more in common than certain letters of the alphabet. Everywhere an idea, in its intellectual content, is a projection of what something existing may come to be. One may report a quality already sensed in a proposition, as when standing before the fire I remark upon how hot it is. When seeing something at a distance, I judge without sensible contact that it must be hot; "hot" expresses a consequence which I infer would be experienced if I were to approach close enough; it designates a possibility of what is actually there in experience. The instance is a trivial one, but it sets forth what happens in every case where any predicate, whether quality or relation, expresses an *idea* rather than a sensibly perceived characteristic. The difference is not between one mental state called a sensation and another called an image. It is between what is experienced as being already there and what marks a possibility of being experienced. If we agree to leave out the eulogistic savor of "ideal" and define it in contrast with the actual, the possibility denoted by an idea is the ideal phase of the existent.

The problem of the connection or lack of connection of the actual and the ideal has always been the central problem of philosophy in its metaphysical aspect, just as the relation between existence and idea has been the central theme of philosophy on the side of the theory of knowledge. Both issues come together in the problem of the relation of the actual and the possible. Both problems are derived from the necessities of action if that is to be intelligently regulated. Assertion of an idea or of an ideal, if it is genuine, is a claim that it is possible to modify what exists so that it will take on a form possessed of specifiable traits. This statement as it relates to an idea, to the cognitive aspect, takes us back to what has been said about ideas as designations of operations and their consequences. Its bearing upon the "ideal" concerns us at this point.

In this basic problem of the relation of the actual and ideal, classic philosophies have always attempted to prove that the ideal is already and eternally a property of the real. The quest for absolute cognitive certainty has come to a head in the quest for an ideal which is one with the ultimately real. Men have not been able to trust either the world or themselves to realize the values and qualities which are the possibilities of nature. The sense of incompetency and the sloth born of desire for irresponsibility have combined to create an overwhelming longing for the ideal and rational as an antecedent possession of actuality, and consequently something upon which we can fall back for emotional support in times of trouble.

The assumption of the antecedent inherent identity of actual and ideal has generated problems which have not been solved. It is the source of the problem of evil; of evil not merely in the moral sense, but in that of the existence of defect and aberration, of uncertainty and error, of all deviation from the perfect. If the universe is in itself ideal, why is there so much in our experience of it which is so thoroughly unideal? Attempts to answer this question have always been compelled to introduce lapse from perfect Being:—some kind of fall to which is due the distinction between noumena and phenomena, things as they really are and as they seem to be. There are many versions of this doctrine. The simplest, though not the one which has most commended itself to many philosophers, is the idea of the "fall of man," a fall which, in the words of Cardinal Newman, has implicated all creation in an aboriginal catastrophe. I am not concerned to discuss them and their respective weaknesses and strengths. It is enough to note that the philosophies which go by the name of Idealism are attempts to prove by one method or another, cosmological, ontological or epistemological, that the Real and the Ideal are one, while at the same time they introduce qualifying additions to explain why after all they are not one.

There are three ways of idealizing the world. There is idealization through purely intellectual and logical processes, in which reasoning alone attempts to prove that the world has characters that satisfy our highest aspirations. There are, again, moments of intense emotional appreciation when, through a happy conjunction of the state of the self and of the surrounding world, the beauty and harmony of existence is disclosed in experiences which are the immediate consummation of all for which we long. Then there is an idealization through actions that are directed by thought, such as are manifested in the works of fine art and in all human relations perfected by loving care. The first path has been taken by many philosophies. The second while it lasts is the most engaging. It sets the measure of our ideas of possibilities that are to be realized by intelligent endeavor. But its objects depend upon fortune and are insecure. The third method represents the way of deliberate quest for security of the values that are enjoyed by grace in our happy moments.

That in fortunate moments objects of complete and approved enjoyment are had is evidence that nature is capable of giving birth to objects that stay with us as ideal. Nature thus supplies potential material for embodiment of ideals. Nature, if I may use the locution, is idealizable. It lends itself to operations by which it is perfected. The process is not a passive one. Rather nature gives, not always freely but in response to search, means and material by which the values we judge to have supreme quality may be embodied in existence. It depends upon the choice of man whether he employs what nature provides and for what ends he uses it.

Idealism of this type is not content with dialectical proofs that the perfect is already and immutably in Being, either as a property of some higher power or as an essence. The emotional satisfactions and encouragements thus supplied are not an adequate substitute for an ideal which is projected in order to be a guide of our doings. While the happy moment brings us objects to admire, approve and revere, the security and extent in which the beautiful, the true and the revered qualify the world, depend upon the way in which our own affections and desires for that kind of world engage activities. Things loved, admired and revered, things that spiritualistic philosophies have seized upon as the defining characters of ultimate Being, are genuine elements of nature. But without the aid and support of deliberate action based on understanding of conditions, they are transitory and unstable, as well as narrow and confined in the number of those who enjoy them.

Religious faiths have come under the influence of philosophies that have tried to demonstrate the fixed union of the actual and ideal in ultimate Being. Their interest in persuading to a life of loyalty to what is esteemed good, has been bound up with a certain creed regarding historical origins. Religion has also been involved in the metaphysics of substance, and has thrown in its lot with acceptance of certain cosmogonies. It has found itself fighting a battle and a losing one with science, as if religion were a rival theory about the structure of the natural world. It has committed itself to assertions about astronomical, geological, biological subject-matter; about questions of anthropology, literary criticism, and history. With the advances of science in these fields it has in consequence found itself involved in a series of conflicts, compromises, adjustments and retreats.

The religious attitude as a sense of the possibilities of existence and as devotion to the cause of these possibilities, as distinct from acceptance of what is given at the time, gradually extricates itself from these unnecessary intellectual commitments. But religious devotees rarely stop to notice that what lies at the basis of recurrent conflicts with scientific findings is not this or that special dogma so much as it is alliance with philosophical schemes which hold that the reality and power of whatever is excellent and worthy of supreme devotion, depends upon proof of its antecedent existence, so that the ideal of perfection loses its claim over us unless it can be demonstrated to exist in the sense in which the sun and stars exist.

Were it not because of this underlying assumption, there could be no conflict between science and religion. The currency of attempts to reconcile scientific conclusions with special doctrines of religion may unfortunately suggest, when such a statement is made, the idea of some infallible recipe for conciliation. But nothing is further from its meaning. It signifies that a religious attitude would surrender once for all commitment to beliefs about matters of fact, whether physical, social or metaphysical. It would leave such matters to inquirers in other fields. Nor would it substitute in their place fixed beliefs about values, save the one value of the worth of discovering the possibilities of the actual and striving to realize them. Whatever is discovered about actual existence would modify the content of human beliefs about ends, purposes and goods. But it would and could not touch the fact that we are capable of directing our affection and loyalty to the possibilities resident in the actualities discovered. An idealism of action that is devoted to creation of a future, instead of to staking itself upon propositions about the past, is invincible. The claims of the beautiful to be admired and cherished do not depend upon ability to demonstrate statements about the past history of art. The demand of righteousness for reverence does not depend upon ability to prove the existence of an antecedent Being who is righteous.

It is not possible to set forth with any accuracy or completeness just what form religion would take if it were wedded to an idealism of this sort, or just what would happen if it broke away from that quest for certitude in the face of peril and human weakness which has determined its historic and institutional career. But some features of the spirit of the change which would follow may be indicated. Not the least important change would be a shift from the defensive and apologetic position which is practically compulsory as long as religious faith is bound up with defense of doctrines regarding history and physical nature; for this entanglement subjects it to constant danger of conflict with science. The energy which is thus diverted into defense of positions that have in time to be surrendered would be released for positive activity in behalf of the security of the underlying possibilities of actual life. More important still would be liberation from attachment to dogmas framed in conditions very unlike those in which we live, and the substitution of a disposition to turn to constructive account the results of knowledge.

It is not possible to estimate the amelioration that would result if the stimulus and support given to practical action by science were no longer limited to industry and commerce and merely "secular" affairs. As long as the practical import of the advance of science is confined to these activities, the dualism between the values which religion professes and the urgent concerns of daily livelihood will persist. The gulf between them will continually grow wider, and the widening will not, judging from past history, be at the expense of the territory occupied by mundane and secular affairs. On the contrary, ideal interests will be compelled to retreat more and more to a confined ground.

The philosophy which holds that the realm of essence subsists as an independent realm of Being also emphasizes that this is a realm of possibilities; it offers this realm as the true object of religious devotion. But, by definition, such possibilities are abstract and remote. They have no concern nor traffic with natural and social objects that are concretely experienced. It is not possible to avoid the impression that the idea of such a realm is simply the hypostatizing in a wholesale way of the fact that actual existence has its own possibilities. But in any case devotion to such remote and unattached possibilities simply perpetuates the other-worldliness of religious tradition, although its other-world is not one supposed to exist. Thought of it is a refuge, not a resource. It becomes effective in relation to the conduct of life only when separation of essence from existence is cancelled; when essences are taken to be possibilities to be embodied through action in concrete objects of secure experience. Nothing is gained by reaching the latter through a circuitous course.

Religious faith which attaches itself to the possibilities of nature and associated living would, with its devotion to the ideal, manifest piety toward the actual. It would not be querulous with respect to the defects and hardships of the latter. Respect and esteem would be given to that which is the means of realization of possibilities, and to that in which the ideal is embodied if it ever finds embodiment. Aspiration and endeavor are not ends in themselves; value is not in them in isolation but in them as means to that reorganization of the existent in which approved meanings are attained. Nature and society include within themselves projection of ideal possibilities and contain the operations by which they are actualized. Nature may not be worshiped as divine even in the sense of the intellectual love of Spinoza. But nature, including humanity, with all its defects and imperfections, may evoke heartfelt piety as the source of ideals, of possibilities, of aspiration in their behalf, and as the eventual abode of all attained goods and excellencies.

I have no intention of entering into the field of the psychology of religion, that is to say, the personal attitudes involved in religious experience. But I suppose that no one can deny that the sense of dependence, insisted upon, for example, by Schleiermacher, comes close to the heart of the matter. This sense has taken many different forms in connection with different states of culture. It has shown itself in abject fears, in practice of extreme cruelties designed to propitiate the powers upon which we depend, and in militantly fanatical intolerance on the part of those who felt that they had special access to the ultimate source of power and a peculiar authorization to act in its behalf. It has shown itself in noble humilities and unquenchable ardors. History shows there is no one channel in which the sense of dependence is predestined to express itself.

But of the religious attitude which is allied to acceptance of the ideally good as the to-be-realized possibilities of existence, one statement may be made with confidence. At the best, all our endeavors look to the future and never attain certainty. The lesson of probability holds for all forms of activity as truly as for the experimental operations of science, and even more poignantly and tragically. The control and regulation of which so much has been said never signifies certainty of outcome, although the greater meed of security it may afford will not be known until we try the experimental policy in all walks of life. The unknown surrounds us in other forms of practical activity even more than in knowing, for they reach further into the future, in more significant and less controllable ways. A sense of dependence is quickened by that Copernican revolution which looks to security amid change instead of to certainty in attachment to the fixed.

It would, moreover, alter its dominant quality. One of the deepest of moral traditions is that which identifies the source of moral evil, as distinct from retrievable error, with pride, and which identifies pride with isolation. This attitude of pride assumes many forms. It is found among those who profess the most complete dependence, often preeminently among them. The pride of the zealously devout is the most dangerous form of pride. There is a divisive pride of the learned, as well as of family, wealth and power. The pride of those who feel themselves learned in the express and explicit will of God is the most exclusive. Those who have this pride, one that generates an exclusive institutionalism and then feeds and sustains itself through its connection with an institution claiming spiritual monopoly, feel themselves to be special organs of the divine, and in its name claim authority over others.

The historic isolation of the church from other social institutions is the result of this pride. The isolation, like all denials of

246 THE QUEST FOR CERTAINTY

interaction and interdependence, confines to special channels the
power of those who profess special connection with the ideal
and spiritual. In condemning other modes of human association
to an inferior position and role, it breeds irresponsibility in the
latter. This result is perhaps the most serious of the many products of that dualism between nature and spirit in which isolation
of the actual and the possible eventuates. The sense of dependence that is bred by recognition that the intent and effort of
man are never final but are subject to the uncertainties of an indeterminate future, would render dependence universal and
shared by all. It would terminate the most corroding form of
spiritual pride and isolation, that which divides man from man
at the foundation of life's activities. A sense of common participation in the inevitable uncertainties of existence would be
coeval with a sense of common effort and shared destiny. Men
will never love their enemies until they cease to have enmities.
The antagonism between the actual and the ideal, the spiritual
and the natural, is the source of the deepest and most injurious
of all enmities.

What has been said might seem to ignore the strength of those
traditions in which are enshrined the emotions and imaginations
of so many human beings, as well as the force of the established
institutions by which these traditions are carried. I am, however,
engaged only in pointing out the possibility of a change. This
task does not require us to ignore the practical difficulties in the
way of realizing it. There is one aspect of these difficulties which
is pertinent at this point. It is appropriate to inquire as to the
bearing of them upon the future office of philosophy. A philosophy committed to rational demonstration of the fixed and antecedent certainty of the ideal, with a sharp demarcation of
knowledge and higher activity from all forms of practical activity, is a philosophy which perpetuates the obstacles in the way
of realization of the possibility that has been pointed out. It is
easy both to minimize the practical effect of philosophic theories
and to exaggerate it. Directly, it is not very great. But as an intellectual formulation and justification of habits and attitudes already obtaining among men its influence is immense. The *vis inertiae* of habit is tremendous, and when it is reinforced by a
philosophy which also is embodied in institutions, it is so great

as to be a factor in sustaining the present confusion and conflict of authorities and allegiances.

A final word about philosophy is then in place. Like religion it has come into conflict with the natural sciences, or at least its path has diverged increasingly from theirs since the seventeenth century. The chief cause of the split is that philosophy has assumed for its function a knowledge of reality. This fact makes it a rival instead of a complement to the sciences. It has forced philosophy into claiming a kind of knowledge which is more ultimate than theirs. In consequence it has, at least in its more systematic forms, felt obliged to revise the conclusions of science to prove that they do not mean what they say; or that, in any case they apply to a world of appearances instead of to the superior reality to which philosophy directs itself. Idealistic philosophies have attempted to prove from an examination of the conditions of knowledge that mind is the only reality. What does it matter, they have said in effect, if physical knowledge recognizes only matter, since matter itself is mental? Idealism in proving that the ideal is once for all the real has absolved itself from the office, more useful if humbler, of attempting that interpretation of the actual by means of which values could be made more extensive and more secure.

General ideas, hypotheses, are necessary in science itself. They serve an indispensable purpose. They open new points of view; they liberate us from the bondage of habit which is always closing in on us, restricting our vision both of what is and of what the actual may become. They direct operations that reveal new truths and new possibilities. They enable us to escape from the pressure of immediate circumstance and provincial boundaries. Knowledge falters when imagination clips its wings or fears to use them. Every great advance in science has issued from a new audacity of imagination. What are now working conceptions, employed as a matter of course because they have withstood the tests of experiment and have emerged triumphant, were once speculative hypotheses.

There is no limit set to the scope and depth of hypotheses. There are those of short and technical range and there are those as wide as experience. Philosophy has always claimed universality for itself. It will make its claim good when it connects this universality with the formation of directive hypotheses instead of with a sweeping pretension to knowledge of universal Being. That hypotheses are fruitful when they are suggested by actual need, are bulwarked by knowledge already attained, and are tested by the consequences of the operations they evoke goes without saying. Otherwise imagination is dissipated into fantasies and rises vaporously into the clouds.

The need for large and generous ideas in the direction of life was never more urgent than in the confusion of tongues, beliefs and purposes that characterizes present life. Knowledge of actual structure and processes of existence has reached a point where a philosophy which has the will to use knowledge has guidance and support. A philosophy which abandoned its guardianship of fixed realities, values and ideals, would find a new career for itself. The meaning of science in terms of science, in terms of knowledge of the actual, may well be left to science itself. Its meaning in terms of the great human uses to which it may be put, its meaning in the service of possibilities of secure value, offers a field for exploration which cries out from very emptiness. To abandon the search for absolute and immutable reality and value may seem like a sacrifice. But this renunciation is the condition of entering upon a vocation of greater vitality. The search for values to be secured and shared by all, because buttressed in the foundations of social life, is a quest in which philosophy would have no rivals but coadjutors in men of good will.

Philosophy under such conditions finds itself in no opposition to science. It is a liaison officer between the conclusions of science and the modes of social and personal action through which attainable possibilities are projected and striven for. No more than a religion devoted to inspiration and cultivation of the sense of ideal possibilities in the actual would it find itself checked by any possible discovery of science. Each new discovery would afford a new opportunity. Such a philosophy would have a wide field of criticism before it. But its critical mind would be directed against the domination exercised by prejudice, narrow interest, routine custom and the authority which issues from institutions apart from the human ends they serve. This negative office would be but the obverse of the creative work of the imagination in pointing to the new possibilities which knowledge of the actual discloses and in projecting methods for their realization in the homely everyday experience of mankind.

Philosophy has often entertained the ideal of a complete integration of knowledge. But knowledge by its nature is analytic and discriminating. It attains large syntheses, sweeping generalizations. But these open up new problems for consideration, new fields for inquiry; they are transitions to more detailed and varied knowledge. Diversification of discoveries and the opening up of new points of view and new methods are inherent in the progress of knowledge. This fact defeats the idea of any complete synthesis of knowledge upon an intellectual basis. The sheer increase of specialized knowledge will never work the miracle of producing an intellectual whole. Nevertheless, the need for integration of specialized results of science remains, and philosophy should contribute to the satisfaction of the need.

The need, however, is practical and human rather than intrinsic to science itself; the latter is content as long as it can move to new problems and discoveries. The need for direction of action in large social fields is the source of a genuine demand for unification of scientific conclusions. They are organized when their bearing on the conduct of life is disclosed. It is at this point that the extraordinary and multifarious results of scientific inquiry are unorganized, scattered, chaotic. The astronomer, biologist, chemist, may attain systematic wholes, at least for a time, within his own field. But when we come to the bearing of special conclusions upon the conduct of social life, we are, outside of technical fields, at a loss. The force of tradition and dogmatic authority is due, more than to anything else, to precisely this defect. Man has never had such a varied body of knowledge in his possession before, and probably never before has he been so uncertain and so perplexed as to what his knowledge means, what it points to in action and in consequences.

Were there any consensus as to the significance of what is known upon beliefs about things of ideal and general value, our life would be marked by integrity instead of by distraction and by conflict of competing aims and standards. Needs of practical action in large and liberal social fields would give unification to our special knowledge; and the latter would give solidity and confidence to the judgment of values that control conduct. Attainment of this consensus would mean that modern life had reached maturity in discovering the meaning of its own intellectual movement. It would find within its own interests and activities the authoritative guidance for its own affairs which it now vainly seeks in oscillation between outworn traditions and reliance upon casual impulse.

The situation defines the vital office of present philosophy. It has to search out and disclose the obstructions; to criticize the habits of mind which stand in the way; to focus reflection upon needs congruous to present life; to interpret the conclusions of science with respect to their consequences for our beliefs about purposes and values in all phases of life. The development of a system of thought capable of giving this service is a difficult undertaking; it can proceed only slowly and through cooperative effort. In these pages I have tried to indicate in outline the nature of the task to be accomplished and to suggest some of the resources at hand for its realization.

Syllabus for the Gifford Lectureship in Natural Theology

"The Quest for Certainty: A Study of the Relation of Knowledge and Action"

Summary

First Edition Pagination Key

Scholarly studies in the past have usually referred to the American edition of *The Quest for Certainty*—either the 1929 Minton, Balch and Company edition or the 1960 G. P. Putnam's Sons Capricorn edition. The list below relates that pagination to the pagination of the present edition. Before the colon appear the 1929–1960 edition page numbers; after the colon are the corresponding page numbers from the present edition.

3:3	28:22–23	53:43–44	78:63–64
4:3–4	29:23–24	54:44	79:64
5:4–5	30:24	55:44–45	80:64–65
6:5–6	31:25	56:45–46	81:65–66
7:6–7	32:25–26	57:46–47	82:66–67
8:7	33:26–27	58:47–48	83:67
9:7–8	34:27–28	59:48	84:67–68
10:8–9	35:28–29	60:48–49	85:68–69
11:9–10	36:29	61:49–50	86:69–70
12:10–11	37:29–30	62:50–51	87:70–71
13:11	38:30–31	63:51–52	88:71
14:11–12	39:31–32	64:52	89:71–72
15:12–13	40:32–33	65:52–53	90:72–73
16:13–14	41:33	66:53–54	91:73–74
17:14–15	42:33–34	67:54–55	92:74
18:15	43:34–35	68:55–56	93:75
19:15–16	44:35–36	69:56	94:75–76
20:16–17	45:36–37	70:56–57	95:76–77
21:17–18	46:37	71:57–58	96:77–78
22:18–19	47:37–38	72:58–59	97:78
23:19	48:38–39	73:59	98:78–79
24:19–20	49:40	74:60	99:79–80
25:20	50:40–41	75:60–61	100:80–81
26:21	51:41–42	76:61–62	101:81–82
27:21–22	52:42–43	77:62–63	102:82–83

103:83
104:83–84
105:84–85
106:85–86
107:86
108:87
109:87–88
110:88–89
111:89–90
112:90–91
113:91–92
114:92
115:92–93
116:93–94
117:94–95
118:95
119:95–96
120:96–97
121:97–98
122:98–99
123:99
124:99–100
125:100–101
126:101–2
127:102–3
128:103
129:103–4
130:104–5
131:105–6
132:106
133:107
134:107–8
135:108–9
136:109–10
137:110
138:110–11
139:111
140:112
141:112–13
142:113–14
143:114–15
144:115–16
145:116

146:116–17
147:117–18
148:118–19
149:119–20
150:120
151:120–21
152:121–22
153:122–23
154:123–24
155:124
156:124–25
157:125–26
158:126–27
159:127–28
160:128
161:128–29
162:129–30
163:130–31
164:131
165:131–32
166:132–33
167:133–34
168:134–35
169:135
170:136
171:136–37
172:137–38
173:138–39
174:139
175:139–40
176:140–41
177:141–42
178:142–43
179:143
180:143–44
181:144–45
182:145–46
183:146–47
184:147
185:147–48
186:148–49
187:149–50
188:150

189:150–51
190:151–52
191:152–53
192:153–54
193:154
194:154–55
195:156
196:156–57
197:157–58
198:158–59
199:159
200:159–60
201:160–61
202:161–62
203:162–63
204:163
205:163–64
206:164–65
207:165–66
208:166–67
209:167
210:167–68
211:168–69
212:169–70
213:170–71
214:171
215:171–72
216:172–73
217:173–74
218:174
219:174–75
220:175–76
221:176–77
222:177
223:178
224:178–79
225:179–80
226:180–81
227:181–82
228:182
229:182–83
230:183–84
231:184–85

232:185–86
233:186
234:186–87
235:187–88
236:188–89
237:189–90
238:190
239:190–91
240:191–92
241:192–93
242:193–94
243:194
244:194–95
245:195–96
246:196–97
247:197
248:198
249:198–99
250:199–200
251:200–201
252:201–2
253:202
254:203
255:203–4
256:204–5
257:205–6
258:206
259:206–7
260:207–8
261:208–9
262:209–10
263:210
264:210–11
265:211–12
266:212–13
267:213
268:213–14
269:214–15
270:215–16
271:216–17
272:217
273:217–18
274:218–19

Checklist of Dewey's References

This section gives full publication information for each work cited by Dewey. Books in Dewey's personal library (John Dewey Papers, Special Collections, Morris Library, Southern Illinois University at Carbondale) have been listed whenever possible. When Dewey gave page numbers for a reference, the edition has been identified by locating the citation; for other references, the edition listed here is his most likely source by reason of place or date of publication, general accessibility during the period, or evidence from correspondence and other materials.

Aristotle. *The Metaphysics of Aristotle.* Translated by John H. M'Mahon. London: George Bell and Sons, 1889.

Barry, Frederick. *The Scientific Habit of Thought.* New York: Columbia University Press, 1927.

Bergson, Henri. *Creative Evolution.* Translated by Arthur Mitchell. New York: Henry Holt and Co., 1911.

Berkeley, George. *A Treatise concerning the Principles of Human Knowledge.* In *The Works of George Berkeley.* London: Thomas Tegg and Son, 1837.

Bridgman, Percy Williams. *The Logic of Modern Physics.* New York: Macmillan Co., 1927.

———. "The New Vision of Science." *Harper's Magazine* 158 (March 1929): 443–51.

Eddington, Arthur Stanley. *The Nature of the Physical World.* New York: Macmillan Co.; Cambridge: At the University Press, 1929 [c1928].

Einstein, Albert. *Relativity: The Special and General Theory.* Translated by Robert W. Lawson. New York: Henry Holt and Co., 1920.

Hegel, Georg Wilhelm Friedrich. *Philosophy of Right.* Translated by S. W. Dyde. London: George Bell and Sons, 1896.

Heine, Heinrich. *Religion and Philosophy in Germany.* Translated by John Snodgrass. Boston and New York: Houghton, Mifflin and Co., 1882.

James, William. *Pragmatism: A New Name for Some Old Ways of Thinking*. New York: Longmans, Green, and Co., 1907.

———. *The Principles of Psychology*. Vol. 1. New York: Henry Holt and Co., 1890.

Kant, Immanuel. *Critique of Judgement*. Translated by J. H. Bernard. 2d ed., rev. London: Macmillan and Co., 1914.

———. *Critique of Practical Reason*. Translated by Thomas Kingsmill Abbott. 3d ed. London: Longmans, Green, and Co., 1883.

———. *Critique of Pure Reason*. Translated by F. Max Müller. London: Macmillan and Co., 1881.

Laplace, Pierre Simon. *A Philosophical Essay on Probabilities*. Translated from the 6th French ed. by Frederick W. Truscott and Frederick L. Emory. New York: John Wiley and Sons, 1902.

Locke, John. *An Essay concerning Human Understanding*. In *The Works of John Locke*, 10th ed., vols. 1–3. London: J. Johnson, 1801.

Maxwell, J. C. *The Scientific Papers of James Clerk Maxwell*. Edited by W. D. Niven. Vol. 2. Cambridge: At the University Press, 1890.

Mead, George Herbert. "Scientific Method and Individual Thinker." In *Creative Intelligence: Essays in the Pragmatic Attitude*, by John Dewey et al. New York: Henry Holt and Co., 1917.

Newman, John Henry. *Lectures on Certain Difficulties Felt by Anglicans in Submitting to the Catholic Church*. London: Burns and Lambert, 1850.

Newton, Isaac. *The Mathematical Principles of Natural Philosophy*. Translated by Andrew Motte. Vol. 2. London: Benjamin Motte, 1729.

———. *Opticks: or, A Treatise of the Reflections, Refractions, Inflections and Colours of Light*. 3d ed., rev. London: William and John Innys, 1721.

Noble, Edmund. *Purposive Evolution: The Link between Science and Religion*. New York: Henry Holt and Co., 1926.

Peirce, Charles S. "How to Make Our Ideas Clear." *Popular Science Monthly* 12 (January 1878): 286–302. Republished in *Chance, Love, and Logic*, edited by Morris R. Cohen. New York: Harcourt, Brace, and Co., 1923.

Spinoza, Benedict de. *The Ethics*. In *The Chief Works of Benedict de Spinoza*, translated by R. H. M. Elwes, vol. 2. London: George Bell and Sons, 1884.

———. *Tractatus de Intellectus Emendatione*. In *Opera Quotquot Reperta Sunt*, recognoverunt J. Van Vloten and J. P. N. Land, 3d ed., vol. 1. Hagae Comitum: Martinum Nijhoff, 1914.

Index

Authority, 76, 110, 245; of Church, 203, 204, 205; conflict of, 40–59, 247; imposition from, 155, 182, 248, 249; means of gaining, 200, 201; from science, 157; for values, 210, 215, 217, 218, 221, 222, 225, 226, 227, 250. *See also* Control; Standards

Axioms, xix–xx, 113, 145*n*

Barry, Frederick, 78–79, 79*n*, 122–23, 128*n*

Behavior. *See* Conduct

Beliefs: conflict with science, 76, 85, 86; formation of, 209, 211; function of, 221–22; integration of, with conduct, 200, 201–2, 204, 205; kinds of, 6, 11; vs. knowledge, 15, 17, 21, 22, 66, 249, 250; pathology of, 109, 181–82; reconstruction of, 226; validity of, 32

Bentham, Jeremy, 146

Bergson, Henri, 73–74

Berkeley, George, 98, 113

Body: inferiority of, 66; and mind, 184, 233

Bridgman, Percy W.: Dewey praises, xii; on observation, 163; on operations, xvii, 89 and *n*, 90*n*

Catholicism, 57

Causality, 127

Certainty: generation of quest for, x, 5, 7, 16, 17, 18, 203; Kant on, 49, 50; means of attaining, 21, 24, 28, 29, 58, 67, 163, 231; nature of quest for, 176, 185, 226, 240, 243, 245; realm of, 41, 96, 103. *See also* Control; Security

Chance. *See* Luck

Change: correlation of, 103, 104, 105–6, 107–8, 158, 197, 198, 219; effecting of, 181, 186, 188, 189; as evil, 82, 148, 200, 234; importance of, to science, 67, 68, 70–71, 76, 80–82; Newton on, 95, 96, 114–15; realm of, 6, 15, 16, 17, 66, 67, 170; regulation of, 84, 163, 165, 168, 170, 171, 231, 232, 236. *See also* Immutables

Christianity. *See* Religion

Church: authority of, 203, 205, 220, 225; doctrine of, 233; expansion of, 61; isolation of, 245–46

Cicero, Marcus Tullius, xxi

Classification, 80, 145, 200, 212

Cohen, Morris R., 90*n*

Communication, 36, 121, 174, 214

Compossibility, 128

Conception of conceptions: empirical, 132–33, 207; and laws, 167; operational, 112, 113, 116, 117–18, 118*n*, 153, 176–77; rationalistic, 144. *See also* Ideas; Operations; Thought

Concrete: meaning of, 123–24, 125

Conduct: analysis of, xiv; direction of, 209–13, 216–17, 218, 225, 249

Consciousness, 69, 181, 182, 191, 196

Consequences: of directed action, 120, 125, 157, 158, 160, 164, 178, 183, 187, 190, 195–97; and means, 130, 238; of operations, 103, 116, 149, 155; relationship of, to values, 207, 208, 212–15, 217, 218, 220–22; test ideas, 110, 132, 230, 231, 240, 248. *See also* Antecedents; Ends

Good: beliefs about, 242–45;
perception and attainment of,
30n, 42, 43, 82, 203–28;
realm of, 12, 27–28; Spinoza
on, 44. *See also* Ends; Values
Greek philosophy and science,
13, 14, 46, 203; concept of
good in, 45; on experience, 21,
22, 23; geometry in, 122–23,
125; on knowledge, xiv–xv,
xvi, 17, 24, 40, 41, 42, 44, 79,
88, 148, 164; metaphysics of,
96, 97; on nature, 43, 184; on
reason, 170; role of observation in, 71–74

Habit: inertia of intellectual, 69,
109, 141, 166, 183, 190, 209,
224, 246, 247, 250
Hartshorne, Charles, 199n
Hebrew theology, 42–46, 49, 50
Hegel, Georg Wilhelm Friedrich,
50–52
Heidegger, Martin: compared
with Dewey, ix, xii and n, xvii
Heine, Heinrich, 48
Heisenberg, Werner: on indeter-
minacy, ix, xi, xiv, xvi, xvii,
160–63, 198
Helmholtz, Hermann Ludwig
Ferdinand von, 131, 222
Hermagoras, xxi
Heterogeneity and homogeneity:
of experienced objects, 76, 77,
78, 85, 107
History, xv, 242; described, 196,
197, 211, 245
Holy, 9–10
"How to Make Our Ideas Clear"
(Peirce), 90n
Hume, David: on mathematical
truths, 125; skepticism of,
xix–xx, 113
Huygens, Christiaan, 78

Hypostatization: significance of,
123, 132, 174, 190, 198, 211,
244. *See also* Substance
Hypotheses, 86; beliefs as,
221–22; concerning knowl-
edge, 138, 140, 143, 144, 147,
149; defined, 63, 132, 133; of
Galileo, 77; of Kant, 231; necessity of, 247, 248; of Newton, 93; verification of,
152–53, 155

Idealism: of action, 243; defined,
133; vs. empiricism, 142; error
of, 221; generating conditions
of, 186; heart of, 27; motif of,
87, 88, 111, 113; systems of,
50–52; theory of knowledge
in, xi, xxii, 18, 151; theory of
real and ideal in, 235, 240,
241, 247; values of, 205–6
Idealization: three modes of,
240–41
Ideals: formation of, 86, 119, 134,
205, 211, 219; function of, 166,
167, 222–25, 227, 237; Hegel
on, 51; nature of, 63, 130, 131,
215, 220; as possibilities, 239–
45, 248; as targets of skepticism, xx
Ideas, 3, 4, 21; denote possibilities, 132–35, 239–40; development of, 86, 87, 88, 91, 98,
155, 183, 214; directive office
of, 48, 224, 226, 230, 247,
248; free, and mathematics,
112–35; as operational,
xvii–xviii, 70, 87–111, 181,
182; of Plato, 74; as source of
knowledge, 137–40, 142; Spinoza on, 167; theories of, 92,
210; validity of, 103–4,
109–10, 112, 154. *See also*
Reflective thinking

INDEX 269

xvii–xviii, 87–111 passim, 157, 158, 160, 164, 172, 173, 176, 240; function of, 68, 100–101, 137–39, 142, 144, 147–51, 153–55, 181–83, 185, 189, 192–94, 198, 199; origin of, 95, 99–100; types of, 122–30, 146

Opinion: defined, xx, 17, 66, 67, 76, 216

Participation: in knowledge, 163, 195, 232; in social affairs, 169, 246

Pathology: of beliefs, 181

Pearson, Karl, xiii

Peirce, Charles S.: compared with Dewey, ix, xviii; on conceptions, 90n, 117

Perception: interpretation of, xiii, xvii, 229, 231, 235; nature of, 72, 113, 165, 184, 192, 221, 239; role of, in knowledge, xxii, 66, 136, 137, 140–43, 213, 214; subject-matter of, 73, 80, 97, 98. See also Observation; Sense

Peril: attitude toward, 3–20, 62; escape from, x, 26, 226, 243; source of, 27, 67, 178, 187, 194

Peripatetic philosophy, 75, 77, 78

Phenomena, 48, 49, 118, 193; explanation of, 73, 74, 77, 78, 80–82, 113–16, 148, 205; laws of, 161, 165; nature of, 83–84, 240

Phenomenalism, 154

Philosophy: attitude of, toward knowledge and action, 4, 5, 7, 11, 12, 16–20, 136, 140, 149, 154, 238; attitude of, toward nature, 195, 197, 198; Dewey's position in, ix, x, xix; history of, xix, 203; impact of science

on, ix, xvii, 76–77, 103, 111; metaphysical problem of, 239; modern problem of, 20, 21–39, 40, 53–55, 58–59, 83, 85–86, 105, 156, 163–64, 175, 176, 226–28; procedures of, 63–64, 69; role of conceptions in, 87–89, 112, 113, 117, 120; role of experience in, 66, 79; theories of values in, 205–6; as topic of Gifford Lectures, viii; true problem of, xviii, 37, 61–62, 134–35, 201–2, 204, 216, 246–50. See also Tradition, classic

Physical: defined, 17, 52, 98, 149, 173–76, 190–93, 215. See also Objects; Science

Plato: ideal realm of, xx, 112, 120, 125, 145, 219; on knowledge, ix, x, 214; structure of, xxi, 13, 74

Politics (Aristotle), xxi

Politics: beliefs about, 5, 136, 200, 207, 218, 221; realm of, 15, 81, 169, 194, 225, 226

Popper, Karl, xv

Possibility, xx; of control, 170, 180, 220–21; defined, 239–44, 246–48; of operations, 124–31; of values, 207, 214. *See also* Symbols

Practice: depreciated, 4–5, 7, 11, 14, 16, 22, 24, 28, 30 and n, 41, 56, 58, 65, 69, 85, 171; experimental method in, 219; meaning of, 25–26; modes of, 203; relationship of, to knowledge, ix, x, xiii, xvi, xvii, xix, 157, 163, 204, 223–24, 226, 227

Pragmatism: of Dewey, vii, viii, ix, xvii, xviii, xix, xxii; essence of, xiii, 30n, 90n; of Peirce, 117

Time, 151; relationships involving, 102, 107, 116, 206, 230, 231; role of, 76, 78, 81, 189, 217; theories of, 113–15, 117, 120
Tools: development of, 8, 10, 176; function of, 119, 123, 132, 217, 221–23; knowledge as, 149, 150; reality of, 193; of science, 68, 70–73, 99–100, 185, 186, 200; of thought, 122, 166; value of, 108–9, 152–53, 238
Topics (Aristotle), x, xix, xxi
Tradition, classic: absorbed by religion, 61–62; advantages of, 62–63; destruction of, 64; doctrines of, 7, 14–16, 21–23, 27–28, 52, 57, 103, 107, 113, 170, 171, 184, 186, 234, 240; indictment against, 29, 57–58, 159–60; Kant furthers, 229–30; values in, 34
Transcendentalism: defects of, 48, 207, 210; values determined by, 63, 205, 206, 227
Truth, 47, 55. *See also* Consequences; Test

Uncertainty: locus of, 178–82, 184, 185, 188, 194, 199, 212; perception of, 31, 53, 240, 246
Uniformity, 130, 166
Universals, 16; nature of, 129, 130; position of, 124, 136, 145 and *n*; proof of, 113
Utilitarianism, 25, 205
Utility, 32; defined, 118, 123; of

experienced objects, 84–85, 177, 190

Validity, 79; determination of, 59, 116, 132; of ideas, 48, 88, 90, 98, 103–4, 154; of judgment, 230; of operations, 157; of purpose, 196; of reflective thought, 112, 117; of values, 34, 210, 213. *See also* Test
Values: beliefs about, 15, 18, 40–48, 56–59, 201; development of, 83, 84, 86, 155, 203–28; as possibilities, 240–43; realm of, 52–54, 63, 76, 110, 186; relationship of, to knowledge, 20, 105, 106, 237, 238; search for, 248–50; security of, 23–29, 31, 33–35, 37–38, 106–7, 247
Verification. *See* Test
Vision, xvii; as knowledge, x, 19, 157, 162, 170, 195

Whewell, William, xxi
Will: in Kant, 47; nature of, 171, 180, 186, 199; relationship of, to values, 214; role of, in religion, 42
Wittgenstein, Ludwig: compared with Dewey, ix, xii and *n*, xiii, xiv, xvii–xviii, xix
Women, 7–8
Woodbridge, F. J. E., viii
Work: as curse, 4, 12; as material, 4